THE
THRILL
OF
Repulsion

EXCURSIONS INTO HORROR CULTURE

WILLIAM BURNS

Schiffer Publishing Ltd®

4880 Lower Valley Road • Atglen, PA 19310

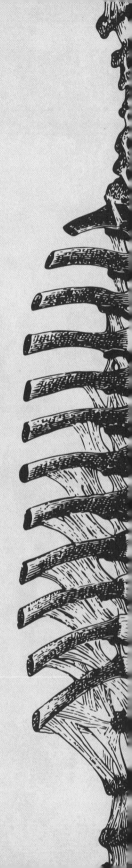

Library of Congress Control Number: 2016936413

Cover & interior designed by Justin Watkinson
Type set in Flyerfonts/Trajan Pro/BauerBodni BT/Minion Pro
ISBN: 978-0-7643-5143-3
Printed in China

Cover illustration by Gustave Dore

Published by Schiffer Publishing, Ltd.
4880 Lower Valley Road
Atglen, PA 19310
Phone: (610) 593-1777; Fax: (610) 593-2002
E-mail: Info@schifferbooks.com
Web: www.schifferbooks.com

Other Schiffer Books on Related Subjects:
Devils and Demonology: In the 21st Century, by Katie Boyd, ISBN 978-0-7643-3195-4

Gorgeous & Gory: The Zombie Pinup Collection, by Jessica Rajs, ISBN 978-0-7643-4784-9

Grim Shadows Falling: Haunting Tales from Terrifying Places, by Benjamin S. Jeffries, ISBN 978-0-7643-4708-5

For our complete selection of fine books on this and related subjects, please visit our website at www.schifferbooks.com. You may also write for a free catalog.

Schiffer Publishing's titles are available at special discounts for bulk purchases for sales promotions or premiums. Special editions, including personalized covers, corporate imprints, and excerpts, can be created in large quantities for special needs. For more information, contact the publisher.

We are always looking for people to write books on new and related subjects. If you have an idea for a book, please contact us at proposals@schifferbooks.com.

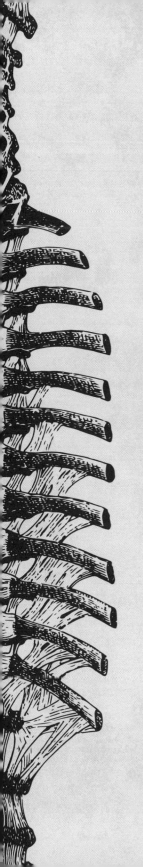

Acknowledgments

Several of these pieces started life as articles for *Horror News Network* (http://horrornewsnetwork.net/), and I would like to express my sincere appreciation to the creators of *HNN*—Rob Caprilozzi and Christine Bucci-Caprilozzi—for their support and encouragement.

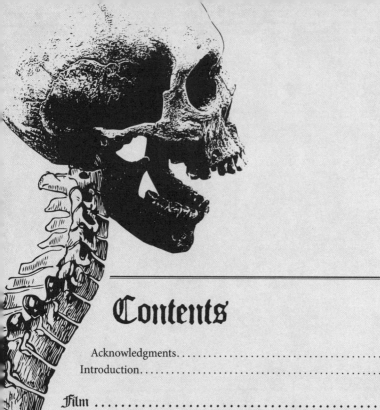

Contents

Acknowledgments 3

Introduction 6

Film 11

CH1: The 13 Most Disturbing Films That Aren't Horror Movies 12

CH2: The 13 Most Sickening Art House Horror Movies 23

CH3: The 13 Most Deranged Horror Director Debuts 37

CH4: The 13 Horror Films that Deserve Better 50

CH5: The 13 Most Phantasmagorical Fantastique Films 61

CH6: The 13 Most Glorious Godzilla Films 77

CH7: The 13 Most Satanic Horror Films 86

CH8: The Horror Film Primer: Witchcraft Movies 98

CH9: *Saw*: The Wrecker of Civilization? 111

CH10: We Blew It: The Death of the '60s on Film 115

CH11: Fear and Head-Spinning: Kierkegaard and *The Exorcist* 123

CH12: We'll Turn the Light Out on Ya: *Halloween*, Sex, and Suburbia 128

CH13: Forty Years and Still Guessing: *Black Christmas* and the Accidental Birth of the Slasher .. 132

CH14: Confessions of a Battered Horror Fan: Dario Argento's *Dracula* 138

Television 142
CH15: The 13 Scariest Horror TV Shows 143
CH16: The 13 Scariest Made-for-TV Horror Films. 158

Literature and Comic Books 169
CH17: The 13 Horror Movie Adaptations That Are Better Than the Book 170
CH18: The 13 Most Important H. P. Lovecraft Stories 189
CH19: The 13 Most Lovecraftian Stories. 202
CH20: The 13 Most Ghastly Horror Comic Artists 215

Music 227
CH21: The 13 Most Terrifying Horror Film Soundtracks 228
CH22: The 13 Most Riotous Horror Bands/Musicians 239
CH23: The UK Occult Sound Revival: An Overview 255

Selected Discographies. 276

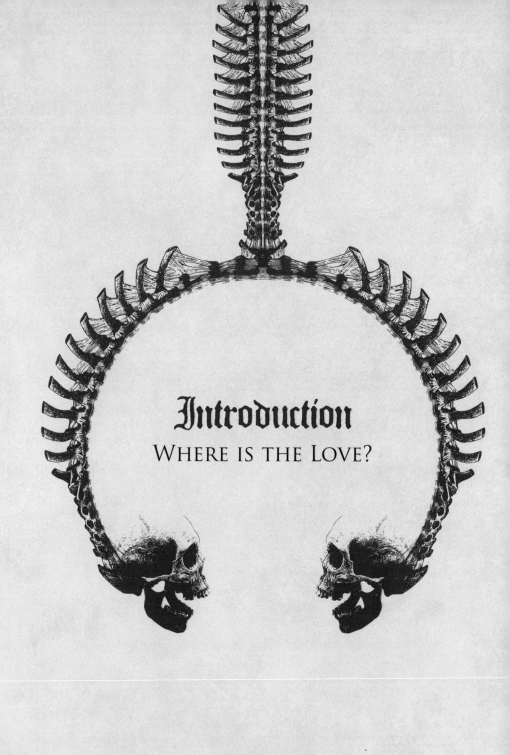

Introduction

WHERE IS THE LOVE?

"Herein lies the reason for the equivocal effect of grotesque art on many people: the material is unfamiliar, and, by ordinary standards, unpleasant; yet it calls forth a deep instinctive response. Thus they are torn between repulsion and attraction . . . Therefore, the picture that claims our attention most immediately and completely is the one that, in its first impression, relates itself to ancestral fear."

—William Mortensen

The vast majority of books on horror criticism open with an almost masochistic need to justify why a book on horror criticism should exist. Long dismissed by academics and intellectuals, horror has now become the thesis/conference paper du jour, and yet a feeling persists among scholars that the genre is inadequate to withstand serious study. Horror fans don't feel this insecurity or embarassment. They already understand the thrill of repulsion that starts at the eye and moves through the body and mind, arriving at the void at the center of existence. This subliminal awareness that horror is the most genuine artistic metaphor for the human condition over the last 10,000 years must lie at the heart of its continued significance—more so than what postcolonial, race, gender, Marxist, or new historical criticism has offered us. This is not to say that Foucault, Kristeva, Adorno, and Fanon cannot tell horror fans something important about the genre. However, authors such as Denis Gifford, William K. Everson, David Pirie, Carlos Clarens, Barrie Pattison, Phil Hardy, Danny Peary, S. S. Prawer, and Robin Wood have already validated horror's place as a literary genre, not to mention works that would be seen as academically dubious yet have contributed far more to the study of horror than any theorist: *Castle of Frankenstein*, *Midi Minuit Fantastique*, *Photon*, *Cinefantastique*, *Midnight Marquee*, and *Little Shoppe of Horrors*, plus magazines and fanzines that stretched the boundaries of what horror cinema was and what horror journalism could cover.

The next wave of independent horror criticism took these aesthetic, historical, cultural, and psychological readings and pushed them well beyond the genre's limits (limits that were imposed from outside as well as self-imposed), as witnessed in the pages of

Psychotronic Video, Film Threat, Video Watchdog, European Trash Cinema, Deep Red, Sleazoid Express, Videooze, Gore Gazette, Shock Xpress, Ecco, and *Eyeball.* These publications exponentially deepened and expanded what horror was, is, and could be. As more and more books were devoted to the horror phenomena, two in particular beautifully epitomized this horror studies glasnost: Christopher Golden's *Cut! Horror Writers on Horror Film* (1992) and Cathal Tohill and Pete Tombs' *Immoral Tales: European Sex & Horror Movies, 1956–1984* (1995). Both of these books redefined the scope of horror criticism to encompass multiple genres and media, displaying writing that is smart, fun, and culturally informed, and doesn't make excuses for the sometimes glorious ridiculousness of the genre. These books share a passion for both the absurd lows and the transcendent highs that the horror genre is capable of.

This book was written in that spirit, looking at the phenomenon of horror in popular culture and connecting horror to other genres and cultural movements that have influenced and been influenced by horror: surrealism, existentialism, punk rock, the occult, heavy metal, industrial music, graphic arts, experimental cinema, trash culture, modernism, and postmodernism. The thread that connects these artistic, philosophical, political, and social expressions is the concept of transgression. Horror fulfills the need to push against, through, and beyond aesthetic, moralistic, and ideological boundaries to critique, define, and redefine what it means to exist, to be human, to explore states of being, to understand ourselves and the world around us (and perhaps the next world, too). The essays in this book cover horror films, music, television, literature, graphic arts, popular culture, and comic books—mediums that are the dominant forms of cultural expression in the late twentieth and early twenty-first centuries. (I have left out one medium: video games, not because of any arrogant dismissal but, rather, because of my own embarrassed ignorance. Surely, horror video games, like the infamous enigma *Sad Satan,* will be one of the most important horror media in the next decade, if they aren't already.) Works of horror deserve to be situated in the same rarefied air as the most challenging art forms of the last century, spoken of in the same awed yet nervous tones as the Dadists, William Burroughs, Francis Bacon, the Futurists, Throbbing Gristle, the Vienna Actionists, Philip K. Dick, and the *Apocalypse Culture* cadre.

The purpose of this book is to break down the opposition that has denied horror its place in the intellectual conversations of the last century. Horror writers, directors, musicians, and graphic artists have created masterpieces, but because their subject matter has been outside the post-Enlightenment, pragmatic, humanist, and scientific views of reality, these works are at best marginalized and at worst scapegoated as the wreckers of civilization. This book looks at social and artistic points of concurrence within the history of horror as well as throughout the cultural and intellectual landscape of the last century.

Horror might be the only genre that allows artists to express the full potential of cinema, literature, and the arts, insisting on a cathartic mix of the visceral and the philosophical, the instinctual and the contemporary, the beautiful and the repulsive, life affirming and life denying, demanding its practioners push the limits of imagination beyond previously acceptable boundaries. Horror is a perspective, a way of seeing, a way of knowing, a way of feeling, a way of existing (or not existing) when faced with a malevolent and uncaring universe. You can have your James Wan, Joss Whedon, J. J. Abrams, and Christopher Nolan, all examples of the genus that Gram Parsons would call "plastic dry fucks." Raise high the roof beams and welcome Ed Wood, Andy Milligan, and Ray Dennis Steckler, filmmakers that make up for their technical deficiencies and stylistic idiosyncrasies with skewed visions, individuality, and personal investment; broken muses full of ecstasy and pain.

Too many things make sense in modern horror: logical, explanations and motivations, A+B=C plots and characters that validate an ordered, positivist empirical world view in the end. Even the fascinating concept of eternal recurrence has been run into the ground by artistically bankrupt filmmakers who can't come up with a decent ending. Many recent horror films have interesting premises but falter in their clichéd

> Horror is a perspective, a way of seeing, a way of knowing, a way of feeling, a way of existing (or not existing) when faced with a malevolent and uncaring universe.

execution (the one exception is Fede Alvarez's *Evil Dead* remake, as the premise is old hat but the execution is anarchy incarnate). The contemporary horror film is a slave to realism rather than its destroyer; just count how many horror movies now include the obligatory "my cell phone has no service" or internet search scenes.

There is a thin line between suspending disbelief and insulting intelligence. That's why films and TV shows like *The Lords of Salem*, *Here Comes the Devil*, *Antichrist*, *Beyond the Black Rainbow*, *Berberian Sound Studio*, *Witching & Bitching*, *Only Lovers Left Alive*, *Under the Skin*, *It Follows*, *Hannibal*, and *True Detective* are the true crucibles for the current horror fan. If a work of horror is conservative in its message and expression, is it still horror? If it hasn't fucked your mind good (to paraphrase Captain Beefheart), you've been cheated. If it makes sense, it has failed. If it's quickly decipherable using a graduate-school ontological, epidemiological, or phenomenological approach, it's worthless. Perhaps horror's most valuable insight is to show us that truth and reality are not the same thing, that an obsession with what is "real" distances us from ourselves and keep us from having an authentic experience in the world.

The future of the horror genre must insist on rejecting banal, repressive realism and exploring Andre Breton's irrational superrealism, "the dream of the raw," throwing open the doors of the abattoir and drowning conventions and expectations in tidal waves of blood, releasing the inmates from the asylums, and allowing paranoia, the unconscious, and delusions free rein. Horror needs to subordinate the ordinary human perspective to the absurd, the fantastique, the kosmische. Horror must be the eternal rebel against imposed reality and the confines of civilization, descending into the wretched and debased in order to attain the heights of artistic expression and human awareness.

Film

Chapter 1

The 13 Most Disturbing Films That Aren't Horror Movies

The horror film is often criticized for glorifying the dark side of humanity, reveling in our basest desires and fears in order to produce some cheap thrill of repulsion. This is a rather unfair judgment, as many films outside the genre hold a terrifyingly lucid mirror up to our own worst thoughts and behaviors. Transgressive films can come in any guise or flavor, just as long as they offend dominant belief systems. These films explore the forbidden so we don't have to; they show how arbitrary and contingent "taste" is and how supposedly objective regulations on freedom of expression are used to control, oppress, and exploit. Transgressive cinema (not to be confused with the equally glorious Cinema of Transgression) is an approach to film that refuses any set form, structure, or content, blurring the boundaries of high and low art where prurient delights and deep insight walk hand in hand. Through their blasphemy, immorality, and illegality, these movies reject the commodification of deviance and the buying and selling of a radical agenda. This is art that can't be easily absorbed into the culture industry or appropriated into the social hierarchy as a token of upper-class elitism.

Srđan Spasojević's *A Serbian Film* may have taken cinema to its most nihilistic, dead-souled zenith, but when torture, child abuse, necrophilia, incest, mur-

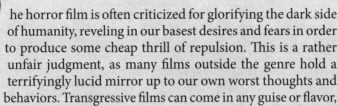

The more gore, the easier it is to look away, to dismiss, to laugh.

der, vicious sexual assault, and "newborn porn" are constantly shoved in your face, even death by raped eye socket (an interesting metaphor for the effect of transgressive media) seems meh. Perhaps the true secret of an effective disturbing film is not an endless deluge of shocking images but showing a bit of restraint, pulling back a bit before pushing us to the edge, never forcing us all the way over but offering us no other option except to step off the ledge under our own volition. The more gore, the easier it is to look away, to dismiss, to laugh. The transgressive might end in the graphic, but it must start with an agenda to subvert and expose. What separates these films from the most stomach churning, chunk-blower flicks is that the truly transgressive film has a philosophy, and that's what makes it dangerous (as noted by Lynne Gorman in Cronenberg's genre-destroying masterpiece *Videodrome*). Here are thirteen of the most disturbing films that aren't horror movies, that take the viewer to places that once ventured into can never be forgotten. But remember that when you gaze into the abyss, the abyss gazes back.

13.

To Be Twenty (1978)—Fernando Di Leo

This Age of Aquarius meets *Deliverance* Italian shocker chokes the life out of any hope for the Love Generation. Misogyny, animalistic voraciousness, and cruel ignorance consistently win out over the idealism, acceptance, and gentle civility of the protagonists. Two women hitchhike across Italy, exploring the sensual freedoms that come with youth, but find only hatred, greed, and much worse. Still they strive in the anticipation of finding a hippie utopia of peace, love, and understanding, or at least finding themselves and having a good time before giving in to the harsh world of adulthood. The world crushes them, but that inevitability involves the characters being harassed, hunted down, and finally violently assaulted. A group of rustic brutes beat the young women savagely, stripping and humiliating them. One woman has her skull caved in, while the other is raped with a tree branch. The film ends with one of the assailants stepping on the girls' cassette player, causing it to turn on and play an insipid disco song, a requiem for the flower children. Di Leo's experience directing heartless crime films sets the downer tone for *To Be Twenty*, but whereas the viewer's expectations for a Poliziotteschi helps to mitigate the astonishing violence of that genre, seeing the same level of brutality visited on two innocent women is almost too much to bear.

12.

White Lightnin' (2009)—Dominic Murphy

White Lightnin' is a fire-and-brimstone bio pic about Jesco White, the so-called "dancing outlaw." If even half of the events in the film actually happened to poor Jesco, it's astounding that he's still alive, never mind still dancing. Murphy's film presents life in rural West Virginia as a Darwinian nightmare where only huffing every chemical available and committing every crime imaginable makes existence bearable. Jesco's youth is a lesson in abject cruelty as he is victimized in reform school, addicted to sniffing lighter fluid and gasoline, and chained to his bed to prevent further delinquencies. His struggles to stay on the straight and narrow path to Jesus drive him to the brink of madness, which is redeemed only by dancing and his love for his common-law wife. Jesco's apotheosis comes when he leaves the grim realities of Appalachian life and descends into an unimaginable realm of suffering, masochism, and self-mutilation—the only way to salvation. Edward Hogg is amazing as Jesco, but child actor Owen Campbell, playing Young Jesco, is a revelation. The soundtrack, using the unhinged music of Hasil Adkins to stunning effect, almost gives us too much insight into the tortured and unstable psyche of Jesco White.

11.

Repulsion (1965)—Roman Polanski

No stranger to life's horrors, Polanski's first English language film is a nauseating indictment of how men drive women insane. The protagonist Carol is leered at, judged, and bullied into paralyzing neurosis. As she mentally decomposes (like the skinned rabbit left on a plate in her apartment), the walls crack, an unknown man molests her, and disembodied hands reach out to violate her. She lashes out against these hallucinations by killing her boyfriend and then slashing to death her lecherous landlord. But even these desperate acts of violent resistance can't stop the gazes that haunt her. Catherine Deneuve proves why she is one of the greatest actresses of all time by bringing a deep pathos to a psychotic, catatonic victim who has no hope of regaining her identity. The final scene in which Polanski hints at the true cause of Carol's tragedy is particularly devastating. *Repulsion* is the first entry in Polanski's so-called "apartment trilogy," which also includes *Rosemary's Baby* and *The Tenant*—films showing that living in the city doesn't guarantee a cultured existence. While the latter two films in the trilogy are masterworks, *Repulsion* is in a class by itself in terms of indicting the viewer in the main character's victimization.

10.

Bug (2006)—William Friedkin

Based on Tracey Letts's play, *Bug* is a paranoiac's dream come true: conspiracy thinking that sucks in all those within the obsessive's sphere of influence. Agnes (Ashley Judd) is a used-up shell of a waitress who has been kicked around by life and her ex-husband. She meets Peter (Michael Shannon), a recently discharged solider, who responds to her need to feel some sort of connection to another human being. That aching desperation blinds her to Peter's psychosis, delusions that involve government experiments, mysterious phone calls, and the infestation of microscopic bugs meant to torment and spy on the couple. Peter's insistence and earnestness draws Agnes deeper into madness as they isolate themselves through sealing up their room. Peter is convinced that the insects have now invaded his body, pulling out a tooth to "prove" it. As they become more erratic and paranoid, they lose all sense of self and reality. But was Peter crazy or just in a heightened state of total awareness? What makes this film so terrifying is the notion that loneliness and the need to be loved by anyone can so easily be used to manipulate and dominate another human being. No one is immune to Peter's persuasive rhetoric; even the viewer can start to feel the itch. Skin-crawling, to say the least.

9.

Gummo (1997)—Harmony Korine

If any film makes a case for the destructive power of a tornado, this is it. *Gummo* provides a sickening laundry list of things to do in a go-nowhere, poverty-stricken Mid-western town: abuse drugs, pimp out handicapped family members, torture animals, sell dead cats to a Chinese restaurant, wrestle chairs, put duct tape on your nipples to make them puffy, assault children, gay bash, burglarize homes, tape bacon to bathroom walls, euthanize old people. The film basically rapes the American dream. Following a bunch of degenerate characters around an almost post-apocalyptic landscape (I wonder if these people would even know that the apocalypse happened), *Gummo*'s aesthetic is a slurred collage of 8mm, 16 mm, 35mm, VHS, Polaroid, and digital film that captures real people and real environs, some so cockroach-infested that the film crew demanded hazmat suits. These characters don't live; they barely exist, and you are left wondering why they even bother to go on. You know a film is horrific when suicide seems like a viable option. Bombarded by scene after scene of downhome repugnance set to a cacophony of black metal, *Gummo*'s luckiest character ends up being a young woman who finds out she has cancer and needs a mastectomy. Korine's directorial debut is one of the most devastating portraits of America that you can ever bear to watch. No wonder Jean Luc Godard loved it.

8.

Bring Me the Head of Alfredo Garcia
(1974)—Sam Peckinpah

None of Peckinpah's movies are a walk in the park, but this 1974 downer has to be his most nihilistic. It offers viewers not a single character with a redeeming quality unless you count the decapitated head. Warren Oates plays Bennie, a down-on-his-luck piano player rotting away in Mexico. Lured by the bounty on Alfredo Garcia's head, Bennie finds out that Garcia has died in a car accident and all he has to do to get his money is dig up the body and behead the corpse. As in all Peckinpah's films, things go from bad to holocaust pretty quickly, as Bennie must fend off the mob and Garcia's family to claim his prize. Every character is a user, has an angle, and is willing to shoot his own mother in the back if it will give him even a slight advantage in life. Trust is nearly impossible to come by in Peckinpah's world, and if you need to rely on another person, you'd better keep one eye on them at all times. Oates is incredible in his role (basically imitating Peckinpah) as he has overwrought conversations with Garcia's head, confessing his feelings of guilt and self-loathing to the decomposing, fly-encrusted cabaza. In the end, Bennie finishes his ghastly quest, but all that is left for those involved in this tale of revenge is disgrace. Violence doesn't bring honor, only tragedy and meaninglessness.

7.

Titicut Follies (1967)—Frederick Wiseman

Documentaries, by nature, have the potential to be disturbing because we expect them to offer unflinching veracity. Not that all documentaries live up to this ideal, but some shove our faces into the filth of human existence. Wiseman's documentary reveals conditions inside the Bridgewater State Hospital for the Criminally Insane in Massachusetts. Incredibly, the correctional superintendent agreed to let Wiseman shoot there, and what Wiseman filmed caused the governor of Massachusetts to get an injunction banning the film, a court case that lasted until 1991. This showcase of horrors seems neverending: patients humiliated, tortured, and neglected. The force-feeding of inmates is particularly grueling to witness, especially as you see cigarette ashes dropping into the food tube. To see people treated as disposable things, arbitrarily punished and degraded, is not only shocking but indicts all of humanity in the crimes of these supposed "guardians" of the weak and infirm. The "follies" of the title refers to a talent show that the inmates are forced to participate in, but it could also represent the absurdity of power and the idiocy of human progress.

6.

Caterpillar (2010)—Koji Wakamatsu

Movies about war are often the most brutal depictions of human behavior. Yet films about the consequences of war seem more disturbing than the battlefield itself. Based on a banned short story by the immortal Edogawa Rampo, Wakamatsu's film eviscerates militancy and nationalism as the viewer is confronted with a soldier reduced to existing like a "caterpillar," without arms and legs. Horribly wounded in WWII, Lieutenant Kurokawa returns to his village as a "god warrior," deified by the emperor as a symbol of Japan's determination and sacrifice. Although this living (barely) god is venerated

THE 13 MOST DISTURBING FILMS THAT ARENT HORROR MOVIES

by his fellow countrymen, his wife's life becomes a hell on earth, a condition made unbearable by her husband's total reliance on her for his basic needs, including constant demands for sex. As husband and wife try to cohabit, feelings of anger, disgust, guilt, and resentment build to a revolting and suffocating height as the husband drains the life from his wife.

Although *Caterpillar*'s story may lend itself to a comparison with Dalton Trumbo's *Johnny Got His Gun*, Wakamatsu's film denies the viewer any hope for the main characters or even a shred of compassion for them. The film incorporates archival news reels and propaganda films to highlight that the true causalities of war are often human dignity, compassion, and reason. Wakamatsu's incredible cinematic career has never shied away from the controversial, political, and wretched, but *Caterpillar* doesn't even offer the catharsis of transgression, just a body and soul-destroying numbness.

5.

Irreversible (2002)—Gaspar Noe

Lumped with the new French extremity movement, *Irreversible* is about much more than the blasé inhumaneness of so many contemporary "extreme" movies. Told in reverse chronological order, Noe makes the motives and justifications for revenge illogical, irrational, and even more selfish than they usually are. Looking to avenge the sexual assault of his girlfriend (Monica Belluci), Marcus (Vincent Cassel) becomes the very horror he hopes to destroy as he rampages across Paris searching for the perpetrator. Infamous for its scene in which a fire extinguisher is used to bash in a victim's head (Nicolas Winding Refn paid tribute to this attack in *Drive*) and the seemingly endless rape scene, Noe's film never glorifies violence but portrays it as a sickening cancer that eats away at victim and perpetrator alike. The takes prolong the action unmercifully until one has to look away. Proving that some deeds are irreversible, the film acts as a terrible warning to those who would fight monsters not to become monsters themselves. Noe's approach seems more socially responsible than other revenge fantasies that coerce the audience into desiring bloody vengeance, and yet the acts of violence are so graphic, one gets the sense that there is some glee in rubbing our faces in it.

4.

Star of David: Beauty Hunting (1979)—Noribumi Suzuki

Probably the most disreputable film in the already morally objectionable Roman Porno series, *Star of David: Beauty Hunting* suggests that violent perversity is inherited and inescapable, so you may as well embrace it and give in to the natural impulses of biology. Tatsuya is a respectable young gentleman from a good home who seduces women and then tortures, humiliates, and rapes them in his basement (one of his brutal escapades involves the use of a German shepherd). The reason for his sadism is that his mother was assaulted and impregnated by a serial rapist, thus dooming the unborn child to a life of cruelty and crime. This son of a rapist feels no guilt; in fact, he thrives on his heredity and uses it to justify his lusts and atrocities. Coming off like a Japanese De Sade or Peter Sotos, Tatsuya sees sexual violence as his right to impose his will on lesser humans (alluded to in the title's reference to the anti-Semitism in Nazi Germany). When one of his victims escapes and finds help in a random person on the street, we think Tatsuya's days of carefree torture are over, and yet in one of the worst examples of movie serendipity ever, the poor woman has actually run into Tatsuya's deranged natural father. The father and son reunion soon escalates the viciousness and depravity of their crimes. Suzuki's nauseating combination of Darwinism, national socialism, Christian martyrdom, and pornographic nothingness is blasphemous on every level. This is truly a film in which there is no hope for humanity.

3.

Eraserhead (1977)—David Lynch

Teen pregnancy is a national concern, and the proposed strategies for addressing it through education or abstinence have been ineffectual. I propose that we show all teenagers *Eraserhead*. Not only would it stop them from having pre-marital sex, it would cause them to mutilate their sexual organs to prevent even the potential for sex. David Lynch's anxieties over fatherhood resulted in his first full-length film, a grotesque meditation on the body, sexual desire, and the revulsion that comes from it. Poor Henry (Jack Nance) is forced into a loveless marriage because his girlfriend is pregnant. Meeting your significant other's parents is often nerve-racking, but Henry has to deal with epileptic seizures, a bleeding-chicken dinner, and sexual come-ons from his future mother-in-law. Once the baby is born,

THE 13 MOST DISTURBING FILMS THAT AREN'T HORROR MOVIES

it is a repulsive monstrosity resembling a crying, screaming, puking penis. His wife leaves him to take care of Junior and his only escape is with the Lady in the Radiator (whose ovaries are on her cheeks and who steps on sperm to destroy them) and the alluring next-door neighbor. The pressures of fatherhood are just too much for Henry and the only way out is to kill his progeny before it kills him. *Eraserhead*'s industrial environment is as bleak as its message, suggesting that our instinctive urge to procreate is a ticking time bomb ready to blow up in our crotches and leave us chained to the horrors of family forever. *Eraserhead* has to be the most tactile film ever made (not that you would ever touch anything in this film). The cracks, bumps, ridges, crevices, and goo threaten to entrap both characters and viewers in its libidinal maelstrom.

2.

The Act of Seeing with One's Own Eyes (1971)—Stan Brakhage

Forget *Faces of Death* or any of those mondo sleazoid shockumentaries; this is the real thing. Filmed in a Pittsburgh morgue, Brakhage documents actual autopsy procedures with no commentary or special effects (the title of the film is a translation of the ancient Greek word *autopsia*). There is no morbid philosophizing or grim humor attempting to rationalize or sensationalize. It is a direct encounter with our own mortality. The scalpel cuts through skin, fat, and tissue with no hesitation. Scalps are pulled back to expose the skull and brain in a businesslike manner. Brakhage demystifies the body through the static depiction of organ removal and embalming. If cinema is about its power to show us things that are hidden or obscured in everyday life, then *The Act of Seeing with One's Own Eyes* is one of the purest examples of moviemaking ever. Although disgusting, the theme is liberating and asks viewers to confront their own existential condition. Brakhage's films often decontextualize seemingly universal human experiences (his *Window Water Baby Moving* shows us the birth of his daughter up close and personal), turning them into moments of wonder and splendor divorced from any social, cultural, or political ideologies. Plus, you get to see a face peeled off.

1.

Salo (1975)—Pier Paolo Pasolini

Pasolini's ruthlessly honest depiction of the devastating abuse of power is inspired by De Sade, structured like *The Inferno*, and hits like a razor-covered 2x4. The film focuses on four fascist power brokers in the final days of Mussolini's Italy. Wealthy sadists abduct teenage boys and girls and use their bodies to satisfy every carnal perversity imaginable. The depravity sinks both predator and prey through the Circle of Manias, the Circle of Shit, and the Circle of Blood (Coil's epic *Horse Rotorvator* could sound-track these circles of the abject). Human beings are turned into mere receptacles for any violent fantasy or sexual whim. The victims are totally debased: severely raped, viciously branded, horribly mutilated, and made to consume feces. Power is revealed as the ultimate dehumanizing corruption that informs not only politics but human relationships as well. The victims have no savior or recompense; they are merely used, abused, and thrown away in the most efficient manner. Even worse, they start to turn on each other and implicitly justify the control and domination of their cruel masters. Though there might be more graphic and extreme films when it comes to the rending of the body's sanctity, no other film so thoroughly eviscerates the human condition, revealing a bottomless depravity that objectively cuts across time, space, class, and rank. The film is banned in Iran, Vietnam, Malaysia, Sri Lanka, and the United Arab Emirates. A video store owner in Cincinnati was arrested on obscenity charges for offering it for rent. Pasolini, always a controversial character, avoided having to defend his film when he was murdered by a male prostitute shortly before *Salo* was unleashed on the world. God rest his sick soul.

THE 13 MOST DISTURBING FILMS THAT AREN'T HORROR MOVIES

Honorable Mention

Taxi Driver
Visitor Q
Calvaire
In a Glass Cage
Angst
The Life and Death of a Porno Gang
Henry: Portrait of a Serial Killer
Martyrs
Michael
The White Ribbon
Kurutta Ippêji
Cruising
Ravenous

Chapter 2

The 13 Most Sickening Art House Horror Movies

The art house is a fading phenomenon in American culture. Maybe it's more accurate to say the art house has been transformed by the proliferation of home media, online viewing options, on-demand, torrent sites, and prestige video labels like Criterion, Eclipse, and Kino. The thrill of going to see an obscure foreign or experimental film just isn't as magical when you can download the entire oeuvres of Fellini, Bergman, and Cassavetes onto your hard drive. Though the internet does provide unbelievable access, there was something special about going to a small independent theater to see arty, off-the-wall movies surrounded by fellow cineastes (okay, maybe not surrounded—there were lots of empty seats). The seats were kind of uncomfortable, but that made you concentrate all the more on the film. They served coffee instead of Coke, scones instead of Sour Patch Kids, and there were no nachos nor mini-pizzas in sight. Certainly, this was not for the masses; it was a journey to an extraordinary place unconcerned with commercial appeal, sort of like making an excursion to a gallery or museum installation. These were challenging niche films focused on aesthetics and style. If the film wasn't daring, indecipherable, intellectual, or shocking, it shouldn't be shown.

On the surface, you might think that these types of films are the antithesis of horror's visceral grittiness. And yet when you realize that art house films deal with life and death, reality and fantasy, splendor and disgust, violence and sex, and the ecstasy and despair of human existence, the correlation starts to make sense.

There is no middle ground…

These two worlds have overlapped in some of the most audacious horror films ever to grace the screen, whether it was in a Greenwich Village repertory cinema or a Tuscaloosa drive-in. These directors were creating great art whether they knew it or not, and it was through art houses that these incredible films were brought to screaming life to terrify, amaze, and inspire all who seek out these rare gems. There is no middle ground: either they are highly stylized, symbolic, and phantasmagorical or unbearably primal and grotty. Hollywood seems another world away from the universe these films occupy. Art house horror isn't concerned with entertaining you or providing an escape from your problems; rather, it rubs your face in the joys and miseries of being; it has one foot in Cannes and the other in the sewer. Not just a kind of film, art house horror is a sensibility, an informed approach to cinema, reality, and the self. Here are thirteen specimens of that curious genus: art house horror.

13.

Fascination (1979)—Jean Rollin

The works of Jean Rollin are a crucible for art house horror fans. Either you will be enraptured by the pure poetry of his films or you will want to slash your wrists so that something actually happens during your viewing. There's a fine line between mesmerizing and boring, and Rollin treads that line nimbly. On the surface, the amount of nudity, sex, and viciousness in the average Rollin film would send it straight to the top of any horror lover's must-see list, but Rollin's tendency to wander and drift, fixating on images for inordinate amounts of time, can test even a Tarkovsky fan's patience. Rollin's cinematic rhythms are an acquired taste, but 1978's *Fascination* achieves a sophisticated balance of elegance and barbarity. In the early 1900's, rich Parisians drink the blood of animals as therapy for anemia. In the countryside, four criminals are on the lam with stolen booty and force their way into a chateau staffed by two young maids awaiting the return of the mistress of the house. Taken hostage, the captive women turn their amorous attentions to the leader of the gang, which creates jealousy and dissension among the criminals. The promiscuous maids are not as welcoming as they appear, and when the mistress returns, their trap is sprung, giving the women the perverse opportunity to remedy the lack of iron in their blood. In Rollin's films sex never heals; it's a mode of deception and entrapment, lulling one into a false sense of security and connection. The only thing that can be trusted is blood, and *Fascination* offers plenty of it. The violence is gracefully presented yet ghastly in its consequences, as the licentiousness of these acts poisons every character in the movie. The ugliness of their behavior hides behind the beauty of Rollin's images, no more so than in the iconic image of euro-goddess Brigitte Lahie swinging a scythe, a bare creamy white thigh juxtaposed with the cold metal blade. I've always wondered if Rollin's naturalistic psycho-sexual surrealism had any influence on Louis Malle's Ionesco-meets-Wild-Kingdom bizzaro flick *Black Moon*. The score by Philippe D'Arm is a droning masterpiece as enchanting and disarming as the film it complements.

12.

Marebito (2004)—Takashi Shimizu

A popular art house theme is voyeurism, the salacious gaze, explorations of perception and filmmaking.

Hilarity, heartbreak, brutality, and whimsy are all part of the world according to Miike. Although he is known for the lurid aspects of his filmography, Miike's subdued, character-driven films are some of his most memorable. His 1999 film *Audition* focuses on Shigeharu, a lonely middle-aged man looking for a relationship after his wife dies. With a movie producer friend, he concocts a fake casting audition to meet women. There he meets Asami, a beautiful, soulful woman with whom he feels an instant attraction. Slowly, Asami's lies start to pile up, but Shigeharu's need to have his attraction reciprocated leads him further into her web of deceit. His pursuit of a woman just out of reach leaves him exposed to unimaginable tortures, both emotional and physical.

Audition starts out as a tragic romance, a story of the risk of starting a new relationship. But when severed body parts, a squirming bag, and a dog bowl filled with vomit pop up, the film takes a serious left turn toward the grotesque. Love is the ultimate repulsive horror because we must open ourselves up completely to reap the benefits of the relationship. That openness can lead to control, ownership, and abuse, a threat that *Audition* pushes to an appalling extreme. The film's emotional detachment and methodical pace make the eruption of violence and madness all the more sickening. Miike's camera never flinches from the atrocities, but it is the sadistic glee of the perpetrator that truly disturbs. In the proud art house shocker tradition of Nagisa Oshima, *Auditon* is the crowning jewel in Miike's expansive halo of genius.

10.

Don't Look Now (1973)—Nicolas Roeg

Supposedly, Nicolas Roeg's mantra on the set of *Don't Look Now* was "anything can happen." The randomness of the universe is at the heart of this film's terror, and a misreading of coincidence can have horrible consequences, especially when fixation on the past and obsession with the future blinds one to present dangers. *Don't Look Now* is a modern-day Greek tragedy: A couple travel to Venice to heal after their daughter accidentally drowns. The husband buries himself in his work restoring an old church but is distracted by glimpses of his dead daughter, a psychic who claims the daughter's spirit is trying to alert him to something, and a killer stalking the winding streets. Adapted from a Daphne du Maurier short story, the film is as labyrinthine as the city in which it takes place. Roeg's intuitive, magical editing style suggests that time is cyclical. Past, present, and future run parallel, occasionally crossing over each other and leaving paradoxical a-synchronistic traces that recur across our lives. The couple's sorrow shackles them to the past.

THE 13 MOST SICKENING ART HOUSE HORROR MOVIES

Symbols, objects, and signs warn them of the peril of being "stuck" in one time stream (the film's dominant color is danger-signalling red). But their inability to recognize these messages leads to disaster.

Roeg's patterns create a looping, doubling resonance that can't be broken until the characters' grief and guilt are met head-on rather than sublimated to work or sex. In this "stuck" environment, everything is reversed: certainty is unreliable, sight is blindness, water is death. Characters are constantly falling, items are constantly breaking, and no one can clearly express themselves or understand the events unfolding around them. The mosaic of life only comes together at the moment we lose our grip. Death is inescapable and cannot be banished to the past or projected into the future. *Don't Look Now* is a self-fulfilling prediction of mortality and chance: the more the characters try to impose a structure on the universe, the more it unravels. Roeg's challenging but invigorating films in this genre have consistently incorporated elements of horror and dread, culminating in the delightful *The Witches* in 1992.

9.

Dark Waters (1993)—Mariano Baino

One of the most difficult challenges in horror cinema is constructing a successful H. P. Lovecraft adaptation. His atmospheric, philosophical prose doesn't easily fit into the narrative structure of your average film, and so cinema inspired by the great author is often Lovecraftian rather than a straight adaptation. The Lovecraftian mood demands style, patience, and the artistry of the weird temperament. A Lovecraftian film has to negotiate the physical, psychological, and existential, starting on the human scale and expanding to the cosmic, dwarfing the individual and our place in the universe. *Dark Waters* begins with a young woman's journey to a remote island convent in search of her mother. Soon she discovers that these nuns are not part of any orthodox sect, but practice the worship of ancient creatures who are treated like gods.

Tapping into the eerie vibe of *The Shadow over Innsmouth* and *The Festival*, the secret primeval rites performed in catacombs beneath a decrepit chapel make you feel like you are watching something not meant for the uninitiated. The authenticity of the convent's deformed inhabitants and their arcane iconography seem to invoke an antediluvian veracity that rends the veil of our human-centered reality. Much like Lovecraft, Baino's style is his substance, meticulously composing his shots for maximum effect, willing to sacrifice logic and plot points to create startling images that delve deep into the unconscious. Shot on location in the Ukraine, *Dark Waters* radiates an old-world, esoteric primitivism that doesn't require words, reason, or explanation. Bypassing rational thought, you can feel the elemental truth of Baino's themes.

8.

Possession (1981)—Andrzej Zulawski

Relationships are hell, to misquote Sartre. The highs can be heavenly but the lows can be agonizing and soul- destroying. Most movies are about the trials of love in one form or another, but *Possession* has to be the most fraught, high-strung, emotionally draining drama ever. Documenting the breakup and breakdown of Mark and Anna, ex-pats living in Berlin, *Possession* drags its characters through the mud, over broken glass, and into an acid bath of passion, despair, and pain. As the couple careen toward divorce, the extremes of loving and loathing unleash frenzied violence, self-mutilation, murder, doppelgangers, and a tentacled creature that evolves as it copulates. The film's characters embody the good, bad, and ugly aspects of Mark and Anna's personalities. Sam Neil gives an amazing performance as Mark, vacillating from dutiful father to abusive stalker to murderer, but it is Isabelle Adjani's Anna, a frenzied, hysterical explosion of neuroses, that transcends film and breaks through into another realm. Adjani's struggle to be an individual and escape the confines of marriage leads her to lash out at the men who attempt to lock her into one identity. Although the violence she wreaks on the male species is savage, it is nothing compared to the violence she does to herself: cutting her throat with an electric knife, throwing herself against subway walls as she miscarries, and allowing a slimy monster to continually violate her. (Adjani's performance is so raw that a rumor spread that the emotional toll caused her to attempt suicide.)

Everything breaks down in *Possession*: personalities, relationships, language, reality, even the Cold-War-divided landscape of Berlin looks devastated. The finale links personal annihilation with the US and Soviet Union's wish for mutual annihilation. Żuławski wrote the script while going through his own angst-ridden divorce, and his nihilism and agony infect every frame. Graced with creepy special effects from Carlo Rambaldi, *Possession* is an exorcism of personal trauma using art and horror as the catharsis they were meant to be. This film must have influenced Von Trier's extraordinary *Antichrist*.

7.

Cemetery Man (1994)—Michele Soavi

Cemetery Man (or the more aesthetically pleasing title *Dellamorte Dellamore*) is the culmination of thirty years of Italian horror cinema. It brings together all the strands of this regional genre of fantastique film and is second only to the US in originality,

THE 13 MOST SICKENING ART HOUSE HORROR MOVIES

imagination, and influence. It is both comedy and tragedy, illuminating the beauty of decay, the abyss of existence, and the edge of sanity. Most important, the film erases the line between life and death, Eros and Thantos, and suggests that we fashion our own reality. Based on a novel by Dylan Dog fumetti author Tiziano Sclavi and directed by wunderkind Michele Soavi, *Cemetery Man* is the saga of Francesco Dellamorte, a grave digger in a rural Italian village. His job description involves killing returners—the recently revived denizens of the cemetery. Ridiculed by the townspeople, saddled with a mentally challenged subordinate, and unable to share his lonely life with the living, Dellamorte falls in love with Anna, an attractive widow who happens to be turned on by ossuaries.

This graveyard romance sets off a chain of events that include a jealous zombie husband, a wedding involving a decapitated living head kept in a TV, and recurring characters and situations that suggest Dellamorte's sanity is deteriorating. As his mind starts to come undone, Dellamorte's fears, desires, and frustrations are projected onto all the characters in his warped construction of reality. Unable to deal with these horrid fragments of his personality, he eliminates them until he is face to face with Death. Even then, he can't tell the difference between the living and the dead. In the end, Dellamorte can't escape himself and can only retreat into blissful negation and mental degeneracy.

Soavi's film is remarkably complex, yet exquisitely simple. It explores the foundational experiences of life, death, love, and sex, showing that these binaries are more closely aligned then we would like to admit. The scene between Dellamorte and Anna in the ossuary is a delirious deconstruction of taboos: skeletal hands ripping her tight dress, colored scarves billowing and preventing Dellamorte from attaining his desire, the fetishizing of rot, and the petite morit of carnality. The Italian title perfectly encompasses this strange connection between love and death, perhaps the two most seminal themes of the art house.

6.

Lemora: A Child's Tale of the Supernatural (1973)
—Richard Blackburn

The literary device of the bildungsroman, the journey from innocence to experience, is another popular art house trope. A young protagonist goes out into the world and finds only vice, hypocrisy, and evil. Will the protagonist hold on to youthful ideals or become jaded and corrupt? *Lemora: A Child's Tale of the Supernatural* falls into this category through the story of Lila Lee, a thirteen-year-old orphan raised by a preacher in the warm bosom of the church. Lila receives a letter asking her to visit her dying father in the far-off, wicked town of Astaroth. Warned by the preacher not to leave, Lee runs away, beginning a journey of realization and temptation involving budding sexuality, predatory men, vampiric creatures, and the sensually enthralling Lemora, an enigmatic woman who seeks to shield Lila from the outside world. Lemora is revealed to be a vampire, feeding on children and holding Lila's father hostage as bait to lure Lila into her mysterious realm. Two types of vampires try to claim Lila: savage, animalistic males and sophisticated women. Vampirism is the metaphor for maturation and Lila needs to choose between patriarchal servitude (which includes the preacher's religious control) and matriarchal dominance. Either way, Lila will be initiated into relationships that will use her in some fashion, and she must decide whether to take the passive or active role.

Blackburn's film echoes the work of Bruno Bettleheim, seeing fairy tales as cautionary parables that warn vulnerable children about the horrors of adulthood and the rapacious motives of grown-ups who should be protecting them but could end up exploiting them. Including the Catholic church in its critique of the predatory machinations of the adult world supposedly got the film condemned by the Catholic Film Board. Interestingly, Blackburn references Lovecraft in several scenes, specifically the terrifying bus ride to Astaroth, which alludes to *The Shadow over Innsmouth*, another story of self-discovery and transformation. *Lemora: A Child's Tale of the Supernatural* introduced the world to the talents of actress Cheryl Lynn "Rainbeaux" Smith, who went on to grace such exploitation classics as *Caged Heat*, *Phantom of the Paradise*, *The Swinging Cheerleaders*, *Revenge of the Cheerleaders*, *The Pom Pom Girls*, and *Laserblast*, as well as drumming in a Runaways side project with Joan Jett.

5.

House (1977)—Nobuhiko Obayashi

When Toho Studios asked director Nobuhiko Obayashi to make an action film that would rival the popularity of *Jaws*, not even Criswell could have predicted the surreal, phantasmagorical concoction that Obayashi whipped up. *House* (or *Hausu* in its original tongue) filters the trials and tribulations of being a teenage girl through an absurdist, pop-art ghost story in which the young women protagonists are basically consumed by a haunted house. Dealing with her father's remarriage, Gorgeous travels to her aunt's home for summer vacation, bringing along her school chums Prof, Melody, Kung Fu, Mac (as in stoMACh), Sweet, and Fantasy—spunky girls who embody their nicknames. They soon realize that all is not kosher with the

THE 13 MOST SICKENING ART HOUSE HORROR MOVIES

mysterious aunt and her creepy house. Evil spirits, a ghost cat, and various household items terrorize the houseguests, devouring and absorbing them into the bizarre surroundings. The events almost defy description: a disembodied head bites a girl's behind, a mattress commits a deadly assault, fingers are bitten off by a piano, a malevolent light fixture attacks, plasma-spewing paintings create a maelstrom of blood, severed body parts take on a life of their own, and there is a spiteful grandfather clock. You'll never look at a watermelon the same way.

Although the events are exceedingly ridiculous, Obayashi (with help from his daughter who gave him script ideas) takes seriously childhood fears that are routinely dismissed by adults, staging them the way a child would perceive the supernatural. Ignoring logical explanations, the movie's set pieces are enlivened by a wondrous, anything-can-happen innocence that would seem very real and make total sense to the wild, unspoiled imagination. In an amazing show of cinematic confidence, Obayashi stunningly mixes and matches genres and styles constantly, jumping from teen melodrama to music video to newsreels to historical romance to comedy to martial arts to gory horror. The plot of this anarchic film also contains a somber message about the effects of war and tragedy on successive generations. Amazingly, this off-kilter, wabi sabi of a film was a box office hit in Japan but didn't threaten the status of Spielberg's blockbuster.

4.

The House with Laughing Windows (1976)
—Pupi Avati

The works of Pupi Avati have been neglected by many genre fans put off by the lack of overt sex, butchery, and flash typical of most Italian horror films. Avati's films are measured, deliberate, and morose. They are enigmatically moody exercises in trepidation and menace, like if you asked Bresson to make a giallo. The physical violence is rough, but the psychological and emotional cruelty is even worse. The theme of discovery underpins his horror films, especially *The House with the Laughing Windows*, in which the protagonist's dawning awareness unlocks a mystery that brings hideous, self-destroying knowledge. Stefano is an artist who has been hired to work on a peeling fresco decorating an old church in a rural town. The original artist went mad and disappeared, and the painting's subject is obscured by the extensive damage. As Stefano slowly restores the image, he disentangles the strange relationships and personalities of the village residents, personified by two creepy sisters who seem to have more facts about the fresco than they let on.

Filmed in the stark, sun-baked Emilia-Romagna region in northern Italy, *The House with the Laughing Windows* may sound like a typical giallo, but its documentary realism and dour attitude toward viciousness puts it more in the realm of Pasolini than Argento (Avati did uncredited work on Pasolini's infamous *Salo*). The unrelenting sun illuminates everything except Stefano's ability to see past the surface of things, ironic given his task in the village. The tone of desperation and isolation hangs heavily over the film, with the sardonic, "laughing" windows commenting on the history of secret brutality that poisons the town. In 1983, Avanti made another art house horror masterpiece called *Zeder*, a chilling meditation on the thin line between life and death.

3.

Kwaidan (1964)—Masaki Kobayashi

One of the seminal art house horrors, *Kwaidan* is the cinematic equivalent of a haiku. It is a controlled, elegiac film that reflects the seasonal imagery of the traditional Japanese poetic form. *Kwaidan* is an anthology consisting of four adaptations of uncanny Japanese folk tales taken from the work of story collector Lafcadio Hearn. All four stories are haunted by revenants and/or spirits that become involved in the lives of humans, often delivering a tragic karmic balance to their indiscretions or hubris. The most famous sequence is probably "Hoichi the Earless," the story of a blind musician plagued by the vengeful ghosts of warriors demanding to hear epic ballads (John Milius paid homage to this segment in *Conan the Barbarian*). But the most exquisite sequence is "The Woman of the Snow," in which a woodcutter is burdened with a beautiful yet terrible secret. The set design and cinematography (Yoshio Miyajima truly paints with light) are mesmerizing: wide-angle, vibrant, expressionistic landscapes with abstract colors and ethereal shapes dwarf the actors, emphasizing our miniscule status in the natural and supernatural world. In this frozen fairy-tale realm, a giant eye looks down upon the vast icy stillness—a gorgeous but deadly environment, much like the apparition who stalks the winter frost.

The four stories reflect the balance of the seasons, and Kobayashi combines natural imagery with obvious stylized imitations of flora and fauna. *Kwaidan*'s spectral ambiance is enhanced with the melding of Toru Takemitsu's eerie score (silence, dissonance, primitive earthy folk rhythms) and the unsettling use of diegetic sounds. *Kwaidan* won the Special Jury Prize at the Cannes Film Festival and was nominated for Best Foreign Language Film at the 1965 Oscars, proving that art house horror can even satisfy the snobs on award committees.

2.
Vampyr (1932)—Carl Dreyer

Vampires are a popular trope in art house horror, as they can be used as a metaphor for a number of philosophical, metaphysical, and sexual themes. Master director Carl Theodor Dreyer uses the notion of the living undead to meditate on the in-between-ness of existence—moments where reverie and reality, natural and supernatural, past and present, and life and death occur simultaneously, blending and bleeding into one another. Pushing the horror film into the dominion of experimental cinema, Dreyer's *Vampyr* is an impressionistic, lucid dream that ebbs and flows, blurring and slowly fading away like dusk crossing over into night (the movie was shot through a piece of gauze in front of the camera).

Loosely based on the work of legendary horror author J. Sheridan Le Fanu and influenced by Poe and Goya, *Vampyr* is the tale of Allan Grey and his arrival in the cursed hamlet of Courtempierre. Weird omens warn Grey that a vampire and his minion are preying on the inhabitants of a local manor. Grey must use his occult knowledge to prevent the undead from possessing the lovely, innocent Gisele. One of the most atmospheric films ever made (achieving what doomed writer Ryunosuke Akutagawa would call a "vague uneasiness"), *Vampyr* is all shadows, fog, and haze, a bleary twilight zone that stretches time in a similar style to the subconscious revelations of Maya Deren's *Meshes of the Afternoon*. Dreyer projects prescient, resonant images that are stunning in their simplicity and grandeur: a weather vane, a farmer with a sickle, an old mill, a boat on misty water. The scenes where the protagonist envisions his own internment and burial are frighteningly moving as he stares out a small window of his coffin, forced to mutely accept the nightmare. Shot on location in a creepy French village and utilizing the dawning technology of sound to unsettling effect, *Vampyr* is not only a classic horror film but a classic film, period. Plus, the main actor looks like H. P. Lovecraft, so one can fantasize about what would have happened had the iconic author abandoned writing and become a movie heartthrob.

1.
Santa Sangre (1989)—Alejandro Jodorowsky

Alejandro Jodorowsky deserves an Oscar, an Eisner, a star on the Hollywood Walk of Fame, a Pulitzer, a Library of Congress Living Legend, a Kennedy Center Honor, and the Nobel Peace Prize. Though he has made only seven feature-length films (one of which, *The Holy Mountain*, may be the greatest achievement in cinema history), Jodorowsky is an absolute god of cinema, a true alchemist who can delve deep into the collective unconscious and conjure up shocking archetypes that will never leave your mind's eye. Along with Jean Genet, Jodorowsky is a genius at interchanging the sacred and profane, sanctifying the abject and debasing the holy. A true original, Jodorowsky sees no genres, no boundaries, no limits. Perhaps the most Jungian filmmaker ever, Jodorowsky seeks a balance between the personal and cosmic, conscious and unconscious, and body and the soul in a way that enlightens and initiates one into the occult wonders of the universe. Blood is a key motif in the Jodorowsky constellation—a transformative fluid that mediates between existence and death and that flows through the past, present, and future. *Santa Sangre* is a paean to the divine and filthy properties of that body fluid, which is necessary for the transubstantiation of all aspects of the human condition.

The film follows the life of Fenix, a disturbed man who witnessed the mutilation of his mother (her arms were chopped off) and the neutering and suicide of his philandering father. The disabled, religiously maniacal mother uses her son to commit murders against women who she sees as polluting the purity of the world. This deranged relationship is even more twisted by Fenix's own psychosis and fugue states. Although *Santa Sangre* is filled with ghastly scenes of violence, twisted sex, and unimaginable grotesqueries, the real horror is the influence, control, and dominance that parents can exert over their children through familial obligations placed, often unfairly and selfishly, on helpless innocents. Fenix's parents represent the worst binaries that a child can be exposed to: his father is a savage, boorish womanizer forcing his son to be tattooed to prove he is a man, while his mother is a religious zealot who forces her son to take on her disgust with sexuality. The enticing carnality of the circus and the chaste spirituality of the church pull young Fenix apart as he struggles to construct a fully developed psyche and rise from the ashes of his ruined childhood.

Santa Sangre contains some of the most outrageously poetic imagery ever committed to film: a gigantic, dead elephant is torn apart in a mass frenzy; Fenix literally becomes the arms of his mutilated mother; mentally challenged patients visit a prostitute; a cross-dressing wrestler is murdered, and a pool of holy blood is a shrine to a raped and disfigured young girl. Incredibly, the film has a happy ending with Fenix emerging as a balanced human being (a remarkable performance by Jodorwsky's own son Axel). *Santa Sangre* is the ultimate art house horror, as it uses the horror genre as an ordeal through which individual and collective enlightenment is achieved. Out of darkness comes light.

THE 13 MOST SICKENING ART HOUSE HORROR MOVIES

Honorable Mention

Onibaba
Antichrist
Persona
Eyes without a Face
The Strange Case of Dr. Jekyll and Miss Osbourne
Pan's Labyrinth
Messiah of Evil
Duffer
Singapore Sling
Master of the Gensenkan Inn
White of the Eye

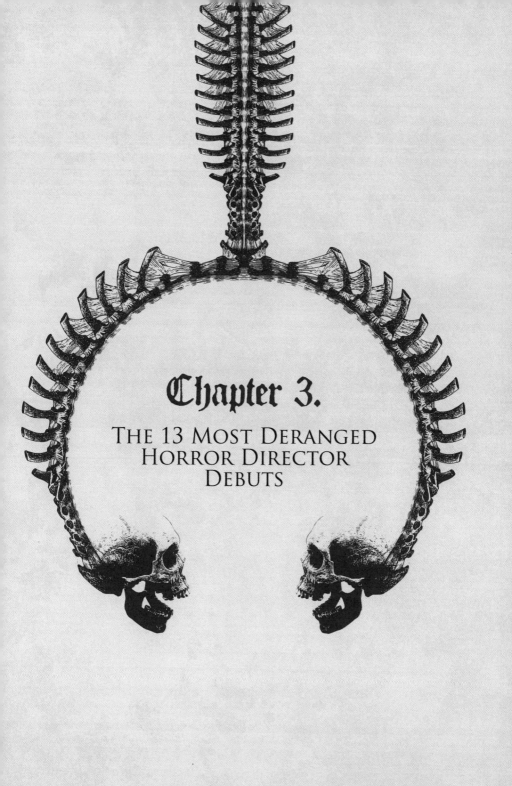

Chapter 3.

THE 13 MOST DERANGED
HORROR DIRECTOR
DEBUTS

The rabid consumption of horror films is both a blessing and a curse for a filmmaker: first-time horror directors are assured a ready-made audience eager to be frightened, but to stand out in a flood of product, one needs to be audacious and original, not just shocking and prurient. Unfortunately, there is a stereotype of the average horror film fan that will accept any offering with gore, nudity, and jump scares galore. Though the content of horror films may seem transgressive and taboo, horror film fans are imagined to be rather conservative in their tastes, preferring formula to innovation—hence the epidemic of sequels and remakes that have plagued postmodern horror. Thanks to the growing affordability of cameras and editing programs, some of these single-minded enthusiasts make their own films, which regurgitate the very clichés that fans rail against. After viewing the vast majority of contemporary horror films, the discriminating aficionado is often left asking: Why was that movie made? Did we really need another derivative? Indie films are just as bad, if not worse than, big studio offerings.

The independent horror filmmaker used to be a hell-bent individualist, an insane savant obsessed with bringing a feverish nightmare to the screen, without regard for obstacles or popular opinion. Given the cutthroat tactics of the film business, lots of first-time horror directors were one and done, creating amazing inaugural terror flicks but never getting the chance to make another. The filmmaker who comes back for more, even in the face of commercial and critical disinterest or even outright hostility, is the true artist, striving in the face of financial, personal, and technical adversity to create a work that will undoubtedly be chewed up and spit out by the gorgers at the horror movie buffet (Uwe Boll, you have my begrudging respect). So to be inventive and take risks, to have the courage to fly in the face of convention and trust one's creative instinct, and then do it over and over again, is worthy of applause. Here are the debut films of thirteen non-conformist, eccentric rebels that truly changed horror and/or kicked off engaging directing careers that pushed (and continue to push) the boundaries of the genre.

> So to be inventive and take risks, to have the courage to fly in the face of convention and trust one's creative instinct, and then do it over and over again, is worthy of applause.

13.

Bad Taste (1987)—Peter Jackson

In 2003, Sir Peter Robert Jackson won an Academy Award for best director. Jackson has collected three Oscars over his remarkable career, produced films, and helped to inform the world of the terrible injustice of the West Memphis 3. And yet this incredible force began with *Bad Taste*—one of the most disgusting, outrageous, low-brow film debuts in the history of cinema. Self-written and produced on a miniscule budget, Jackson transmutated his love of the detritus of movie history into a sick missive aimed right at the industry. *Bad Taste* posits that one aspect of the aliens' agenda is to use our planet as a cheap, plentiful food source for their universe-spanning fast food franchise. Four New Zealanders aren't about to become intergalactic Happy Meals and launch a guerrilla counterattack on the interstellar venture capitalists. The film is a non-stop splatterthon: brains blown out of heads and stuffed back in, chainsaw butchery, Three Stooges-esque beheadings, rocket attacks on sheep. The plot's absolute insanity belies an astute critique of consumer culture and the wholesale rape-for -profit strategies of multinational corporations. Jackson's next films would refine and sharpen his splatterstick satiric style, culminating in the undead body fluid armageddon *Braindead* (a.k.a. *Dead Alive*, 1992). With nowhere else to go in the comedic gore genre, Jackson took a left turn into the subtle, psychological true-crime drama of *Heavenly Creatures* (1994) and the dark witticisms of *The Frighteners* (1996). Jackson's stately adaptations of Tolkien's *Lord of the Rings* saga made him a worldwide phenomenon, but those of us who remember *Bad Taste's* aliens dining on vomit know where his true allegiances lie.

12.

Testuoi, The Iron Man (1989)–Shiniya Tsukamoto

Japanese cinema is often unfairly characterized as being inaccessible, weird, cold, and sexually perverse. For those who see these traits as assets and not deficits, *Testuo: The Iron Man* is gloriously all of the above. Launching the cinema of cyberpunk extremism, Shiniya Tsukamoto's underground 16mm full-length debut melds dream and nightmare, sex and violence, and flesh and metal into an alchemized black-and-white hyperkinetic video game. The film is a series of scenes that portray the awakening of a new species: a hybridized man-

THE 13 MOST DERANGED HORROR DIRECTOR DEBUTS

machine with biotechnical protuberances and infernal devices bursting out of soft, weak skin. While some of these evolutionary harbingers embrace this new stage of development, others are horrified by their involuntary transformation. Filled with futuristic imagery and a Nietzschean technological will to power, *Testuo, The Iron Man* is a prophetic vision of the next wave. Sexuality and libido are the electricity that drives this fetishism of metal, portraying the rise of new techno gods and monsters. Body-violating tube probes, penis power drills, and interlocking iron couplings delete traditional expressions of attraction, gender, and intercourse. The theme of metamorphosis runs through all of Tsukamoto's impressive cinematic projects, whether it be supernatural (*Hiruko the Goblin*, 1991), emotional/physical (the brilliant *Tokyo Fist*, 1995), or personality-based (*Gemini*, 1999). *Tetsuo 2* (1992) and *3* (2010) followed the evolutionary trajectory established in the first film but lacked the sheer irrationality and recklessness of the original. Tsukamoto is also an actor in several gonzo Japanese films, such as Takashi Miike's punishing *Ichi the Killer* (2001), Teruo Ishii's *Blind Beast vs. the Dwarf* (2002), and, most significantly, in Takashi Shimizu's extraordinary *Marebito* (2004).

11.

Stage Fright (1987)—Michele Soavi

Michele Soavi had the ultimate Italian horror film education. He acted in *Alien 2: On Earth* and Fulci's apocalyptic *City of the Living Dead*. He worked on films by illustrious directors like Joe D'Amato, Dario Argento, and Lamberto Bava, even directing a short documentary on the great Argento. With these types of professional influences, it's no wonder that Soavi's first feature-length film would be an amalgam of the giallo, slasher, and horror films on which he apprenticed. *Stage Fright* focuses on an acting troupe working on a musical about the cheerful exploits of a serial killer called the Night Owl. When someone in an owl costume starts to imitate art imitating life by viciously killing the cast, a frantic search for the culprit unravels as the body count escalates. Though the influence of Argento can't be denied, Soavi shows original flashes of brilliance. Instead of following Argento's 1980s style of cold, brutal realism, Soavi's depiction of murder is informed by dramatic absurdities: Pick axes shoved in mouths, disembowelings, screwdrivers in the eye, and incineration can be quite theatrical and gleeful when perpetrated by a killer in a giant owl mask. Soavi moved through his Argento period, directing the incredible *The Church* (1989) and the occult-infused *The Sect* (1991), achieving his own distinct contribution to the genre with the final masterpiece of Italian horror *Dellamorte Dellamore* (1994), a magically existential adaptation of the Dylan Dog fumetti. Family obligations have kept Soavi from making as many films as he should have, but every now and then there are hopeful murmurings (*Dellamorte Dellamore* sequel anyone?) that he will make a triumphant return as the savior of Italian horror.

10.

Cronos (1993)—Guillermo del Toro

Not only is Guillermo del Toro one of the most innovative creators of contemporary fantastique films, he is one of the genre's most eloquent and insightful critics as well. His vision of horror as beautifully savage fairy tales that engage the monstrous, the metaphysical, and the wonderful have made a significant impact on how people think about what the genre should be. His passion for horror is in full flight with his debut feature *Cronos*, a radical revision of the tired vampire mythos that expands both the characterization and metaphor of the bloodsucker. *Cronos* is concerned with the lure of eternal life and a living clockwork device that grants immortality but demands a terrible price for this gift. The obsession with possessing this talisman corrupts all who come in contact with it, changing their physical constitution and relationship with reality. Thirst, feeding, and transformation are shown to be both spiritual and biological. Names like Jesus, Angel, and Aurora mix with insect-like, parasitic, mechanized characters and symbols. Here is the core of del Toro's works: the reverence of the fantastic and the supernatural crashing down into the terrifying truth of carnality and mortality. This collision of imaginary escapism and ruthless maturation informs *The Devil's Backbone* (2001) and *Pan's Labyrinth* (2006), and even the more mainstream *Hellboy* series. Del Toro also produces films and writes screenplays and novels that resonate with his core values of horror and fantasy. *Pacific Rim* (2013) continues his streak of beautifully shot, awe-inspiring, exhilarating genre movies. His mix of entertainment, artistry, and intellect brings to mind the winning formula of Hitchcock. Far above the overrated Abrams, Whedon, and Nolan and approaching the rarefied air of Haneke, Von Trier, and Aronofsky, Guillermo del Toro could go beyond even these contemporary geniuses and achieve all-time greatness as a master of fantastique cinema.

9.

The Bird with the Crystal Plumage (1970)—Dario Argento

Reviewing the first films of genre icons is always a fascinating experience. Did these mavericks come out of the box fully formed or was there a period of trial and error

THE 13 MOST DERANGED HORROR DIRECTOR DEBUTS

in working toward their signature styles and themes? The premiere of an instant genius seems somehow unfair to those directors who have to make fledgling, stumbling steps into the cinematic world. Case in point: Dario Argento's *The Bird with the Crystal Plumage*. Argento was a movie critic and screenwriter (helping to write the immortal *Once Upon a Time in the West*) with a passion for film. Inspired by the great maestro Sergio Leone, Argento decided to do to the thriller what Leone did to the western. Rejecting the traditional slow buildup, subtle violence, and objective point of view of the traditional mystery film, Argento dragged the thriller into the modern era with explicit, expressionistic, extremely stylized depictions of murder, deception, and sexual assault. Rarely had the savagely erotic component of crime been so exposed as Argento lingered over the salacious aftermath of rape and torture, exemplified in a killer ripping the panties off his victim. Argento synthesized the krimi, film noir, psychological suspense, art house horror, and the new cinema of the late '60s (like a mélange of Hitchcock, Leone, Bava, Antonioni, and Peckinpah) to rewrite the genre of the giallo. All the elements of the giallo can be seen in Argento's debut: a troubled protagonist, misdirected perception, an obsessed killer, lurid sexuality, ineffectual police, blood-red herrings, odd clues, black gloves, and frenzied, well-choreographed brutality. The film is an adaptation of Frederic Brown's pulp novel *Screaming Mimi*, but the plot really isn't that important; it's like the clothesline on which billowing, blood-sprayed sheets flap seductively in the wind. What is the bird with the crystal plumage, and why is its call crucial to solving the mystery? Who cares when it is such a singularly striking image? Though Argento's vision is particularly notable for a debut director, one can't ignore the contributions of famed cinematographer Vittorio Storaro and the modern-day Mozart Ennio Morricone. Having those two aces in the hole could make any debut shine a bit brighter. Argento's film not only kickstarted the directing career of a horror/suspense giant, it also inaugurated a genre revolution in Europe as the giallo became one of the most popular types of film made during the '70s. The influence of Argento can also be seen in *Black Christmas*, *Halloween*, *Friday the 13th*, and pretty much the entire slasher film genre. Argento's brilliance didn't stop with just one paradigm shift. In 1977 he would transform the artistry of the genre once again with the simple tale of a young woman attending a dance academy in Germany.

8.

The Nameless (1999)—Jaume Balagueró

Spain has a fascinating relationship with the horror film. Ravaged by civil war, ruled by a fascist dictator, repressed by the Catholic church, real-life terrors seemed enough for the citizens of Andalusia. With the pioneering work of Paul Naschy, Armando D'Ossorio, and Jess Franco, Spain became a leading light for the genre in the '70s.

That light has dimmed and flared over the last four decades, but the current Spanish horror renaissance has been a vital force in contemporary fantastique films. One of the premier voices of this movement is Jaume Balagueró, and his first feature-length film, *The Nameless*, was the catalyst. Based on a novel by the criminally under-adapted Ramsey Campbell, the film centers on the abduction and murder of a six-year-old girl, which devastates the lives of the child's parents. Five years later, as the girl's mother attempts to deal with her loss through addiction, she receives a phone call from her "dead" daughter stating that she is still alive and needs to be rescued. This call begins a journey into the heart of darkness symbolized by a cult called the Nameless. Led by an imprisoned madman and practicing child sacrifice, the Nameless cult is emblematic of the chaotic evil that lies in wait to disrupt and destroy our neatly ordered lives. The cult dwells in the cracks and crevices of the modern family, waiting for the moment when frazzled, overburdened parents take their eyes off their progeny.

Exacerbating Campbell's domestic dread, Balagueró's film sees family as both a blessing and a curse, a bait-and-switch proposition that can bring joy but also vulnerability and tragedy. The need to belong, to be connected and protected, breeds a certain madness and paradoxical drive to smother rather than solidify. After *The Nameless*, Balagueró made other films in the genre such as *Darkness* (2002) and *Fragile* (2005), but would make his most significant contribution with the *Rec* series, a new twist on both the docu-terror and possession sub-genres of horror.

7.

Hellraiser (1987)—Clive Barker

Let me take you back to 1987 and the dark days of horror. The serious genre fan is being inundated with cookie-cutter sequels, unimaginative franchises, and the diluting of horror with bad comedy. Out of nowhere, a new film appears as if from the bowels of hell itself. Tearing through the bloated belly of '80s horror, *Hellraiser* would cement Clive Barker's reputation as the most important fantastique artist of the 1980s. Already heralded as "the future of horror" by Stephen King, Barker's *Books of Blood* series of short stories melded a post-punk willingness to experiment and blur genres with a return to the primordial viscerality of fear. Adapting his own *The Hellbound Heart*, Barker's audacious cinematic debut transgressed the limits of pain and pleasure and illustrated the shocking extent to which people will go to satisfy their appetites. Most famous for introducing an unsuspecting world to the Cenobites and its Faustian leader Pinhead, *Hellraiser* tapped into the growing interest in BDSM, body modi-

THE 13 MOST DERANGED HORROR DIRECTOR DEBUTS

fication, and divergent sexuality as important lifestyle statements rather than merely the perverse behaviors of select deviants. (Barker's vision of Pinhead was also influenced by the creative weirdoes of the group Coil.) Barker's visual sense fetishized iron hooks, chains, piercings, and mutilation, culminating in the mechanical decadence of the Lament Configuration, a puzzle box that unleashes desire and destruction simultaneously.

Hellraiser was like no other '80s horror film and instantaneously made the period's genre offerings obsolete. Barker's later films *Nightbreed* and *Lord of Illusions* would perform autopsies and revitalizations of such traditional horror tropes as the outsider, monsters, magic, and the supernatural. *Hellraiser* would spawn many sequels with only the second *Hellbound: Hellraiser II* (1988) approaching the power and ferocity of the first film. Barker produces horror films through his Midnight Picture Show company (responsible for the impressive *The Midnight Meat Train*), but it is when Barker is in the director's chair that viewers can truly feel they are in the presence of greatness.

6.

House of a 1000 Corpses (2003)—Rob Zombie

I can't imagine a bigger supporter of the horror genre than Rob Zombie. His unconditional love was first manifested in his mega popular music career as the mastermind behind White Zombie, whose sound, lyrics, and look are deeply steeped in the history of horror cinema. It would only make sense that Zombie would transition from referencing horror movies to making them, and, when he got the opportunity, he infused seventy years of terror (both real and fictional) into *House of a 1000 Corpses*. Zombie projects all his cinematic, pop culture, and true crime obsessions into the story of four young people searching for weird American roadside attractions. This leads to a deadly encounter with the Firefly clan, a sadistic family.

Alluding to Charles Manson, *The Munsters*, Ed Gein, Universal Horror, Aleister Crowley, and late-night horror hosts, just for starters, Zombie's directing style comes straight out of the sleazy, anything-goes shockers of Lewis, Hooper, and Craven. Stocked with legendary character actors, memorable personages like Captain Spaulding, Baby, Otis, and Dr. Satan, as well as graphic torture and bloodletting, *House of 1000 Corpses* was too much for Universal Pictures, which ended up shelving the film for fear of offending post 9/11 audiences. In a show of guts and vision rarely seen in the contemporary (spineless) movie industry, Zombie bought the rights from those wussies at Universal and shopped the film until he found a studio willing to release it in the form that honored his passion for the rebellious potentials of horror. Unfortunately, this commitment to the purity of the genre rubbed some horror enthusiasts the wrong way, and Zombie became an extremely polarizing figure in fandom.

The financial success of *House of 1000 Corpses* would lead to a sequel that saw Zombie move from the satanic darkness of his first film to the oversaturated, sun-bleached dread of *The Devil's Rejects* (2005), a tribute to the ultraviolent epics of Peckinpah, Hill, and Leone. Zombie compounded his controversial position in horror fandom by remaking John Carpenter's epochal *Halloween* (2007) and then directing a sequel that was poorly received yet allowed him to try out a few ideas that would come to fruition in his next film. Any fears that Zombie had been co-opted by the suits was put to rest with the release of his masterpiece *The Lords of Salem* (2013), a film that was unceremoniously dismissed by most, but understood by the chosen few.

5.

Black Sunday (1960)—Mario Bava

As the primary architect of the Italian horror phenomenon, Mario Bava was both the genre's technical genius and savior, salvaging movies that had been abandoned such as *The Giant of Marathon* (1959), *Caltiki the Immortal Monster* (1959), and, most significantly, *I Vampiri* (1956), considered the first contemporary Italian horror film. As a show of gratitude, Galatea Films gave him the chance to make his own film. Choosing to loosely adapt Gogol's weird tale "Viy," Bava used all his cinematic skills to create *Black Sunday*, an atmospheric, lushly photographed black-and-white fairy tale involving the resurrection of a vampiric witch looking for revenge on the descendants of those who imprisoned her.

The film begins with some of the most memorable imagery in horror cinema. A huge, shirtless masked executioner (who looks a bit like one of the Mentors) wields an enormous hammer and smashes a spiked iron mask onto the face of a beautiful woman as blood spurts out of her eye sockets. As fog swirls, the faceless inquisitors watch the witch being burned, enveloped in darkness so thick and black it gives the appearance of perpetual sorrow, as if Bergman had made *The Seventh Seal* for Universal Studios in the '40s. *Black Sunday* is the most Gothic film ever made: a ruined crypt, a violated tomb, secret passages, a haunted castle, ancient curses, and a threatened romance. Bava's eye for the macabre is unparalleled, with images such as scorpions scurrying out of a corpse's eyes and a reanimated vampire crawling out of his unsanctified grave. The presence of euro-cult queen Barbara Steele, playing both the wicked Aja and the virginal Katia, elevates *Black Sunday* from classic to godhead status as her decadent beauty (like a living Edward Gorey

THE 13 MOST DERANGED HORROR DIRECTOR DEBUTS

drawing) personifies elegance and corruption—the attraction/ repulsion that illuminates so much of European horror. Bava would make a litany of amazing films that influenced the next generation of horror, from *Friday the 13th* to *Sleepy Hollow*. Even Martin Scorsese paid tribute to the maestro in his masterpiece *The Last Temptation of Christ*, proving that Bava's rococo power extends well past the dark recesses of the horror genre.

4.

Re-Animator (1985)—Stuart Gordon

The year 1985 was critical for zombie cinema. Three films were released that rewrote the rules of the genre: Dan O'Bannon's *The Return of the Living Dead*, George Romero's *Day of the Dead*, and the best of the best, Stuart Gordon's *Re-Animator*. Mixing unbelievable gore, gallows humor, unorthodox sex, and an irreverent attitude, *Re-Animator* set the bar so high that it wouldn't be approached until Peter Jackson's *Dead Alive* seven years later. Gordon had toyed with the idea of adapting H. P. Lovecraft's serial "Herbert West: Re-Animator" as a stage play or TV series, but after meeting producer Brian Yuzna, a feature film was born. Teaming with the mighty Charles Band and his Empire Pictures, Gordon cast the irrepressible Jeffrey Combs as Herbert West, a brilliant but immoral scientist driven by his egomaniacal need to prove that life is just a chemical reaction that can be rejuvenated even after death with his glowing reanimating reagent. West and his sidekick, Dan Cain, fly in the face of the medical establishment at the hallowed Miskatonic University, raising the ire of the eminent Dr. Carl Hill, whose ego is as enormous as West's. A slight misunderstanding between the two doctors results in murder, the resuscitation of a decapitated head, and tons of revivified corpses running amuck. There are just too many outrageous moments to recount, and the joy of a first-time viewing is the sheer chutzpah of Gordon trying to outdo the previous scenes of depravity.

The *Re-Animator* saga would extend over two sequels, but neither have the daring of the original. Gordon would become the most sympathetic cinematic interpreter of Lovecraft, making a series of adaptations that largely succeed in conveying the essence of the Old Gent from Providence's work: *From Beyond* (1986), *Castle Freak* (1995), *Dagon* (2001), and "Dreams in the Witch House" (2005). And he finally got to produce a *Re-Animator* musical in 2011.

3.

Shivers (1975)—David Cronenberg

David Cronenberg is the greatest living genre filmmaker. The fact that he hasn't made a true genre film in a long time should indicate how influential his contributions have been to fantastique films. One of the paramount conceptualists in all of cinema, Cronenberg doesn't just examine the Cartesian mind-body split; he encourages the mutiny and insurrection of flesh, breaking away from the dictatorship of consciousness. His films suggest that evolution and metamorphosis won't be nice, clean, and pretty, and the future will be severe for those who aren't willing to adapt. The new humanity will be hard, cruel, and predatory.

This bleak outlook began in his two short films, *Stereo* (1969) and *Crimes of the Future* (1970), and exploded on to the world with *Shivers*, his first feature film. The film dissects the lives of the empty, disillusioned inhabitants of an ultramodern high-rise (shades of J. G. Ballard) plagued by sexual parasites that eventually fill the voids in their bored lives by awakening their polymorphous perversity. These characters are so alienated by their privileged ennui that the parasites easily gain entry through the desperate, emotionless physical couplings that the inhabitants engage in just to feel something. Cronenberg shows his mastery of style and content right from the opening scenes, balancing the clinical sterility of a commercial touting the high-rise's luxury lifestyle with the anarchic frenzy of a murder-autopsy-suicide. Transferring William S. Burroughs's theory of language to film, Cronenberg's cinema is a virus that infects and replicates through repeated viewings and discussion, which then passes on the contagion to the next viewer. His subsequent films certainly spread the Cronenbergian pathogen through such challenging experiments as *The Brood* (1979), *Videodrome* (1983), *The Fly* (1986), *Dead Ringers* (1988), and *Crash* (1996). Maybe he got bored reinventing genres every few years and now sees a greater test in directing more conventional (but very well made) movies. Hopefully with his son making films now, the Cronenberg legacy will continue.

2.

The Evil Dead (1981)—Sam Raimi

An English major, a college dropout, and an economics student decided to make a low-budget horror movie that would combine furious drive-in flick insanity with the sublime supernatural terror of Lovecraft. To scare up enough money to make a feature film, they shot a short sample called *Within the Woods*, which did the

THE 13 MOST DERANGED HORROR DIRECTOR DEBUTS

trick. The resulting film was *The Evil Dead*, which would revolutionize horror around the world and begin the long careers of Sam Raimi, Bruce Campbell, and Rob Talpert.

The humble story of two couples spending time in a remote cabin and reading from a malevolent book that summons evil spirits resulted in one of the most inventive and scary horror films of all time. Raimi threw out the accepted rules for directing a horror movie by constantly keeping his camera moving, utilizing dizzying cuts and off-kilter editing to keep the audience as unsettled as the besieged characters. Most of the film is just sustained demonic attacks, and the fact that each consecutive sequence increases the manic energy and massive blood-flowing is a testament to Raimi's abundant imagination. Tapping into the primal fear of the forest but adding an exploitation sensibility, *The Evil Dead* certainly merits Stephen King's compliment, boldly splashed across its video cover, that the film is "the most ferociously original horror movie I have ever seen." And yet not all the credit for the film's success gets dumped in Raimi's lap. Bruce Campbell's performance as Ash, the put-upon protagonist, created an entirely different kind of horror hero—courageous yet klutzy, resourceful but often his own worst enemy.

The last gasp of 1970s-style guerilla horror moviemaking, *The Evil Dead* would spawn two vastly different but immensely entertaining sequels and propel Raimi to Hollywood blockbuster status with the *Spider-Man* franchise. Along the way, Raimi made some underrated films such as *Crimewave* (1985), *Darkman* (1990), and *The Quick and the Dead* (1995) and produced some fun horror movies including the respectable remake of his own *The Evil Dead*. Just forget about *For Love of the Game*.

1.

Night of the Living Dead (1968)—George Romero

It's hard to believe that the world survived the year 1968. Assassinations, wars, riots, rebellions, governments nearly overthrown (France), social and economic bedlam—what else could go wrong? Revolution was in the air and a group of novice filmmakers was channeling the zeitgeist into a movie about the dead returning to life to feed on the living. How would the establishment deal with this threat to the old order from the upstart dead? Inspired by Richard Matheson's masterful novel *I Am Legend*, George Romero made a film about people dealing with their own obsolescence. *Night of the Living Dead* illustrates the terror of change and the desperate survival strategies of one way of life when confronted with a competing, hostile form of living death. Romero had previously filmed commercials and industrial films, and that objective, dead-eyed perspective gives *Night of the Living Dead* its documentary realism which, when merged with flashes of noir-like expressionism, results in a deeply disquieting viewing experience. This is especially apparent as his camera lingers over the ghouls as they tear apart and consume flesh, much like the nightly newscasts showing young bodies being blown apart in Vietnam. *Night of the Living Dead* cuts across class, race, gender, ethnicity, and creed, showing how meaningless these classifications are in a world where one can't even depend on death anymore. The film was a hit and ignited a worldwide zombie phenomenon that would encompass fiction, comic books, TV shows, video games, music, and of course film. (Ironically, the word "zombie" is never mentioned in *Night of the Living Dead*). You could fill an entire book cataloguing the movies inspired by Romero's debut; it seems that every country that has ever made a horror film has made at least one *Night of the Living Dead* clone, whether serious or comical.

If Romero had only made *Night of the Living Dead*, he would have left an indelible mark in horror movie history, but he continued to make exciting and thought-provoking genre films like *The Crazies* (1973), *Martin* (1978), *Knightriders* (1981), *Creepshow* (1982), *Monkey Shines* (1988), and *Two Evil Eyes* (1990). He has also continued to explore the world of the living dead with sequels like the equally influential *Dawn of the Dead* (1978), the politically informed *Day of the Dead* (1985) and *Land of the Dead* (2005), and the somewhat redundant *Diary of the Dead* (2008) and *Survival of the Dead* (2009). Hopefully, Romero can escape the zombie apocalypse ghetto and return to making more confrontational, provocative, and personal films that could change the horror genre once again.

Honorable Mention

Jan Svankmajer, *Alice*
David Lynch, *Eraserhead*
Xavier Gens, *Frontieres*
Frank LaLoggia, *Fear No Evil*
Peter Sasdy, *Taste the Blood of Dracula*
John Llewellyn Moxley, *Horror Hotel*
Carlos Aured, *Horror Rises From the Tomb*
Jose Larraz, *Whirlpool*
Dan O'Bannon, *The Return of the Living Dead*

THE 13 MOST DERANGED HORROR DIRECTOR DEBUTS

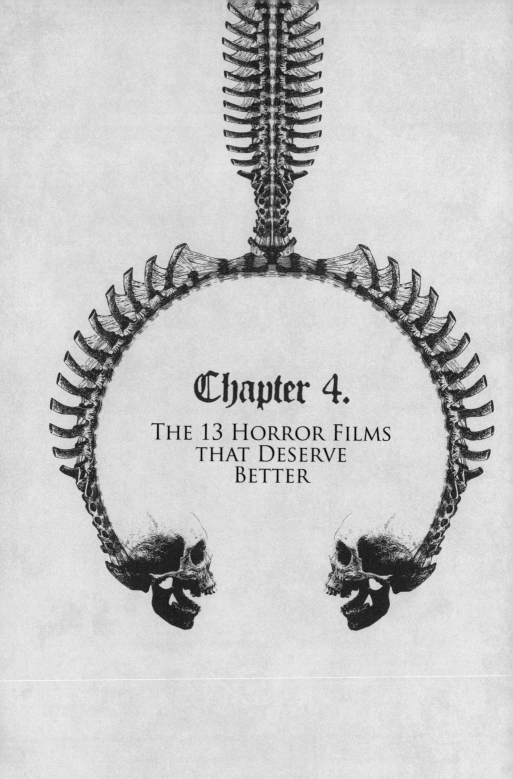

Chapter 4.

THE 13 HORROR FILMS THAT DESERVE BETTER

n our switched-on information age where everyday minutiae is recorded, posted, shared, viewed, and commented on immediately, it's inconceivable that some films still haven't made their way into the digital realm on DVD or Blu-Ray. With more rare films at our fingertips than at any other time in history, it seems greedy to demand that the small percentage of un-digitized movies be presented to us post haste, but it is a nasty habit of collectors to dwell on what they don't have rather than the riches that they do have. Often when these neglected gems are finally released, expectations have been raised so high that they can never live up to their reputation as diamonds in the rough. Even with this cycle of disappointment, collectors are eternal optimists, holding out a Tantalus-like hope that these seemingly forever-out-of-reach films will result in a life-changing cinema extravaganza. For the horror fan, this is best exemplified in the *London after Midnight* snipe hunt that has obsessed macabre cineastes for almost ninety years.

So why are these films not more readily available on DVD or Blu-Ray? And if they are, why not in the deluxe editions they

> Didn't the Berlin Wall come down because the East Germans had enviable access to pirated VHS copies of *Police Academy*?

so sorely deserve? Is it a matter of neglect, indifference, ignorance, rights, economics? And why are some films released only in some countries and not in others? With globalization and technological advances breaking down geographical and cultural borders, the fact that there are different video systems and region codes is ludicrous. Whatever happened to the democratizing of home video? Didn't the Berlin Wall come down because the East Germans had enviable access to pirated VHS copies of *Police Academy*? Though some say that the hunt is better than the catch (tell that to Captain Ahab), these continuing frustrations are what make being a horror film collector both a joy and a tragedy. In the spirit of the never-ending quest, here is a list of thirteen horror films that deserve better than their current status in terms of presentation, availability, or preservation. That's not to say that these films are great, but they certainly aren't well served by the bootleg, PAL-converted, YouTube, download, or TV versions that are currently the only ways to see them. Long live the keepers of the flame like Arrow, Code Red, Synapse, Vinegar Syndrome, Severin, Raro, Mondo Macabro, and Scream Factory!

13.

Queens of Evil (1970)—Tonino Cervi

Many euro-cult tour de forces remain un-digitized for us underprivileged US viewers. Case in point: *Queens of Evil*, a.k.a. *Le Regine* or *Il Delitto del Diavolo*. Directed by Tonino Cervi (who also helmed *Today We Kill, Tomorrow We Die*, a spaghetti western co-written by Dario Argento), Ray Lovelock (a few years before he would be fighting *The Living Dead at the Manchester Morgue*) plays David, a young hippie enjoying a leisurely motorcycle drive across a bucolic sylvan glen, where he meets an older Luciferian gentlemen who berates him and sabotages his motorcycle, leading to an accident. David is forced to find shelter in the forest, where he meets three beautiful women who seem to embody the freedom he is searching for. These wood nymphs occupy an elegant country house that offers all the comforts and pleasures anyone could want. As he becomes increasingly seduced by this Garden of Eden, some odd supernatural occurrences start to manifest themselves, and the three ladies get down to some witchy occult business with David as their target. Pagan shrines, naked rituals, and druggy nightmare sequences project that special early '70s euro-trash satanic atmosphere that any true lover of horror seeks out with wild abandon. Somewhere between a giallo, a fairy tale, and a sleazy sex magick ceremony, *Queens of Evil* needs to cast its spell on US terror junkies. Those lucky demoniacs in Japan and Germany have had the pleasure of home video incarnations of this film. Who were the real winners of WWII?

12.

Screams of a Winter Night (1979)—James Wilson

Anthology films are always a crap shoot. Rarely are they more than the sum of their parts, but some do transcend their hodge-podge structure to offer a more holistic experience. Although certainly not perfect, *Screams of a Winter Night* is an above-average low-budget anthology horror film that makes up for a lack of finesse and gore with a clunky authenticity and plenty of atmosphere. Directed by one and done filmmaker James Wilson, the film's premise involves young partiers spending a weekend in a hunting cabin at Lake Durand. Unfortunately, the pre-credit sequence intimates that not all is right at the lake as we hear wailing winds, unearthly howls, bloodcurdling screams, and a violent attack on a family living in the vicinity. Clearly, this piece of real estate has some intense history with wendigos or some sort of Native American revenants. Once at the cabin, the revelers start to trade scary stories and the film consists of dramatizations of these yarns. The tales should be familiar to anyone who went to summer camp and thrilled to counselors' attempts to terrify their young charges (in between getting stoned and heavy petting), but Wilson milks the creepiness of each segment and offers a significant twist to each of these well-known legends: 1. a couple run out of gas on a secluded road, 2. frat initiates have to spend the night in a haunted house, and 3. a college girl is trapped in her room with a murderer. The film ends with the partygoers learning that what lurks around the lake is much worse than anything in their stories. *Screams of a Winter Night* is a golden example of those creaky but lovable regional horrors that provide both shivers and (unintentional) laughs in equal portion.

11.

Blood Beach (1981)—Jeffrey Bloom

Jaws was bad enough, but you know you're in trouble when even the beach isn't safe. Written and directed by Jeffrey Bloom and partly funded by the infamous Run Run Shaw of the god-like Shaw Brothers, *Blood Beach* has an exceptionally vile concept: some kind of gigantic sea worm is living under the sands of Santa Monica, sucking down and devouring hapless beach bums and bunnies. The LAPD comes off as particularly incompetent in uncovering the true culprit of all the disappearances and mutilated body parts (the castration of a rapist is extremely gratifying, though). But when the police finally realize that they are dealing with a carnivorous sea cucumber-like thing, they execute a cunning plan. *Blood Beach* must be the first horror film in which a backhoe plays a pivotal role in the climax. The deaths are gruesome (the sadistic game of burying someone in the sand takes on a whole new level of horror here) and the acting by such B-Movie stalwarts like John Saxon and Burt Young (Paulie!) is wonderfully over-the-top. Add a score from genre maestro Gil Melle, and you have a glorious early '80s killer worm film that deserves a bigger audience.

10.

The Maze (1953)—William Cameron Menzies

Is there such a thing as an atmospheric 3-D film? *The Maze* might be the only 3-D movie that, despite the gimmick, actually sustains mood while literally shoving things awkwardly in your face. Directed by the unsung William Cameron Menzies, the auteur behind *Invaders from Mars*, the film centers on a familial curse, a brooding castle in the Scottish highlands, and a hedge maze that reflects a character's confused

THE 13 HORROR FILMS THAT DESERVE BETTER

mind long before that copycat in Colorado used this element. After learning of his uncle's death, Gerald (Richard Carlson) leaves his fiancée Kitty (Veronica Hurst) and goes into seclusion at his ancestral manor in Scotland. Kitty arrives at the castle demanding answers but finds even more mysteries, including Gerald's premature aging, sinister locked doors, and the legends of an amphibious monster (I always wondered if Ramsey Campbell's "The Room in the Castle" was influenced by this film). Menzies's layered compositions are quite subtle in building the depth required for 3-D. Though displaying a bit of the '50s melodramatic approach to the genre, *The Maze* harkens back to the golden age of horror; maybe not to the heights of Universal, but certainly in the RKO/Val Lewton ballpark. The film can be seen in a non-3-D version on Netflix.

9.

Blood and Roses (1960)—Roger Vadim

Based on J. Sheridan le Fanu's influential story "Carmilla," *Blood and Roses* is Roger Vadim's Gallic take on the female vampire, using vampirism as a metaphor for the predatory and draining aspects of eroticism. Carmilla's (Annette Vadim) jealousy and rage over her best friend Georgia's (Elsa Martinelli) engagement to her cousin leads to a series of murders on the family estate. Does Carmilla's homicidal frenzy come from being an actual vampire, being possessed by the spirit of an ancestral vampire, convey an unrequited love for her cousin, or express her homosexual attraction to Georgia? Vadim's style is lyrical, showing little of his later pop art ridiculousness as displayed in the kitchy but fun *Barbarella*. Cinematographer Claude Renoir (nephew of master director Jean Renoir) works his magic by creating a dreamy, timeless, ambiguous beauty in the midst of the violence. Unfortunately, the English language version deletes much of this ambiguity and adds an unnecessary voice-over narration by Carmilla's vampire ancestor. Regardless of these tinkerings, *Blood and Roses* needs to be more readily available. If all of Jean Rollin's films are accessible to us, then the fount from which they came should be accessible, too.

8.

The Boy Who Cried Werewolf (1973)—Nathan H. Juran

Much like *Phantasm* and *The Lost Boys*, *The Boy Who Cried Werewolf* captures the feelings of exhilaration and terror that most adolescent horror fans experience in their need for adults to take their obsessions seriously. Richie (Scott Sealey) is a young man trying to deal with his parents' divorce and the new relationship he now has with his father, Robert (the eternally cool Kerwin Mathews). On a bonding camping trip, Richie and his father encounter a madman who attacks them. While defending his son, Robert kills the assailant but is bitten by the ferocious marauder. Richie is convinced that they were assaulted by a werewolf, and when his father starts to get feral during the full moon and people end up savagely dismembered, Richie's scoffed-at beliefs begin to be validated. The film touches on many psychological and social issues confronting adolescents as they try to exert their identity in the adult world: distrust, dismissal, confusion, doubt, insecurity. Authority figures like parents, a child psychologist, and a sheriff are no help at all and reject Richie's experiences and feelings. His separated parents' awkward interactions make things worse, leading to an Oedipal struggle manifested in the primal ferocity of the father's transformation into a wolf man. Will the cycle continue with Richie? Often mistaken for a made-for-TV film, *The Boy Who Cried Werewolf* is expertly directed by Nathan H. Juran with Naschy-level transformation effects. Any movie where a werewolf attacks a hippie commune has to be good. Do I even have to say avoid the 2010 Nickelodeon remake at all costs?

7.

Dark Intruder (1965)—Harvey Hart

Originally a pilot for Alfred Hitchcock's television series *The Black Cloak, Dark Intruder* was deemed too violent for TV and so it was released as a second feature in theaters. The film takes place in turn-of-the-century San Francisco as playboy occult expert Brett Kingsford (Leslie Nielsen, yes, the Frank Drebin) investigates a series of Jack the Ripper-type murders confounding the police. Hideous idols are being left at the crime scenes, and Kingsford and his little-person sidekick Nikola discover that the murders are the work of someone or something trying to summon a Sumerian demon. Though only fifty-nine minutes long, *Dark Intruder* has more *Weird Tales* pulp atmosphere than films three times its length. Influenced by Seabury Quinn's Jules de Grandin yarns, the film also has significant connections to the Cthulhu mythos, mentioning such Lovecraftian entities as Dagon, Azathoth, and the Henry Kuttner creation Nyogtha. The Lovecraft influence should come as no surprise, because *Dark Intruder* was produced by Jack Laird, whose contributions to Rod Serling's *Night Gallery* anthology show involved a great adaptation of "Pickman's Model" and the goofy Derlethian "Professor Peabody's Last Lecture." Currently available on a bare-bones DVD two-fer with William Castle's *Night Walker*, *Dark Intruder* deserves a special edition including a CD of Lalo Schifrin's atmospheric score.

THE 13 HORROR FILMS THAT DESERVE BETTER

6.

Angst (1983)—Gerald Kargl

Coming on like a more disturbing *Henry: Portrait of a Serial Killer* (if you can conceive of that), *Angst* is an Austrian film written and directed by Gerald Kargl. Loosely based on real-life mass murderer Werner Kniesek, it illustrates a day in the life of a psychopathic killer recently released from prison. Our hero (played with unnerving intensity by Erwin Leder) takes up where he left off before he was incarcerated, looking for victims to torture, debase, and kill. He happens upon a secluded home and proceeds to cruelly torment and murder a young woman, her disabled mother, and her mentally challenged brother. The violence is sadistic, brutal, and relentless, and although the killer flashbacks to his abusive childhood, no past traumas can rationalize or justify his maniacal drive to demean and destroy. No other film gets into the head of a serial killer quite like *Angst*; between the deranged monologues, disorientating cinematography, and realistic acting, the viewer is repelled yet intrigued by the horrors that collapse in on themselves. Krautrock legend Klaus Schulze's minimalist electronic soundtrack adds immeasurably to the foreboding feeling. Though hard to sit through, *Angst*'s influence is still felt on current cinema as Gaspar Noé (no stranger to transgressive films) has claimed that the film influences his own disconcerting works.

5.

Devil's Express (1976)—Barry Rosen

First of all, any movie that stars an actor named Warhawk Tanzania has to be worth a look, and luckily *Devil's Express* delivers the gonzo goods. Combining three of the greatest genres ever—horror, Blaxploitation, and martial arts—*Devil's Express* starts with Tanzania playing the role of karate instructor Luke Curtis, traveling to China with his protégée Rodan to bone up on their kung fu skills. While in the Far East, they find a mysterious medallion, which Rodan decides to bring home. Unfortunately, the medallion is the property of an ancient demon zombie hybrid, and the rightful owner follows our heroes to New York City to get his property back. Taking up residence in the subways, the light-sensitive monster starts killing hapless strap-hangers. Luke thinks it might be the work of street gangs. His investigation involves integrating members of the Blackjacks and the Red Dragons until he gets the 411 call at an occult store in Chinatown owned by an old Asian dude who was involved in the ritualistic sacrifices that empowered the medallion in the first place. The final battle is an all-out street fight between Luke and the creature, but who would be stupid enough to mess with a guy called Warhawk? No, the plot is not a result of getting zooted on Robitussin; this is a real movie and deserves a place in your collection. The benevolent society that is Code Red DVD released this crazed masterpiece for our viewing pleasure, but where are the commentaries, interviews, deleted scenes, and documentaries? Whatever happened to Warhawk? Could someone please release the groovy soundtrack by Patrick Adams, too?

4.

Eyes of Fire (1983)—Avery Crounse

A treasure that many horror fans first discovered on VHS, *Eyes of Fire* was released to theaters in 1983, but it wasn't until 1987, when the much-lamented Vestron Video released the film on videotape, that it attracted a cult following. Written and directed by Avery Crounse, *Eyes of Fire* was filmed in Missouri under the title *Cry Blue Sky*, but the usually wonderful distribution company Aquarius Releasing cut its 106-minute run time by sixteen minutes. The film takes place in 1750 on the Western frontier, where a group of pioneers is searching for religious freedom. The pilgrims are anything but pure, as adultery, insanity, and witchcraft all problematize their precarious situation. Add to this seething paranoia the threat of hostile Native Americans, a cursed valley, and malignant spirits, and you have the recipe for a morose, gritty period piece that mixes the supernatural with the historical. The wide-open plains of Missouri provide an especially haunting setting for the desperate actions and life-or-death decisions the characters are forced to make. Crounse coaxes nuanced performances from his actors, who succeed in creating a hopeless pathos that infuses every situation. Currently, there are DVD editions available through Brazilian and Thailand retailers, but these versions seem dubiously gray market at best.

3.

Alabama's Ghost (1973)—Fredric Hobbs

The work of outsider genius/savant Fredric Hobbs, *Alabama's Ghost* consists of, in no particular order, the spirit of magician Carter the Great, Otto Max, a vampire concert promoter, a Nazi scientist named Dr. Caligula, a mind-controlling substance called "raw zeta," a nightclub called Earthquake McGoons, a magical mystery tour called the Psychedelic Spirit Show, an acid rock band called The Loading Zone, a hapless audience member named Domingo Burrito, a voodoo witchdoctor, the vanishing elephant trick, a media kingpin that disguises himself

THE 13 HORROR FILMS THAT DESERVE BETTER

as a grandmother, and a vampire production line! Any plot synopsis would be inadequate, but basically the film documents the rise of magician Alabama from his humble beginnings as a nightclub janitor to his fame as the massively popular "Alabama, King of the Cosmos." The film is a horror-sci-fi-comedy-musical-vaudevillian DMT hallucination that could only be the product of a singular artistic vision. When filmmakers try to be bizarre and surreal, it always come across as pretentious and forced. It is when there is a true creative drive to express the inner, no matter how inept the technique, with little regard for commercialism or critical praise, that real art is created. Is *Alabama's Ghost* art? Petition some brave DVD company to release this shoestring masterpiece and find out for yourself.

2.

The Haunting of Julia (1977)—Richard Loncraine

Full Circle (a.k.a. *The Haunting of Julia*) is one of the saddest and eeriest films ever made. Based on the novel *Julia* by Peter Straub, Richard Loncraine's adaptation examines loss, tragedy, recurring evil, and the fragility of existence. Julia (Mia Farrow), her husband Magnus (Keir Dullea), and their daughter Kate (Sophie Ward) are eating breakfast when Kate starts to choke. Exhausting every avenue of helping her asphyxiating daughter, Julia attempts a tracheotomy but Kate bleeds to death from the botched kitchen-table surgery. Devastated, Julia leaves her husband and moves into her own house to deal with her sorrow. The house seems to have a child-like presence that initially asserts itself in innocuous ways but quickly becomes more malicious and destructive. Is it Julia's daughter returning or something much more vengeful and horrific? There are countless ghost films, but *The Haunting of Julia* is one of the few movies (along with *Don't Look Now* and *The Changeling*) that seem to actually be haunted, each frame projecting a spectral influence over the viewer. The film's ethereal terror floats in and out of sight, felt more than seen, especially in the séance sequence and the interrogation of a scared alcoholic, who, in his past, was a young accomplice to a child murderer whose crimes might not have stopped when she was killed by her own mother. The ending is utterly devastating, suggesting that evil is an inescapable energy that can never be destroyed but only transmigrated into another form. Mia Farrow gives another brilliant performance and the score by Colin Towns is sublime.

1.

The Spider Labyrinth (1988)—Gianfranco Giagni

The Spider Labyrinth is one of the last gasps of Italian horror, and what a gasp it was. Director Gianfranco Giagni combines the artistry of Argento with the themes of Lovecraft, with nods to Bava, Fulci, and Carpenter along the way. Although not as innovative as those horror titans, Giagni manages a sickly ambience that filters "The Shadow over Innsmouth" and "The Whisperer in the Darkness" through an '80s euro-trash sensibility. Alan Whitmore (Roland Wybenga) travels to a creepy Eastern European village to find his incommunicado colleague. Alan finds his mentor, but the doomed professor has been driven off the deep end by his research into an ancient spider-worshipping cult and the notion that the cult is trying to revive its hideous god. The standout set pieces are the ominous Escher-like, web-filled hotel run by a witch (*Suspiria*, anyone?) and the eldritch underground lair of the Great Old One arachnoid deity. Though crude, visual effects by the reliable Sergio Stivaletti are extremely effective, like Screaming Mad George meets Al Adamson. Euro cult legend William Berger appears as a Zadok Allen-type character that warns Alan about the strange doings of the native inhabitants. *Spider Labyrinth* should appeal to those mesmerized by the unbelievably arcane *Dark Waters* (1994). Unlike that masterwork, *Spider Labyrinth* is not available as a deluxe DVD edition, and that travesty needs to be addressed immediately.

THE 13 HORROR FILMS THAT DESERVE BETTER

Honorable Mention

Beasts
A Holy Place
Let's Scare Jessica to Death
Centipede Horror
Deafula
Dr. Satan and the Black Magic
Vice Wears Black Hose
The Supernaturals
The Sect
Erotic Witchcraft
Lake of the Dead
Witch Hammer
Night of the Howling Beast

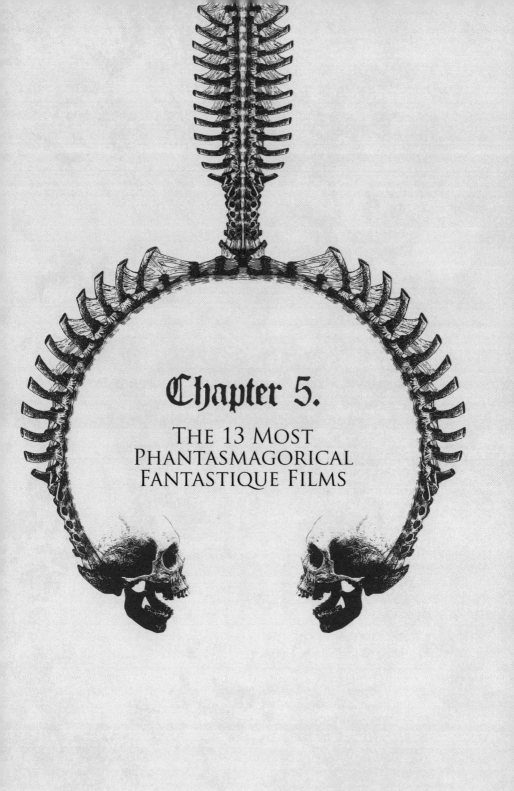

Chapter 5.

The 13 Most Phantasmagorical Fantastique Films

The genre of the fantastique film is vague, but the vagaries of its conventions and categorization are actually assets, allowing it to grow and encompass a variety of moods and emotions. The French literary concept of the fantastique came into its own in the nineteenth century as a beguiling mixture of high and low art: the fairy tale, English Gothic, the ghost story, legends, German romanticism, the Penny Dreadful, the picaresque novel, and the influences of Byron, Hoffman, Poe, and Wilde. Authors like Frederic Soulie, Paul Feval (pere), Octave Mirbeau, and Erckmann-Chatrian flew in the face of naturalism and the Enlightenment by concocting a wickedly decadent mélange of fantasy, science fiction, crime, and horror; and interjections of the unexplained, supernatural, enigmatic, and weird into everyday life. These works could be considered early examples of magical realism. However, the French were more interested in converting the real into the magical and the struggle to understand these strange experiences, than with the bemused contemporaneous acceptance of, say, Garcia-Marquez's characters. Fantastique literature offered cheap thrills and profound ontological concepts simultaneously, making them popular with the working class and the symbolist aesthetes.

> The subject matter of the fantastique is the overturning of a character's frame of reference and connection to certainty and stability.

Underpinning the fantastique is the tension between the protagonists' perspectives and the phenomena unfolding before them—events that are out of their control, engulfing them as they try to rationally understand, process, and deal with a situation that clearly goes beyond their understanding. The subject matter of the fantastique is the overturning of a character's frame of reference and connection to certainty and stability. This results in a reconciliation with the fantastic or an escape into the fantastic, or the destruction of one's sense of reality and self through denying the fantastic. This genre of literature would have a profound effect on the beginnings of cinema as George Melies, a French magician, would see film as an extension of the fantastique, effectively combatting the mind-numbing realism of the Lumiere Brothers. As the twentieth century emerged kicking and screaming from the Victorian Age, the Dadaists, surrealists, psychology, two world wars, and altered consciousness would push the concept of the fantastique away from its literary conventions, suggesting that it was not a genre but an approach—a point of view that had more to do with the look and feel of art than its content. Fantastique filmmakers were not chained to the superstitions and fears of the past: Einstein, Freud, and Hitler had destroyed all the boundaries for expressing, practicing, and experiencing horror, and so everything was fair game.

A fantastique film can be about anything as long as it creates a sense of awe, connects with the sublime, and conjures an immersive environment that operates by its own laws. The viewer is in the director's world and must let go of conventional views of narrative, character, setting, time, and perspective, or nothing wonderful can come of the stories the directors relate to us. Beautiful yet shocking, fantastique films disrupt, challenge, and confront, but not in a polemical or ideological way; the truths these films offer are personal revelations, individualized encounters with the realms of light and darkness, an artistry of birth, sex, death, and transformation. Poetic, joyous, brutal, and sickening: the fantastique film exists between dreams, nightmares, and the mundane as normality and reason deteriorate in the face of the unknown. The irrational is revealed to be the natural state of things; the unconscious is our true identity. The abject and majestic are the same thing, symbolized by the half god/half ape condition of human beings.

This clash between what should be and what is, what we expect and what we experience, results in a worldview that is askew, a sidereal existence that shows us that the magickal is more existentially authentic than a verite documentary. The symbiosis of opposing, competing binaries are shown to be not in opposition but composing a necessary balance that can co-exist and actually inform each other; this fruitful but transgressive juxtaposition is where the fantastique is found. Fantastique directors create cinematic worlds that are recognizable on the surface, but the façade starts to crack as deeper, darker truths are revealed: horrible and grotesque yet redemptive and enlightening, expressed through an alchemical process that forces us through the ordeal of material terror and confusion to the world of higher gnosis and existence. But is even that state an illusion? Artists such as David Lynch, Luis Bunuel, Alejandro Jodorowsky, Orson Welles, Federico Fellini, Andrei Tarkovsky, Kenneth Anger, Maya Deren, Alain Robbe-Grillet, Jean Rollin, Walerian Borowczyk, and Dario Argento have kept the fantastique at the heart of their masterpieces. Here are thirteen more examples of fantastique cinema.

13.

Valhalla Rising (2009)—Nicolas Winding Refn

Cinematic depictions of the past never seem authentic to me. The notion that peoples of the past were just like us except that they wore togas or fur bikinis is ludicrous. Ancient peoples must have experienced their surroundings and themselves in vastly different ways than we do. Invoking the past so that the viewer not only sees but feels the weird otherness of different historical perspectives has been achieved in only a few films: *2001: A Space Odyssey*; *Andrei Rublev*; *Conan the Barbarian*; *The Begotten*; *Aquirre, the Wrath of God*; and *Black Knight* (just kidding). Nicolas Winding Refn's *Valhalla Rising* is one of the precious few. *Valhalla Rising* displays a world of pagan ferocity and mystical transcendence. *Hannibal* hunk Mads Mikkelsen plays One Eye, a silent Viking warrior whose berserker fighting style and bestial sense of vengeance allows him to survive in a harsh, unforgiving environment. Accompanied by a boy who speaks for him, One Eye is promised that his soul will be cleansed if he joins Christian pilgrims on a crusade to the Holy Land. One Eye's journey is one of brutal massacres and metaphysical visions as he arrives either in North America, the Christian hell, or Norse heaven. Refn's visuals range from the poetically vague and ethereal to the explicitly anatomical as myth, reality, and the fantastic intermesh in a state of altered consciousness (it doesn't help that the crusaders imbibe a psychedelic drink that severely affects their perspectives). The struggle between the material and spiritual, church and pagan, civilized and heathen, believer and unbeliever informs *Valhalla Rising*'s depiction of the fantastique, as neither religion nor sheer physicality can save the crusaders. Refn's characters are not just like us; rather, they are a bit more primal and aware as they confront existential problems that humans have struggled with for 2,000 years. Perhaps it's more of a commentary on our modern sensibilities (or lack thereof) that we haven't evolved much from the violent reactions, fearful ignorance, and defeated acceptance found in *Valhalla Rising*. Refn's *Drive*, *Only God Forgives*, and *The Neon Demon* also exist on the reality/fantasy periphery, so there is hope that he will be the next great fantastique director.

12.

Doriana Grey (1976)—Jess Franco

Jess Franco is a genre unto himself. Dabbling in almost every category of film, he appropriates any given genre's conventions and, for better or worse, twists them to fit his own aesthetic purposes. There is something slightly off about his direction, pacing, and editing: painfully slow pans, nauseatingly quick zooms, music that doesn't jive with the scene, cheap special effects, and gynecological close-ups. And yet he is also an auteur; themes, settings, plots, and characters recur continuously across his prodigious oeuvre, always altered but always the same, over and over again. The viewer feels awkward, like being a bit behind and a bit ahead of the narrative at the same time, thrown into these situations with nothing to hold on to except past Franco film viewing experiences. These traits are purposeful, part and parcel of Franco's artistry, doggedly sticking to his idiosyncratic style and unique concerns over a fifty-year career that produced at least 200 films. Because of his refusal to follow anyone else's notions of filmmaking, Franco's films often reflect the fantastique as a melting pot of high surrealist experimentation and the brutal assault of the lowest, most filthy and exploitative aspects of any given genre. Franco's *Doriana Grey* can be considered a reimaging of his earlier languidly erotic masterwork *The Bare Breasted Countess*, a.k.a. *Female Vampire* (Franco's films were frustratingly released with multiple titles and in multiple edits). Franco's wife and muse Lina Romay plays the title role but also plays Doriana's twin sister: Lady Grey is aristocratic but frigid and her twin sister is insane but sexually insatiable. The twins are connected through their ability to feel each other's sexual sensations. With her nymphomaniacal sister locked up in an asylum, Lady Grey must provide her sibling with these erotic thrills, but because she can't feel pleasure, ends up killing her lovers in a quest to reach some sort of climax. Franco keeps his lascivious qualities in check and lets his more poetic and dreamy approach dominate. Like many Franco films, *Doriana Grey* was also prepared with hard-core sequences that explicitly depict real sex acts, but this unnecessarily pornographic focus actually upsets the fantastique ambiance of the movie. Lady Grey seems to live in a world entirely of her own as Franco's camera glides throughout the empty, melancholy rooms of the Chateau Grey, searching for some way out of this self-imposed existential prison (only Antonioni has a greater eye for matching characters' internal states with architecture). Romay is amazing in her roles, displaying a fearlessness and willingness to delve into the darker recesses of sexuality but at the same time reflecting metaphysical, physical, and emotional ennui. Romay's substantial body of work deserves much more praise and attention. *Doriana Grey* is a tribute to Thanatos: an erotic, visual fugue of longing, pain, and death.

11.

Antichrist (2009)—Lars Von Trier

Danish auteur Lars von Trier is so steeped in the fantastique that he had to self-impose his own list of filmmaking rules (the infamous Dogme 95 movement) to force himself out of this aesthetic mindset. Thank goodness he failed and made *Antichrist*, the explicitly fantastic journey into primordial sensuality and contemporary psychoses. Sex and death has always been a controversial pairing, but in *Antichrist*, Von Trier repeatedly pounds the viewer with scenes of graphic sex, vicious disfigurement, and an anthropomorphized Nature that is beautiful yet horribly cruel. The film is a descent into relationship hell as a couple attempt to rebuild and heal after the death of their child, an accident that occurred while they were consumed in a passionate tryst. Retreating to a rural cabin (called "Eden"), "he" (Willem Defoe) soon realizes that his psychological training and medically therapeutic approach to helping his wife cannot account for the forces unleashed by pain, suffering, and biological instinct. Their increasingly frenzied sexual encounters unlock the overwhelming energies of Nature, manifested through freakish weather, animals who can communicate, and humans that cannot. Because the female character is portrayed as a psychotic, nympho sado-masochist, critics have called the film misogynistic, and yet Von Trier seems more interested in revealing the shadow side of all of our psyches—the irrational, the alluring, the dangerous, the animalistic darkness that men are allowed to express but women are forced to repress. Charlotte Gainsborough's performance as "she" is a revelation, madly vacillating between earth mother and devouring monster as her body transcends material reality, becoming a passageway into the fantastique (though she is no stranger to sexual controversy, as she sang "Lemon Incest" with her provocative dad as a pre-teen). Just as civilization has engaged in a futile, mutually destructive campaign to conquer and domesticate Nature, so are women subjugated and annihilated. But as the talking fox states, "Chaos reigns," and any attempt at imposing order on Nature is doomed to failure. Von Trier's *Antichrist* is the final piece in the conceptual fantastique triptych with Roeg's *Don't Look Now* and Zulawski's *Possession*.

10.

Martin (1977)—George Romero

George Romero's *Martin* is a reverse fantastique film as mundane, oppressive reality keeps intruding on a young man's romantic, Universal horror-inspired fantasies. Young Martin is a serial killer with a blood fetish and, in an effort to justify his cravings, often imagines himself as a Bela Lugosi-esque gentleman vampire— seductive, suave, unfairly persecuted for his unfortunate condition by the clichéd pitchfork-and-torch-wielding mob. Martin's great uncle and guardian believes he is a vampire but sees the young man as a disgusting parasite, a true Nosferatu, and tries to contain his nephew with all the usual methods: garlic, crucifix, and religious icons. Though this old-world mentality should help to feed Martin's reveries, he denies these folk repellents as false and not "real magic." Martin needs to have total control over his fantasy world in order to feel powerful, and once reality touches it, the fantastique is gone and he must face the truth of his horrible predilections. There is nothing poetic about Martin's crimes as rendered in gruesomely realistic ways by special effects guru Tom Savini (*Martin* would be the first of Romero and Savini's groundbreaking collaborations), but it is Romero's thoroughly depressing depiction of the rundown, dying, working-class town of Braddock that makes Martin's sickening escapes into fantasy almost understandable. Ironically, it is when Martin gives up his fantasy world that his great uncle's fantasies finally intrude into Martin's reality. John Amplas's schizophrenic performance alternates between shy, withdrawn naiveté and experienced, unemotional predation as Martin's baby face masks a raping, mutilating defiler of lives. Romero's direction moves effortlessly through the drab realism of a town without hope into the lush, nostalgic expressionist imagination of *Martin*, but the fantastique is not enough to redeem this "vampire's" lost soul. Supposedly the rough cut of the film was four hours long and shot entirely in black and white. While the loss of the original version is a tragedy, the use of natural color to make Braddock even more unbearably realistic helps to highlight the alluring artifice of the fantastique.

9.

The Beyond (1981)—Lucio Fulci

In the Italian Horror Trinity, Mario Bava is the father, Dario Argento is the son, and Lucio Fulci is the unholy ghost. Fulci's pushing of the extremes of gore and sadism penetrates the walls of logic and thrusts into the realm of trashy surrealism. From his earliest films (*Massacre Time, Beatrice Cenci*) right through his core '80s masterpieces (*Zombie, City of the Living Dead, House by the Cemetery*), graphic violence and the obliteration of any sense of the human body's integrity have earned Fulci a well-deserved cult following willing to overlook lapses in reason and sanity to experience the visceral thrill of the fantastique. Perhaps his greatest achievement is *The Beyond*, a film in which the supernatural takes a backseat to the multitude of repellent shocks in terms of creating a sense of awe. *The Beyond* (which is probably the greatest fantastique movie title ever) depicts the opening of one of the seven doors to hell and the waves of evil that emanate from its portal. Though the film plays with the stock horror and paranormal components of the genre (zombies, ghosts, the Clark Ashton Smith-created grimoire *The Book of Eibon*, possession, etc.), *The Beyond*'s claim to immortality is found in its relentless Artaudian cruelty and the harrowing

THE 13 MOST PHANTASMAGORICAL FANTASTIQUE FILMS

torture of its characters. Much as pain rituals supposedly alter the consciousness of those enduring them, Fulci's focus on gaping wounds, gushing blood, a chain whipping, a crucifixion, face melting (from acid and quicklime, no less), tarantulas eating a man's tongue, and a little girl having her brains blown out are freakish explorations of body modification and abjection. They become so abstract that familiar components of the body are rendered alien and unidentifiable.

The most interesting character in *The Beyond* is the artist Schweick, whose occult works of art lead him to be killed by an angry mob. His ritual slaughter opens the gate, and so the ignorant rabble's act of censorship actually completes Schweick's masterwork (superstitious townspeople, weird kids, and ocular trauma are Fulci's leitmotifs). The narrative, though a bit wonky, ends on a magnificently fantastique note as our heroes are somehow transported into Schweick's painting, a hellishly bleak setting littered with damaged bodies. Trapped in this miasmic nightmare, the protagonists mercifully go blind and are absorbed into the nothingness of the universe. Only Fulci would claim that this ending was a "not unhappy one."

8.

La Jetee (1962)—Chris Marker

Because of its limitless imagination, you'd think that there would be countless science fiction fantastique films, but because much of sci-fi pays too much attention to the science and not enough to the fiction, there is actually a severe deficit. In a mission to achieve total technical verisimilitude, science fiction can often bypass the wonder and strangeness of other worlds. What is the effect on human consciousness to be able to violate the laws of the universe? Chris Marker's short film *La Jetee* is a brilliant meditation on not only the subjectivity of time and memory but also of the cyclical experiences of life and death, a phenomenon even science can't change. In a post-apocalyptic Paris, a prisoner is used as a test subject in experiments concerning time travel. The hope is that someone from this devastated time can either go back and intervene in the past to prevent WWIII or get help from the future. The prisoner is chosen because he has a particularly strong (yet vague) memory that anchors him to the past. This vision of a woman watching a man dying is actualized with tragic repercussions for the prisoner. *La Jetee* is told entirely through still photographs, replicating the notion of one's life "flashing before your eyes." Our memories and perceptions seem static and beyond our control, yet they emanate from within us. Marker's narrative is not concerned with explaining the theoretical or practical application of time travel because *La Jetee* focuses on the feelings of being out of time, lost between the past, present, and future, thrown from moment to moment, memory to memory, without any stable, objective referent besides the fleeting instant of connection to another human being. The only unifying thread through these confusing, fragmented experiences of time and space is love—the need to bond with another mind, body, and soul. The prisoner's tenderness and vulnerability is juxtaposed with his sterile and unfeeling present, a world of inhumane, unrelenting scientists and jailers. Marker's herky jerky editing makes the viewer feel the terrifying disorientation of existing across multiple spaces and eras and yet, in the end, the circular notion of time will always catch up with us. *La Jetee* inspired *12 Monkeys*, directed by fantastique film artist extraordinaire Terry Gilliam.

7.

Enter the Void (2009)—Gaspar Noe

The specter of death hovers in the background of all fantastique films. The great unknown provides us humans with equal thrills and terrors as we fruitlessly ponder the next phase of existence. What will happen on the other side? Is death the ultimate trip? Exploring the undiscovered country, Gaspar Noe's *Enter the Void* follows a newly liberated consciousness on a first-person, out-of-body drive through the neon-lit labyrinth of Tokyo, substituting strip clubs, bars, hotel rooms, apartments, and bathroom stalls for the Bardos of the *Tibetan Book of the Dead*. Oscar, a young expat drug dealer, is shot dead by police, which begins his spiritual quest to find some meaning in his recently expired life. He moves through space and time, watching the secret lives of friends, acquaintances, and his sister, reliving traumatic incidents of his own personal history before being reincarnated after confronting his place in the universe and given a chance to start again. Yet the fact that Oscar is a stoner and uses hallucinogenics calls into question whether he has attained enlightenment or is having one helluva last DMT trip.

Noe's camera never stops moving because life is motion: above and below, inside and outside, as no spatial or temporal barriers can stop it. Perspectives move from character to character, shifting through memories, dreams, blackouts, and visions, even merging with several people having sex and delving into the body's inner recesses to witness the conception of life. Oscar is killed in a club called The Void, and Noe's film does much with the Buddhist concept of sunyata, the need to erase the ego, attain pure emptiness, and transcend the material realm to attain nirvana. This higher awareness is replicated in Noe's dazzling array of crane shots, visual effects, and collaged points of view. Much like David Bowman's journey into the monolith, *Enter the Void* is pure cinema, merging the psychological, physical, and metaphysical, and taking our feeble minds along for the ride

THE 13 MOST PHANTASMAGORICAL FANTASTIQUE FILMS

6.

The Night of the Hunter (1955)—Charles Laughton

It took a British director to create the first American cinematic fairy tale, a parable of light and dark populated with criminals, murderers, false prophets, angelic children, vulnerable widows, and a compassionate savior. Iconic actor Charles Laughton adapted Davis Grubb's novel *The Night of the Hunter*, creating a film that is both deeply American and universal in its message of good and evil. *The Night of the Hunter* conjures up the feeling of portentous, apocalyptic biblical judgment as Old Testament and New Testament iconography mingle with an expressionistic Southern Gothic atmosphere of American authors like William Faulkner, Flannery O'Connor, and Harry Crews. Two children are the keepers of a secret, pursued by a fanatical preacher who is willing to lie, trick, and kill to learn the whereabouts of a stolen cache of money. The Great Depression hangs over the narrative like the testing of Job, setting in motion the precipitous events but also stripping away the protection, sanctuary, and preservation that any society should offer its inhabitants, especially its most vulnerable. What is left is a lawless, unforgiving environment where only the strong and cunning survive and purity has to be safeguarded from the wolves that look to exploit and tear it apart. Much like Hansel and Gretel, John and Pearl have to navigate a world in which adults can't be counted on and predators will use deception, their authority, and brute force to get what they want.

Robert Mitchum's incredibly crazed performance as the very wrong Reverend Harry Powell (whose knuckles on the right hand are tattooed with "Love" and the left with "Hate"), based on real life psychopath Harry Powers, alternates between smooth, calculated con man and bestial, howling frenzy. Laughton's directing style is right out of the German cinema classics of the '20s: shadowy, spooky, and distorted, while at the same time naturalistic, simple, and lyrical, displaying the balance of both sides of the psyche. The image of Shelly Winters's corpse at the bottom of the river, her face frozen but her hair eerily swaying with the current, perfectly encapsulates the horror and beauty of the fantastique. The soundtrack by Walter Schumann combines moody orchestration with popular songs, but it is Mitchum's intoning of the hymn "Leaning on Everlasting Arms" that creepily resonates (parts of the soundtrack are brilliantly sampled in Coil's "Who'll Tell?"). Unfortunately, Laughton never directed another film, but sometimes the greatest fantastique films exist by themselves in their own world.

5.

Evil Dead 2 (1987)—Sam Raimi

Sequels are often needless extensions of the original or watered down retreads of their progenitors. Sequels are usually also conservative works of art that try to establish and prolong a brand, and so the eccentricities of the original are smoothed out and made to fall in line with whatever cinematic trend is currently profitable. It is rare for a sequel to surpass its predecessor, and even rarer when that sequel transforms the original's intention into the fantastique.

Sam Raimi's "sequel" to his horror classic *The Evil Dead* is a surrealist Tex Avery nightmare with no connection to the laws of cinema or reality. Rebounding after the unfairly neglected *Crimewave*, Raimi reteamed with producer Rob Talpert and the irrepressible Bruce Campbell to venture once more into the woods and encounter Kandarian demons unleashed by the *Necronomicon Ex Mortis*. But instead of continuing the story of the first film, Raimi takes certain key elements of the original and reimagines, expands, and remixes, blowing them out with no thought of internal or external continuity. *The Evil Dead* was the test, the rough draft, the dipping of the toe; *Evil Dead 2* plunges into the ocean, drinks it all in one big gulp and throws it up into astonishingly inconceivable permutations, drowning us along with Ash, the put-upon protagonist. The thin line between horror and comedy is effectively trashed as Ash's sanity is tested by increasingly absurd events that transpire in a cabin, which takes on the dimensions of the TARDIS. Raimi's camera acts like an accomplice to the dark forces, assaulting Ash and the viewer. As each incredible set piece twists our brains, the viewer is left wondering what else could happen and Raimi always manages to terrify and entertain with his next gag. *Evil Dead 2*'s genius is in adding the anarchic, nonlinear virtuosity of the Three Stooges to the horror formula as eye gouges, face slaps, and blows to the body take on a literal life of their own, independent of a human agent. Much of the violent humor and visual puns came from filmmaker Scott Spiegel's participation in the script, a strategy he would also use in his own splatter comedy *Intruder* (which had a cameo from Three Stooges bit player Emil Sitka). The ending of *Evil Dead 2* left room for another sequel, the rousingly entertaining *Army of Darkness*, and there are constant rumors that a fourth Evil Dead film is in the cards. Let's hope it is a return to the splatterstick fantastique of *Evil Dead 2*.

THE 13 MOST PHANTASMAGORICAL FANTASTIQUE FILMS

4.

Phantasm (1979)—Don Coscarelli

Dreams are a crucial element of the fantastique: non-sequitur images created by our own naked fears and desires, filling us with exhilaration and terror. Time is meaningless in dreams: everything flows together in an avalanche of personal and collective memories, projections, and denials. Cinema is often compared to the dream experience, and the metaphor is certainly valid when discussing Don Coscarelli's lucid delusion *Phantasm* (even the title sounds like a synonym for a dream). The film is funneled through a teenage boy's id as he uncovers a supernatural conspiracy behind a rash of recent deaths. The sinister Tall Man (I hesitate to say "played" by Angus Scrimm as I believe it's the other way around) is murdering townspeople and reanimating their corpses with help from interplanetary dwarves and free-floating killer silver spheres. Phantasm is every teenage boy's fantasy come true: a dirt bike, a 1971 Hemmicuda, pretty girls, guitars, a heroic mission to save the town, an evil villain to fight, and no parents to spoil the fun. The only adult that can be trusted is Reggie (who puts aside his lucrative career as an ice cream man to help fight the Tall Man), because all the other grown-ups are either dead, absent, or dismissive.

Phantasm lays bare fears of mortality and maturity but revels in the freedoms and enthusiasms of youth, a state of development where everything, good and bad, is still possible, treated seriously and as a goof at the same time. Young Mike has to confront his own anxieties and insecurities concerning death and growing up (personified in the character of the Tall Man, who only refers to our young hero as "boy") and though Mike appears to have vanquished the malevolent undertaker, can we ever really defeat the reality of our own aging and expiration? The Tall Man character embodies every adolescent's phobia of authority figures, but aren't all adults "tall," as size and stature validate their ability to impose their authority on kids? Filled with bizarre imagery, *Phantasm* is an associative film based around idiosyncratic moments rather than a smooth, linear narrative (though Coscarelli attributes this strange rhythm to the need for extensive editing and a largely improvised script). *Phantasm* has spawned three sequels, but none have captured the in-between waking and dreaming, caught between life and death fantastique feel of the original. Coscarelli saved that absurd ambience for *Bubba Ho-Tep* (2002) and *John Dies at the End* (2012).

3.

The Man Who Fell to Earth (1976)—Nicolas Roeg

Extraterrestrial beings have been a staple of cinema since Melies took us on a trip to the moon. Films told from the perspective of visitors from another world are much rarer. How would we appear to an alien? What would our existence look like from their perspective? Everything would appear fantastique to them. One of the few directors who could create a credible hypothesis on this subject is Nicolas Roeg, a true visionary and fantastique icon who specializes in outsider points of view. Roeg's adaptation of Walter Tevis's novel *The Man Who Fell to Earth* is disjointed, angular, and estranged in its depiction of human beings, as we are revealed to be weak, flawed, selfish, and barbaric to the "visitor." This feeling of disassociation and awkward trepidation is brilliantly conveyed through David Bowie's performance as Thomas Jerome Newton, an alien who comes to Earth to obtain water for his drought-suffering planet. As he amasses wealth, power, and acquaintances, Newton is weighed down and trapped by obligations, machinations, and his own vices—bad habits picked up from his terrestrial companions and used against him by institutions that seek to control him. In the end, Newton fails in his quest and becomes a drunken, jaded pop star who can only compose a requiem for his abandoned family and dying planet. Roeg's imagery and editing techniques achieve a true state of otherness that has not been surpassed: free-floating, gymnastic sex that spews milky liquid from every pore; the blaring of multiple TVs as their images and sounds collide and comment on Newton's plight; lapses in time as Newton's limousine seemingly travels back into the past to a nineteenth-century farm. The most poignant scenes are Newton's memories of his home and family, weird and foreign to us but containing more love and caring then any scene on Earth. The motif of falling—physically, emotionally, mentally, and spiritually (also seen in Roeg's *Don't Look Now*)—affects all the main characters and yet Roeg doesn't fully blame us humans for Newton's ruin. As the visitor quips, "We would have done the same to you."

2.

Brazil (1985)—Terry Gilliam

It takes a truly secure artist to meticulously create a fictional but realistic world and then have the fantastique intrude on and undermine it. Terry Gilliam's *Time Bandits* added dark humor to the fantastique formula, and his masterpiece *Brazil* would push the comedy/tragedy binary to absurdly grotesque heights. *Brazil* is a

THE 13 MOST PHANTASMAGORICAL FANTASTIQUE FILMS

Fellini meets William Sansom meets Orwell dystopian satire uncovering the terroristic control that the bureaucratic capitalist industrial state has over our reality. Sam Lowry is an employee in a Kafkaesque, totaliatarian governmental department who withdraws from his maddeningly regimented life through a fantasy of being a winged superhero knight battling a giant Samurai monster to rescue a fair princess. When a random mistake results in an innocent man being arrested and executed, Lowry is unwittingly drawn into an underground resistance movement seeking to overthrow the fascist regime. The more Lowry tries to straighten out the absurd comedy of errors, the more entangled he becomes in the equally confusing conflict between the forces of repression and freedom. Gilliam's retro-futurist constructivist designs highlight the disorientating and paradoxical aspects of Lowry's world: while the threats of surveillance and state terror advance unheeded, the technology of everyday life constantly breaks down, crushed under its own obsolescence. The film is packed with incredible performances, but Michael Palin's nice-guy torturer—who is so detached from the horrors of his job that he brings his kids to work with him—embodies the banality of evil. The film's central metaphor is escape, the individual soaring above the stifling conformity and obsessive order, procedures, and codification of institutionalization (represented by the strict Bushido code of the Samurai warrior in Lowry's fantasies). The two competing endings—the insipid, studio-imposed "happily ever after" conclusion and Gilliam's stunningly tragic denouement—both critique the delusion of freedom (Gilliam's purposefully, the studio's unknowingly). Lowry's fate is the second greatest ending in cinema history, superseded only by Maggie's defiant threats in Jack Hill's *Switchblade Sisters*. Gilliam's original title was *So That's Why the Bourgeoisie Sucks*, but he wisely decided to use the wistfully exotic appellation *Brazil*.

1.

Apocalypse Now (1979)—Francis Ford Coppola

I'm surprised that there aren't more fantastique war films. Though military campaigns are designed to be as efficient as possible, the mass destruction, nihilistic slaughter, and chaotic aftermath of war changes reality into an anarchic conflagration of annihilation for all who are unfortunately tossed on the rubbish heap of history. Drawing from Joseph Conrad's *Lord Jim*, Michael Herr's *Dispatches*, Werner Herzog's *Aguirre, the Wrath of God*, and most importantly, Conrad's *Heart of Darkness*, *Apocalypse Now* is an exploration of the madness of war, an insanity that is contagious and affects everyone touched by the atavistic delirium of authorized violence. Francis Ford Coppola transformed John Milius's screenplay (originally titled *The Psychedelic Soldier*) into one of the greatest spectacles in the history of cinema, taking Conrad's commentary on colonialization and applying it to US interventionist policy in Southeast Asia, dropping the audience in the middle of the senseless mania of the Vietnam War. Just as colonial powers projected their own dark side onto the colonized to justify their oppressive methods, so does the US military dehumanize the enemy to validate the unprecedented brutality and savagery visited on the Vietnamese people. Captain Willard is given the mission to hunt down and assassinate Colonel Kurtz, a renegade officer who has gone "native," recruiting a guerilla army of Americans and indigenous peoples that kills everyone, and not abiding by the subjective "rules" of war. As Willard and his crew travel up the Nung River into the heart of darkness, objective reality starts to break down as the irrationality and absurdity of war transforms Vietnam and Cambodia into the circles of Dante's Inferno. When Willard finally meets Kurtz, the ceremonial and the ritualistic are enacted in an archetypal transference of power and responsibility. Informed by the allegory of the Fisher King as interpreted by T. S. Eliot and the pagan rites and mysticism found in James Frazer's *The Golden Bough, Apocalypse Now* questions how much progress Western civilization has actually made when it is unable to address or rectify the horror at the core of human existence. While native peoples seem to have made peace with humanity's darker impulses, Westerners are shown to be the ultimate hypocrites. Coppola's direction is both documentarian and surrealistic (miles above his pedestrian style in *The Godfather* series), interweaving the logical and illogical so that it is hard to tell the difference between the two (perfectly personified in Robert Duvall's likable psychotic, Col. Kilgore). Yet it is when Coppola draws the viewer into Kurtz's Angkor Wat-inspired compound that reason goes completely out the window and the fantastique takes over completely. (Any time Dennis Hopper greets you as you arrive, you know you're in for a weird visit.) *Apocalypse Now* is proof that the fantastique can inform not only cult movies but the finest films ever made.

THE 13 MOST PHANTASMAGORICAL FANTASTIQUE FILMS

Honorable Mention

On the Silver Globe
Pan's Labyrinth
Dark City
Barton Fink
Performance
Once Upon a Time in the West
Angel Heart
Jacob's Ladder
In the Mouth of Madness
Carnival of Souls
The Sargossa Manuscript
The Tree of Life
Orpheus
Stalker
La Bête

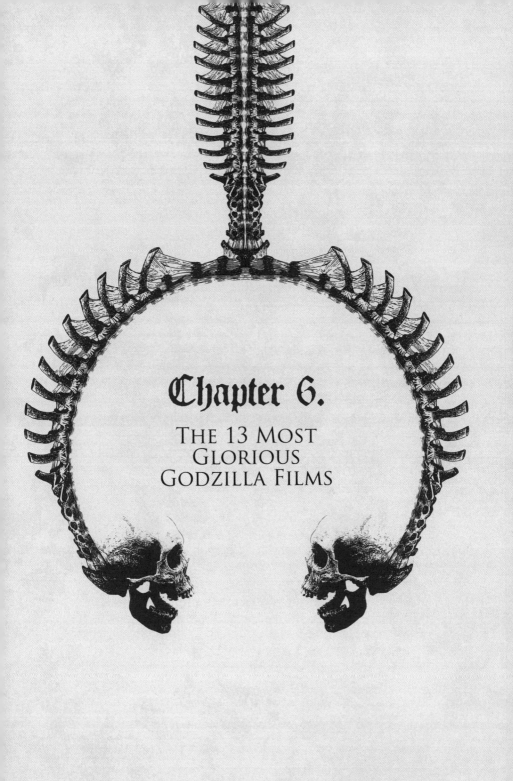

Chapter 6.

THE 13 MOST GLORIOUS GODZILLA FILMS

ith the release of the newest version of Godzilla, the cultural phenomenon of the king of the monsters is back in the public eye. It all started in 1954 when Toho Studios in Japan unleashed the original runaway son of the nuclear A-Bomb in the form of Gonira—Ishiro Honda's devastating metaphor for the Hiroshima and Nagasaki bombings. It's hard to believe that a long-lasting film series and the phantasmagorical genres of kaiju eiga (monster films) and tokusatsu (live action masked hero/giant robot television series) sprang from such a gritty, serious film. The film was imported to the US in an altered version and titled *Godzilla: King of the Monsters*, gaining Raymond Burr as an American journalist narrating the events but losing some of the tragedy and political critique of the United States' unrestricted nuclear weapons testing in the Pacific. From this bleak masterpiece, the Godzilla sensation would catch the public's attention around the world, and as Toho capitalized on the unexpected popularity of its character; the studio watered down the social commentary and gave audiences what they wanted to see: giant monsters destroying cities. From

In the first film, Godzilla is a brilliant metaphor; in subsequent films, he is a character.

the 1950s through the 1970s, Toho would reign supreme, releasing fifteen Godzilla films (the so-called Showa series) as well as many other sci-fi, special-effects extravaganzas that would often cross over with the studio's Godzilla films like *Rodan* (1956) and *Mothra* (1961), along with those that didn't cross over but should have, such as *Dogora* (1964), *Frankenstein Conquers the World* (1965), *War of the Gargantuas* (1966), and *King Kong Escapes* (1967). Toho's two biggest exports in the 1950s and '60s were giant monster films and the world-cinema-defining works of Akira Kurosawa. After a short break, Toho would bring back Godzilla in 1984, kicking off the

Heisei series that culminated with Godzilla's death in 1995's *Godzilla vs. Destoryah*. The turn of the century saw Toho resurrect Godzilla for the controversial Millennium series of films, which ended with the fiftieth-anniversary giant monster battle, 2004's *Godzilla: Final Wars*, the last Toho-produced Godzilla film to date. Ignoring the 1998 Roland Emmerich-directed travesty, there were high hopes for Gareth Edwards's American take on the beloved icon. While the question of whether the emperor of the kaijus can ever be Americanized is still being debated, here are thirteen of the best Godzilla films to get you in the mood for his inevitable return. (Obviously, the first Godzilla film is the greatest giant monster film ever made, and yet its dismal tone and tragic ambience place it in a different aesthetic universe from the rest of the Godzilla series. In the first film, Godzilla is a brilliant metaphor; in subsequent films, he is a character.)

13.

Godzilla vs. Mechagodzilla II
(1993)—Takao Okawara

If hardware, weapons, and other types of techno-gadgets are your thing, then *Godzilla vs. Mechagodzilla II* is mecha-manna from heaven (Kaiju films always had the best vehicles and armaments, like the Maser Cannon). A celebration of the fortieth anniversary of Godzilla, the film brings back beloved kaiju Rodan, introduces a sleeker, revamped Mechagodzilla (though the original, clunky tin-man look is still the coolest), and a baby Godzilla is born. The United Nations Godzilla Countermeasures Center uses the remains of Mecha King Ghidorah to build the ultimate kaiju deterrent: Mechagodzilla, which is quickly put to the test. Though there are some questionable biological explanations for the kaiju (Godzilla has a second brain? Who laid the egg from which baby G hatches? Godzilla left the egg in Rodan's nest?), the film has so much going on that one doesn't have the chance to stop and question the political, scientific, or psychic justifications for anyone's actions, including the monsters'. And Little Godzilla is so darn cute, he'll make you forget all about Minilla and Godzooky.

12.

Godzilla: Tokyo SOS (2003)—Masaaki Tezuka

Although the plot is kind of tough to follow, this Godzilla film has perhaps the most superbly anarchic fight and destruction scenes ever filmed. Picking up from the previous film in the Millennial series, the Japanese government is dealing with the consequences of fusing the original Godzilla's bones with the newest version of Mechagodzilla (called Kiryu) and now has to negotiate with an angry Mothra who wants Godzilla's remains returned to the ocean floor. The latest version of Mechagodzilla has an absolutely killer look, menacing but raggedly glorious, and Godzilla's design is more fearsome than ever as he attacks with a merciless vengeance. *Godzilla: Tokyo SOS* returns to the notion of Mothra as a goddess, a Joseph Campbell/Carl Jung archetype of dying but being reborn to keep the cycles of nature in balance. Everything changes, but everything returns.

11.

Godzilla's Revenge (1969)—Ishiro Honda

Okay, this film is often ridiculed as one of the worst Godzilla films, but many G-fans had their first encounter with kaiju through

Godzilla's Revenge and perhaps identified with the young boy who escapes his lonely, bullied life through fantasizing about the denizens on Monster Island. Padded with lots of stock footage from previous Godzilla films, *Godzilla's Revenge* might not be the most innovative or breathtaking kaiju film, but it has the most heart. It's also never boring, like some of the earlier Showa films where it seems like you are waiting forever to see Godzilla. *Godzilla's Revenge* not only has monsters, but also a kidnapping plot, and a bully gets his comeuppance. Last but certainly not least, Minilla finally musters up an atomic breath blast, making his papa proud. What son doesn't dream about impressing his dad?

10.

Godzilla: Final Wars (2004)—Ryuhei Kitamura

Toho's final Godzilla film (yeah, right) was picked apart by the Godzilla community, but it must have been an example of anticipation being so high that no movie could have met the fans' fevered expectations. *Godzilla: Final Wars* is a loose remake of *Godzilla vs. Monster Zero* (1965) as evil Xiliens use the Earth's kaiju to devastate and conquer the planet, resulting in a glorious concoction of monsters, mayhem, martial arts, and action film clichés. Directed by the flashy but always interesting Ryuhei Kitamura, the film is a cut and paste of all the Toho kaiju and tokusatsu films of the past fifty years (including such rarities as *Atragon* and *The War in Space*), with some unnecessary nods to *The Matrix*. Even with these faults, the film has some of the greatest kaiju ever, with crazy redesigns of Gigan and King Ghidorah. And you get to see Godzilla dispatch his American pretender to the throne in a very satisfying way.

9.

Terror of Mechagodzilla (1975)—Ishiro Honda

The '70s were a strange time for the Godzilla film. Trying to retain a young audience but also attempting to lure those who wanted to see more violence and sex, the final two films in the Showa series saw Toho experimenting with more mature aspects of genre moviemaking, including arterial spray blood effects in *Godzilla vs. Mechagodzilla* (1974) and nudity in *Terror of Mechagodzilla* (1975). The last film of the Showa series, *Terror of Mechagodzilla*, brought back Ishiro Honda to direct. Mechagodzilla is one of the most impressive creations of in all of kaiju eiga and tokusatsu genres, built by aliens in ape masks to conquer Earth and defeat Earth's defender, Godzilla. Its shiny metal sheen and bolted-together armor look like what Rube Goldberg would

THE 13 MOST GLORIOUS GODZILLA FILMS

have created if he had been a mad Japanese scientist. Add in a punk-rock-looking kaiju named Titanosaurus, some Kinji Fukkasaku-esque violent action scenes, and a topless fembot, and you have a helluva movie. *Terror of Mechagodzilla* tries to return to the more serious tone of the early Godzilla films but can never decide which audience it wants to please. Still, it is massively entertaining.

8.

Godzilla and Mothra: The Battle for Earth (1992)—Takao Okawara

Technically, Mothra should be the easiest kaiju for Godzilla to defeat. Outside of its wings and ability to spew out silk when it is in larvae form, Mothra doesn't have much to offer. Yet the oversized bug is one of the most frequently appearing kaiju in the genre, even spawning its own series in the '90s. Maybe the appeal is those haunting songs that the Little Fairies sing as avatars of Mothra. Mothra's return in the Hensei series resulted in a box office smash for Toho and cemented the popularity of kaiju in the '80s. *Godzilla and Mothra: The Battle for Earth* returns to some of the ecological concerns of *Godzilla vs. Hedorah* but does it in a more new age/ mystical context, as Mothra acts as a symbol for a synergistic Mother Earth. That's not to say there aren't some spectacularly destructive action sequences, but this film is a more meditative, character-driven film than others in the Godzilla series.

7.

Godzilla vs. Gigan (1972)—Jun Fukuda

Though one would love to praise kaiju films for their drama, innovative stories, acting performances, and subtext, the truth is that one outrageous-looking monster can make up for deficiencies in any of these categories. Case in point: *Godzilla vs. Gigan*. The plot makes very little sense, the story has been told a thousand times, and the acting is monotonous, but the introduction of the alien kaiju Gigan is just stunning. Built by cockroach aliens, wearing a cool visor, armed with hooks for hands and a buzz saw for a belly, Gigan makes no anatomical sense but looks like an ultramodern death machine. Gigan's attacks on Godzilla are some of the bloodiest in the Godzilla series. The film is a mess, but it never drags and the hero calls his girlfriend a "hard bitch," which you wouldn't expect to hear in such a kid-orientated Godzilla film.

6.

Godzilla, Mothra and King Ghidorah: Giant Monsters All-Out Attack (2001)—Shusuke Kaneko

Director Shusuke Kaneko reinvented the kaiju film with his *Gamera* series in the '90s by juxtaposing anime style and realism in his giant monster movies. Kaneko brought his unique vision to the Godzilla series by making Godzilla a villain again and displaying the human consequences of living among god-like creatures, as well as the shocking after-effects of their clashes for the all-too-vulnerable inhabitants of Japan. People are just as important as the monsters in Kaneko's kaiju films and the characters are well developed here, much more than in any Godzilla film since the original. This is perhaps the most Lovecraftian of the Godzilla series; Kaneko should have been allowed to make more Godzilla films, but the poor box office showing prevented him from returning. The inclusion of the under-used kaiju Baragon is another positive attribute.

5.

Godzilla vs. Megalon (1973)—Jun Fukuda

Once considered the nadir of the Godzilla films, *Godzilla vs. Megalon* has aged quite well and is experiencing a critical turnaround. Yes, there are some cloyingly lame scenes with the annoying little boy (what is that contraption he is riding at the beginning of the film?), but Megalon and Jet Jaguar are some of the best kaiju and tokusatsu characters ever (Jet Jaguar was one of Toho's answers to Ultraman, the other was Zone Fighter), and the tag team battle between Godzilla/Jet Jaguar and Megalon/Gigan is so much fun that you can forgive the pandering to children and just enjoy the great suit work. Plus, there are some nudie pictures plastered all over a truck's cab, displaying the difference between Japanese and American sensibilities when it comes to movies aimed at children. Goofy but funky score by Riichiro Manabe, too.

4.

Destroy All Monsters (1968)—Ishiro Honda

Originally intended to be a celebration and end of the Godzilla series, director Ishiro Honda, genius soundtrack composer Akira Ifukube, and special effects master Eiji Tsuburaya pulled out all the stops for a kaiju battle royale featuring Anguirus, Baragon, Gorosaurus, King Ghidorah, Kumonga, Manda, Minilla, Mothra, Rodan, and

Varan. There are some slow parts and meaningless exposition, but when the monsters rampage, it is a thing of rare beauty. The only thing that bothers me about the film is that Gorosaurus is misidentified as Baragon and shown to be burrowing out of the ground, which is not in his nature. Okay, it's a geeky criticism, but those who love kaiju will understand. The movie has the best title of all the Godzilla films, though.

3.

Godzilla vs. King Ghidorah (1991)—Kazuki Omori

The best of the Hensei series, *Godzilla vs. King Ghidorah* brings back one of Godzilla's most fearsome foes not only in its organic form but in a suped-up, ultra-cool mecha version, too. Using a new twist on *The Terminator/La Jetee's* changing the future by intervening in the past, the film jumps from WWII to the present to the future. Like most time travel films, the implications aren't quite worked out, but it's fun nonetheless. Fusing innovative technology, incredible battle scenes, and an alternative origin story for Godzilla, the film has been criticized as a paranoid, xenophobic allegory for the rest of the world's desire to stop Japan's prosperity. However, Mecha King Ghidorah is so rad one can look past the over-done nationalism.

2.

King Kong vs. Godzilla (1962)—Ishiro Honda

The epic battle between East and West: a WWII rematch as the King of the Apes faces off against the King of the Monsters with only one creature left standing. The crown jewel of Toho's thirtieth anniversary celebration of the founding of its studio, this is the film that made Godzilla a worldwide phenomenon and effectively transformed him from political symbol to action hero. *King Kong vs. Godzilla* is the culmination of the 1950s giant monster genre and laid the groundwork for a new type of sci-fi film that would revolutionize special effects artistry and movie marketing. And contrary to the urban myth, there was only one ending filmed with King Kong emerging victorious (though he does get sloshed in the film).

1.

Godzilla vs. Hedorah (1971)—Yoshimitsu Banno

Hated by Godzilla traditionalists but loved by those who are enamored of insane Japanese films, *Godzilla vs. Hedorah* is a mashup of different film styles, tones, and plots all connected by a hysterically grim yet psychedelic ecological warning, personified by the pollution-spawned Smog Monster who pretty much owns Godzilla. Banno brought a maverick, counterculture aesthetic and a radical political agenda to the Godzilla series, suggesting that there are threats that even Godzilla can't defeat. Featuring acid trips, go-go dancers, hippies playing a free concert, Godzilla's skin dissolving, kooky animation, lectures about the effects of contamination, and the strangest kaiju ever, this film brought Godzilla into the postmodern era. Bring back the sun!

Honorable Mention

Godzilla vs. Mothra
Godzilla vs. Monster Zero
Godzilla vs. Destoroyah
Godzilla X Mechagodzilla
Zone Fighter TV series
Godzilla Island TV series

THE 13 MOST GLORIOUS GODZILLA FILMS

Chapter 7.

The 13 Most Satanic Horror Films

rench philosopher Voltaire once quipped, "If God did not exist, it would be necessary to invent him." The devil is a far more interesting (and cinematic) human invention. As Dostoevsky noted, we made the devil in our own image, and so we couldn't make him a total loser. The eternal underdog, Satan, is the personification of humanity's fears, desires, and vices—all those things we are told to keep in check to be good citizens. Unable to voluntarily indulge in our darker, instinctual, sensual side, we need both a tempter and a scapegoat to blame when we are forced to face the consequences of our uncivilized actions and impure thoughts. Milton and the romantics revised the medieval identification of Satan with the abject and the venal, transforming him into Lucifer, the proud, rebellious anti-hero whose refusal to kneel to the boss made him the ideal symbol of individual liberty fighting against the tyranny of monarchy. The complexity of humanity's relationship with the devil (a combination of fear, envy, admiration, and attraction) make him the perfect literary character, much more approachable than the obscured, distant, self-absorbed, omniscient God. Starting with Melies, Satan has been a perennial bad guy in film, the ultimate antagonist adversary and

> The eternal underdog, Satan, is the personification of humanity's fears, desires, and vices...

fount from which evil flows and infects us poor, helpless, innocent humans. Satanic cinema came into its own during the late '60s/early '70s when the occult revival and counterculture revolution upended conventional views of good, bad, and the metaphysical. The Church of Satan publicized a vision of the devil as a metaphor for a social Darwinism that celebrates worldly materialism, the individual will to power, and satisfaction of all sexual and primal urges. Yet these are not the kind of Satanists that usually populate horror films. Cinematic devil worshipers traffic in actual supernatural entities, murder in the name of their deity, perform blood rituals, wear hooded cloaks, and seek to overthrow the reign of Christianity. Surrounded by pentagrams, black candles, and making the sign of Baphomet during a Black Mass, this is the corrupt, shocking, salacious satanism of exploitation films, horror fumetti, occult pornography, and black metal. It has nothing to do with a liberatory philosophy and everything to do with cheap sex, bad drugs, and trashy rock 'n' roll. Celebrate Walpurgis Nacht with some of these satanically inclined movies.

13.

"Heavenly Puss"
(1949)—William Hanna and Joseph Barbera

Hanna and Barbera should have received a Nobel Prize for their contributions to the cultural landscape. The cartoons they directed and produced from 1939–2006 are an unparalleled body of work in animation. Their Tom and Jerry theatrical short, "Heavenly Puss," ruminates on our existence once we have shuffled off this mortal coil and how our earthly behaviors will affect our lives in the next world. Tom's constant harassment of Jerry leads to Tom being crushed to death by a runaway piano. Tom ascends into the clouds on a golden escalator and tries to board the Heavenly Express train that will lead him to heaven. The only problem is that his past treatment of Jerry prevents him from attaining paradise. The gatekeeper insists that he return to earth and get Jerry to sign a certificate of forgiveness. If Jerry doesn't sign it within an hour, Tom will be cast into the infernal pits of hell, ruled by a satanic bulldog who wants to submerge Tom in a cauldron of molten lava. Tom's efforts to get Jerry's forgiveness are nerve-rackingly tense as a celestial clock ticks away and the canine Lord of Darkness keeps beckoning to Tom and reminding him of the eternal tortures that await if he is unable to get Jerry's pardon. Hanna and Barbera's cartoon is a frightening reminder of the pervasive cultural imagery of hell and the devil: fiery pits of misery and hopelessness governed by a pitchfork-wielding, bright-red, ferocious devil dog that clearly takes glee in his fiendish work. If cartoons have any influence on how children imagine what the afterlife will be like, then "Heavenly Puss" can surely scare even the most delinquent kid straight.

12.

Satan's Wife (1979)—Pier Carpi

Europe embraced the satanic film genre in the 1970s, churning out dozens of unbelievably cool movies mixing sex, violence, and the occult. Reuniting the stars of *Danger: Diabolik*, John Phillip Law and Marissa Mell square off on opposite sides in *Satan's Wife*, a sleazy story of satanic seduction. Lucifer impregnates female cult members in the hope that his devil children will wreak havoc on the world. One of the devil spawn rejects her parentage, while the other revels in her malevolent birthright, tormenting her teachers and burning her horny classmate. A priest attempts to combat this teenaged anti-christ, but her father won't give up on her that easily. The film is a bit of a mess with unexplained plot twists and motivations (it is, after all, an Italian genre film), but it boasts some groovy satanic rituals, a coven of Italian housewives, and the underrated Lara Wendel as the ultimate demonic, petulant teenager. Stelvio Cipriani provides his usual dazzling music to accompany the occult proceedings and that wonderful euro-cult awkwardness that we Americans love so much. If you had to play matchmaker for Satan, the slinky, ice-cold beauty of Marissa Mell would make ol' Scratch a perfect mate.

11.

The Devil's Rain (1975)—Robert Fuest

A perennial late-late show movie, *The Devil's Rain* is an overacting aficionado's dream with over-the-top performances by William Shatner, Tom Skerritt, Ernest Borgnine, Eddie Albert, Ida Lupino, and Keenan Wynn. The great Robert Fuest (responsible for the *Dr. Phibes* masterpieces) conjures up a desolate, sun-baked wasteland as the setting for this tale of a family curse and supernatural betrayal. It seems that coven leader Jonathan Corbis has been searching for a satanic book that was stolen from him in the 1600s. The Preston family stole the book and informed on the coven they were once part of. Swearing revenge, Corbis has hunted down the Prestons after 300 years of searching and is finally within reach of the book. Remembered for its grisly special effects in which a foul rain melts the devil worshippers into gooey puddles of ooze, the film exudes a blasphemous tone, particularly in Borgnine's performance as Corbis channeling the simmering rage of a double-crossed warlock. The scenes of satanic ceremonies feel genuine, perhaps because of head satanist Anton LaVey's work as the film's technical advisor. Fuest uses many creepy props and set pieces to create a foreboding feeling of despair, such as the Hieronymus Bosch opening credits, an abandoned church, a ghost town, the goat-like transformation of Corbis, and the crystal-ball urn of lost souls. Unfortunately, the critics eviscerated the film, ending Fuest's promising movie directing career. Hopefully, there's a special place in hell where those critics are forced to watch *Good Luck Chuck* over and over again.

10.

The House of the Devil (2009)—Ti West

Though the so-called "satanic panic" of the 1980s ruined many lives and almost led to the execution of an innocent man, the devilish zeitgeist of conspiracy, ritual abuse, and occult sacrifices make for perfect horror movie fodder. Expertly recalling that time of doubt and paranoia, Ti West's *The House of the Devil* is a fearsome tribute to not only this cultural

THE 13 MOST SATANIC HORROR FILMS

anxiety but to the horror films of the era as well, seamlessly replicating camera techniques from '80s slashers. Opening with the bogus "based upon true events" disclaimer, the movie focuses on college student Samantha, who, like most college students, needs money and a room of her own. She accepts a babysitting job from a strange couple (played with cult actor excellence by Tom Noonan and Mary Woronov) in a strange house on the strange night of a lunar eclipse. Samantha soon realizes that the job she responded to is not the job she is required to perform and that pretense has lured her into a satanic nightmare. West's direction strikes just the right balance between suspense and full-on demonic mayhem as the tension builds though his use of stillness and quiet, lingering takes that build to a ritualistic crescendo. Jeff Grace's minimalist score complements the invocation of satanic forces as expressed in the shocking climax. How could you not love a film that was also released on VHS in a big clamshell box, a tribute to the days of video store sales based on garish covers?

9.

The Ninth Gate (1999)—Roman Polanski

Roman Polanski's connection to the dark side has resulted in personal tragedies, questionable life decisions, and incredible works of cinema art. *The Ninth Gate* was advertised as Polanski's return to horror, but anyone who follows Polanski's career would know that horror is always there no matter what genre of film he is making. Based on Arturo Pérez-Reverte's novel *The Club Dumas*, the film centers on rare book dealer Dean Corso (Johnny Depp) and his hunt to prove the authenticity of a priceless grimoire called *The Nine Gates of the Kingdom of Shadows*, which can summon Lucifer himself and grant unlimited power to its owner. Corso's search leads to murder, femme fatales, and devil-worshipping decadents who want the book for a satanic ceremony. The movie is a bibliophile's dream: comparing editions, illustrations, and printings of the book comprises pretty much the majority of the film, and before you can think that's as interesting as watching paint dry, Polanski's mastery of tension, misperception, and a vaguely threatening mood creates a compelling quest that leads not to stability but to more confusion. Like a combination of *The Kabbalah* and *The Necronomicon* written by Borges, *The Ninth Gate* is an enigma that can't be solved, and the more one tries to delve into its mysteries, the more lost and disillusioned the searcher becomes. An underrated master work, *The Ninth Gate* is proof that Polanski is still a vital, important artist. Just ignore the bad CGI effects and his criminal record.

8.

All the Colors of the Dark (1972)—Sergio Martino

The giallo is a magnificent Italian invention, and like the Ferrari or Lamborghini, it is a flashy machine that is all about speed, caring nothing about reasonable fuel economy. While most gialli focus on the immorality of the abnormal psyche, some have looked to the occult as a device for propelling the ultra-violent sexual violations on display. Giallo director extraordinaire Sergio Martino recruits a devil-worshipping Manson family-type cult to terrify and brainwash the Queen of the giallo—the gorgeous Edwige Fenech. Edwige is suffering from nightmares that recall her mother's murder and a recent miscarriage. Rejecting the specious advice of medical and psychological professionals, the tormented woman turns to the tried and true cure of satanism and the therapeutic healing of the Black Mass. When Edwige tries to back out of her membership in the coven, her nightmares become a reality of satanic stalking and supernatural danger. But is the peril real or just paranoid delusions? *All the Colors of the Dark* presses all the right gialli buttons with plenty of nudity, viciousness, and incomprehensible plotting, but makes the genius move of adding a psychedelic occult element to the insanity. The coven leader is a beastly maniac who wears long metallic fingernails and flashes his bloody gums to intimidate his followers. The sublime soundtrack by Bruno Nicolai is one of the finest to ever grace a giallo.

7.

The Sect (1991)—Michele Soavi

Wunderkind director Michele Soavi was the last great Italian horror artisan. Mentored by the maestro Dario Argento, Soavi's films project an arcane, demented beauty that is difficult to explain but ravishing to experience. *The Sect* (a.k.a. *The Devil's Daughter*) was co-written and produced by his illustrious patron, but it's still all Soavi, the mind-bending account of a woman (played by Jamie Lee Curtis's sister, Kelly Curtis) who has been chosen, against her will, to be the mother of Satan's son. A satanic sect will stop at nothing to enact this profane consummation: murder, mutilation, torture, face ripping, sacrifices, suicide, possessed washcloths. The film is a series of occult symbols and Cocteau-like images that individually make no sense, but when woven together form an instinctual continuity that activates the third eye. Sacred geometry and Fortean portents create disorientating viewing; for example, when a bug crawls up a character's nostril and we can see her dreams through the bug's perspective or when the

THE 13 MOST SATANIC HORROR FILMS

camera follows a blue substance through a labyrinth of plumbing pipes. Lovers of euro-cult films will have a field day picking out some of the genre's stalwarts like Herbert Lom, Giovanni Lombardo Radice, and Mariangela Giordano. An incredibly unique achievement, I suspect that this demonically transcendent film had a definite influence on Clive Barker's *Lord of Illusions*.

6.

Alucarda (1978)—Juan Lopez Moctezuma

Just the fact that Juan Lopez Moctezuma collaborated with the grand magus Alejandro Jodorowsky should be enough to warrant faith in his bizarro filmmaking abilities. Luckily, Moctezuma makes good on this expectation in *Alucarda*, a testament to the power and glory of satanic emancipation and absolution. Two young orphans, Alucarda and Justine, live an austere, cruel life in a Catholic convent. With only each other to cling to, the teenage girls form a bond that could be construed as unhealthy. Exploring the woods around the convent, the girls discover another world of pagan freedom, which leads them to a pact with Satan. The liberated demoniacs set their sights on the repressive convent that has kept them in bondage for far too long. Moctezuma's film is a DeSadeian attack on organized religion and the abuses of power legitimized in the name of Jesus. *Alucarda*'s sacrilege, perversity, and defilement are mechanisms for deconditioning and deliverance. Inverting every virtue and indulging in every vice, the satanic protagonists turn institutionalized violence and sadism back on their oppressors. The film's imagery transforms the primal, animalistic, and profane into sacred ablutions with the satyr-like Satan personifying the earthly delights of the body and nature. *Alucarda* is an iconoclastic film that sees Satan as the redeemer of humanity. Now, will someone please release this miraculous soundtrack?

5.

Sheitan (2006)—Kim Chapiron

The new wave of French horror rebelled mightily against the Jean Rollin/Georges Franju mode of lyrical terror. An extreme example of this raw tendency is Kim Chapiron's *Sheitan*, a film that rubs the viewer's face in the grotty backwardness of the French countryside with its brutally ignorant, lustful, and superstitious inhabitants. The film begins in the strobing lights and thumping techno of a Paris nightclub. A group of revelers accepts the invitation of a young woman to continue the party at her country home. At the secluded house, the guests meet the strange family that resides there, realizing too late that their presence is required for an immaculate birth. The family is a bit too sexually accommodating, and their fixation on a creepy doll can't be a good thing. The demonic in *Sheitan* (which means Satan in Arabic) is an expression of all those ugly emotions and thoughts that should be kept repressed: sexism, racism, irrationality, spite, selfishness, and insensitivity. It is this kind of permissiveness that encourages evil to grow unchecked, bursting out, and engulfing all within its reach. The film takes place on Christmas Eve, signaling the nativity of a supernatural being, but this demi-god reflects the contemporary mores of a contemptuous, sick society. Driven by a bonkers performance from the impressive Vincent Cassel, *Sheitan* injects an occult ferocity into the rural boogeymen-out-to-get-the-city-slickers genre of horror. This impressive debut from Chapiron suggests that family can be the worst kind of cult.

4.

Prince of Darkness (1987)—John Carpenter

Leave it to the innovative John Carpenter to radically rethink the concept of the devil. Perhaps the most Lovecraftian film not based on a Lovecraft work, *Prince of Darkness* melds quantum physics with gnosticism and adds a bit of Erich von Däniken to tell the story of the awakening of the Anti-Matter Christ. Religion and science form an ineffectual alliance to prevent the Demiurge from crossing over into our universe. Evil is not a metaphor but a tangible substance emanating from the Father of all that is Antithetical, seeking to negate our world. The film has enough ideas and theories to propel a dozen movies, but there are also visceral shocks in the midst of the intellectual conjectures. *Prince of Darkness* contains Carpenter's most surreal imaginings: an ancient canister of sentient fluid, a man devoured by beetles, a woman who metamorphoses into the essence of malevolence, an army of murderous homeless drones, and the submerged mirror dimension of Satan (surely an homage to Cocteau's *Orpheus*). The most frightening scenes contain fragmentary future transmissions beamed into one's dreams, which suggests that present actions are doomed to futility. Carpenter used the pseudonym Martin Quatermass, a tribute to British author Nigel Kneale (who infamously asked to be removed from the credits of *Halloween III*), and yet Carpenter's sci-fi/horror/occult hybrid is better than any of Kneale's creations. Would Nigel ever feature Alice Cooper killing the nerd from *Riptide* with a bicycle frame? Ably staffed with Carpenter's stable of ragtag actors and featuring one of his most intense scores, *Prince of Darkness* might be Carpenter's best film. It is certainly his most underrated.

THE 13 MOST SATANIC HORROR FILMS

3.

The Devil Rides Out (1968)—Terence Fisher

Hammer Films goes satanic in this thrillingly regal adaptation of Dennis Wheatley's novel. Directed by the king of English Gothic, Terrence Fisher, and written by the immensely talented Richard Matheson, *The Devil Rides Out* pits the dashingly heroic Duc de Richleau (Christopher Lee) against the sinister Aleister Crowley clone Mocata (Charles Gray) in a struggle to claim innocent souls. Simon has fallen in with a group of satanists lead by Mocata, and the Duc must use his occult acumen and elegant erudition to save his friend's son. Interrupting a Black Mass that has conjured Satan himself, Richleau and his spunky charges must guard themselves from the demonic vengeance of Mocata. Fisher displays all his cinematic talents as a craftsman of terror, building tension and dread as Mocata tightens the satanic screws on the forces of good, sending menace after menace to the Duc and culminating in a heartstopping visit from the Angel of the Death. The film is suffused with occult symbols and references to Hecate, but the most startling image is the appearance of Lucifer himself, surely the most realistic depiction of the Dark One in film. Gray is fantastic as leader of the coven, a seething, sophisticated antagonist, and Lee has stated that Richleau is one of his favorite performances. Enhanced by James Bernard's rousing soundtrack, *The Devil Rides Out* exemplifies all that is magnificent about Hammer horror.

2.

Race with the Devil (1975)—Jack Starrett

Often mistaken for a made-for-TV movie, *Race with the Devil* is the quintessential satanic cult film. Scary, action-packed, and massively entertaining, this drive-in favorite hits all the devil-worshipping sweet spots: nude sacrifice, robe-clad coven, ritualistic murders, occult books, growing paranoia, and a nihilistic ending. Two couples on vacation inadvertently spy on a Black Mass in the middle of nowhere and are relentlessly hunted by the satanists in order to silence the witnesses. The premise is a horror fan's fantasy: who hasn't wondered what occult activities go on in the dead of night under our noses in our own vicinities? The cult members are anonymous figures that could be anyone, anywhere, at any time. The authorities are suspiciously ineffectual, and the wide open spaces of the Southwest offer only emptiness and death. The two leads, Peter Fonda and Warren Oates, prove why they were two of the best actors of the '70s, and any time we get to see Lara Parker (Angelique from *Dark Shadows*), it's a good day. On top of all the satanic thrills, there are car chases and crashes galore, as if *The Road Warrior* had been pursued by devil worshippers rather than post-apocalyptic punks. Director Jack Starrett keeps the plot moving at a frenetic pace and even hired actual satanists to serve as extras. Kevin Smith stated that *Race with the Devil* was a strong influence on his own *Red State*. Please don't hold this against the original film.

1.

Rosemary's Baby (1968)—Roman Polanski

One of the five films that blueprinted the contemporary horror film (along with *Night of the Living Dead*, *The Exorcist*, *The Texas Chainsaw Massacre*, and *Halloween*), *Rosemary's Baby* is Roman Polanski's masterpiece, a psychologically complex examination of the occult as a ruthlessly manipulating force. Based on Ira Levin's popular novel and produced by horror's great showman William Castle, it is the story of Rosemary and Guy Woodhouse (Mia Farrow and John Cassavetes), a young couple who have recently moved into an old apartment building. Their elderly neighbors are nosey but nice, and soon Guy's acting career takes off—just in time, because Rosemary discovers she's pregnant. As her neighbors try to take control over her life (using the excuse of helping her through her pregnancy), Rosemary starts to believe that their aid is not altruistic but has demonic motivations, notably protecting the devil's child she is unwittingly carrying.

The satanism in *Rosemary's Baby* is a metaphor for any belief system that seeks to dominate, repress, and eliminate individuality. Rosemary's gender and her "condition" make it that much easier to force her to conform and distrust her own instincts. Everyone knows better than Rosemary, and this selfishness masquerading as selflessness begins with Guy's willingness to sacrifice his own wife for personal success and fame. Polanski keeps the audience constantly guessing whether Rosemary is just overreacting or if there is an actual occult conspiracy working against her. The hallucinatory sequences and satanic rape scene are probably the closest any film has come to re-creating the stupefying viscerality of a nightmare. The neighbors (played by Ruth Gordon and Sidney Blackmer) are not your usual satanists; they are more like senior citizen swingers just back from the sleazy side of Boca Raton. The ending is one of the most hauntingly poignant in horror as Rosemary accepts her role as mother of the beast, preferring to side with her victimizers in order to find some form of significance.

THE 13 MOST SATANIC HORROR FILMS

It is a film of frightening coincidences and eerie tragedies that seem to leak off the screen and into reality, from ill-omen pregnancies (Sharon Tate), to murder (the Manson family massacre and John Lennon's assassination in front of the gloomy Dakota), to family breakups (Mia Farrow was served with divorce papers from Frank Sinatra on set), to satanists' attraction to celebrities (Rosemary reads *Yes I Can*, the autobiography of future Church of Satan buddy Sammy Davis Jr.) Heightened by little details like the black bassinet and the upside-down crucifix mobile hanging over the infant anti-christ, filled with phenomenal performances, and capped off with one of the greatest horror film scores ever, *Rosemary's Baby* singlehandedly changed the satanic horror film forever. As the ad campaign requested, "Pray for Rosemary's Baby."

And one extra:

"The Sign of Satan" (1964)—*The Alfred Hitchcock Hour*

Because it is a TV show and was never shown in a theater, Robert Bloch/Barré Lyndon's "The Sign of Satan" falls outside the scope of this article, but if you are a true satanic media connoisseur, you have to see this episode of *The Alfred Hitchcock Hour*, which includes a frighteningly realistic litany to Satan led by Christopher Lee himself. As eerie and atmospheric as any demonic film. Maybe the first time a Black Mass was depicted on TV?

Honorable Mention

The Devil's Nightmare
Invocation of My Demon Brother
Satan's Blood
Satanis: The Devil's Mass
Angel Heart
Nude for Satan
The Devil's Wedding Night
Satanico Pandemonium
The Brotherhood of Satan
Black Candles
Psychomania
Devil Dog: Hound from Hell

Chapter 8.

THE HORROR FILM PRIMER: WITCHCRAFT MOVIES

have noticed that the kind of monster a horror fan likes tells you a lot about the person and their aesthetic. Vampire aficionados are usually romantically elegant, werewolf fanatics more brutally primal, zombie zealots more graphically visceral, ghost obsessives more faithfully anticipative, and satanic enthusiasts more worldly and cynical. Those who prefer the witchcraft category of horror film are a singular kind of epicurean that delights in the ritualistic, ceremonial, ornamental, and diabolical. Now, when I talk about witchcraft, I don't mean those pretentious Wiccan, neo-Pagan, Druid, New Age, White Magic, Mother Earth hold-hands-and-dance-around-a-maypole-on-the-equinox "witches." I mean witches that draw pentagrams and summon Lucifer, demand blood sacrifices to the Goat of Mendes, hold blasphemous orgies of violence and sex, lash out with black magic, and curse the good and righteous. Evil witches like the Queen in *Snow White*, the Wicked Witch of the West from *The Wizard of Oz*, Bathsheba Sherman from *The Conjuring*, the Blair Witch, and the world-shattering coven from *Witching & Bitching* (surely the greatest patriarchy vs. matriarchy movie ever made). Witchcraft is steeped in ancient traditions and lore, an alternative historical account of power and conspiracy. Covens and sabbaths represent secret illuminated cults in league with darker forces and forbidden knowledge. Witches are natural insurrectionists and revolutionaries, embracing the aberrant, esoteric, and profane as instruments of sinful self-fulfillment and rebellious individual empowerment. Clearly, establishment institutions have been threatened by these anarchic primeval forces since the beginning of recorded time, attempting to control, dominate, or eradicate these wickedly potent energies. Witch hunts have resulted in hundreds of thousands of deaths across the globe, but the sparks of disorder, chaos, and malevolence can never be extinguished and continue to spread disorder and pandemonium. Our witch cult grows. Witchcraft films are among the most sinisterly stylish horror films in the canon, exuding a moody, impure yet seductive atmosphere of mysticism, legend, and carnality. Witchcraft can be split into three subgenres: witch-hunting films, warlock films, and witch films.

> Those who prefer the witchcraft category of horror film are a singular kind of epicurean that delights in the ritualistic, ceremonial, ornamental, and diabolical.

Witch-Hunting Films

These films are usually historically based and reveal the corruption and sadism of authorities who attack others in the name of God and country. The evangelic fervor to eradicate deviance has turned the defenders of morality into deviants themselves. Witchfinder films reflect the persecution that hippies felt at the hands of the powers that be: old, lascivious corrupt men secretly lusting after young women and men under the guise of maintaining law and order. The witch-hunting film seemed to hit its stride just as feminism and woman's liberation gained greater attention in the public sphere. Coincidence?

1.

Witchfinder General
(a.k.a. *The Conqueror Worm*, 1968)—Michael Reeves

Witchfinder General focuses on real-life witch hunter Matthew Hopkins, a corrupt sadist who takes advantage of the social upheaval of the English Civil War to prey upon the weak and innocent. Vincent Price gives arguably his best acting performance as the murderous Hopkins, and director Michael Reeves uses this historical personage to brilliantly comment on the nature of institutionalized terror and the cancer-like spread of revenge and violence.

2.

The Demons (1973)—Jess Franco

Jess Franco's gloriously idiosyncratic style perfectly fits this sleazy, libidinous tale of witch hunting, nuns, and demonic vengeance. The testing of the witches is particularly perverted, bordering on BDS&M, allowing Franco to indulge his De Sade fixation. Franco regulars like Howard Vernon, Britt Nichols, and Anne Libert are their usual gloriously licentious selves. Gotta love the anachronistic, wah-wah drenched acid rock soundtrack.

3.

Mark of the Devil
(1970)—Michael Armstrong/Adrian Hoven

An intensely unpleasant film, *Mark of the Devil* moves the witch-hunting premise to scenic eighteenth-century Austria as Herbert Lom and Udo Kier make their way across the countryside, raping and torturing suspected witches. *The Sound of Music* this is not. The hills are alive with the sounds of screams, grunts, burning flesh, and ripped out tongues. Memorable for the gleeful approach to the atrocities inflicted on the voluptuous victims of the witch hysteria.

4.

Cry of the Banshee (1970)—Gordon Hessler

A lower-rent version of *Witchfinder General* crossed with *Blood on Satan's Claw*, *Cry of the Banshee* is more supernatural and weird than your average witch-hunting flick. Lacking the political subtext of Reeves, Gordon Hessler goes for a Gothic approach, using folklore and superstition to cast a spell on the viewer. Cool Les Baxter score, too.

5.

The Bloody Judge (1970)—Jess Franco

Franco's first stab at a witch-hunting film, *The Bloody Judge* mines much of the same territory as *Witchfinder General* but with more sick eroticism. Christopher Lee is witch hunter Lord Chief Justice Jeffreys (a real historical figure), who uses accusations of witchcraft to crush political opposition to King James II. Great Bruno Nicolai soundtrack, but the material is kind of tame for a Franco film. His later films, *The Demons* and *Love Letters of a Portuguese Nun*, would ratchet up the sleaze element that seems integral to the witchfinder genre.

Warlock Films

Traditionally, witchcraft has been a woman's way to power and authority, using supernatural influence when political, economic, and social avenues have been closed to them. In most witchcraft films, men are the servants of the all-mighty females, but there are a few films that allow men to follow the left-hand path.

1.

The Witchmaker
(a.k.a. *The Legend of Witch Hollow*, 1969)
—William O. Brown

This is a perfect movie about a professor of paranormal studies who brings his students into the Louisiana bayou to investigate a string of occult murders. The perpetrator is a warlock with the awesome nomenclature of Luther the Berserk (John Lodge), who drinks the blood of his victims and can raise the dead with his necromantic power. Director William O. Brown makes the most out of the spooky swamp setting and ritualistic crimes to create an atmosphere of trepidation and morbidity.

2.

Halloween III: Season of the Witch (1982)—Tommy Lee Wallace

Tommy Lee Wallace's fantastic ode to All Hallow's Eve, *Halloween III* is often maligned as not being a Michael Myers slasher-thon, but thank Samhain it isn't. The film revolves around the exploits of Conal Cochran, the CEO of the Silver Shamrock Novelties Company, who is seeking to return Halloween to its pagan roots. His plan involves a nasty surprise on Halloween night for all the kiddies who bought his masks. Dan O'Herlihy gives a discreetly insane performance as Cochrane, whose anti-commercialism stance on the holiday likens him to a warlock Charlie Brown. His discourse on the origins of Halloween is one of the most foreboding speeches in film ever. A movie of such witchy ferocity that that wussy Nigel Kneale asked to have his name removed from the credits.

3.

The Wicker Man (1973)—Robin Hardy

One of the true classics of the horror genre, Robin Hardy's *The Wicker Man* is a treatise on the struggle between the naturalistic indulgences of paganism and the unnatural repressions of Christianity, and yet the true target of the film is blind faith in any ideology. Loosely based on the real-life Findhorn community in Scotland, a devoutly Catholic police sergeant (played with righteous indignation by Edward Woodward) is lured to the pastoral municipality of Summerisle in search of a missing girl, but finds a deeper conspiracy of magic and myth informing the lives of the inhabitants. As community leader, Lord Summerisle (Christopher Lee in his greatest role) is a charismatic zealot willing to sacrifice an innocent to prolong the idyllic existence of his utopia. The soundtrack of transcendent folk songs plays a pivotal role in enhancing the aura of animism and old religion that suffuses the film, as well as offering a Greek-chorus-like commentary. If you ever wanted to see an issue of *Man, Myth, and Magic* come alive, here's the next best thing. However, I'd rather burn myself alive in a straw effigy than watch the sequel, *The Wicker Tree*.

4.

Simon, King of Witches (1971)—Bruce Kessler

Made in the confusing aftermath of the '60s, *Simon, King of the Witches* is satirical look at the post-hippie scene, with magic as a metaphor for the idealized dreams of the Love Generation. Directed by Bruce Kessler and starring Andrew Prine as Simon, the self-proclaimed king of the witches desires to be a god but is consistently brought back to earth by the crass hedonism and materialism that has engulfed the selfless liberality of the Age of Aquarius. Loosely based on real-life warlock Alex Sanders, *Simon, King of Witches* is one of the last gasps of the psychedelic film, dragged through the mud of the emerging '70s.

5.

Warlock (1989)—Steve Miner

A thoroughly entertaining time-waster, *Warlock* ties together New England witch trials, time travel, *The Grand Grimoire*, a "Witch Compass," and late '80s LA into one crazy movie. The warlock (portrayed in a casually creepy manner by Julian Sands) is followed by a witch hunter (Richard E. Grant, who also played the irrepressible Withnail) from 1691 to twentieth-century California. The warlock is searching for the pages of a satanic book that will expose the apocalyptic "real" name of God, and the witch hunter has his hands full pursuing his prey and trying to acclimate to '80s culture. It spawned a number of sequels, each one a little worse than the last.

Witch Films

1.

Suspiria (1977)—Dario Argento

The grandmother of all witch movies, *Suspiria* took the horror film to a higher level of artistic expression. Directed by Dario Argento, one of the finest stylists in all of cinema, and co-written by the unsung heroine of Italian horror, Daria Nicolodi, *Suspiria* is a vividly flamboyant ultra-violent phantasmagoria built on sighs, awkward gestures, maggots, razor wire, and art deco peacocks. Ballet dancer Suzy Bannion (Jessica Harper playing at Snow White) arrives at an esteemed dance academy run, unbeknownst to her and her fellow students, by a coven of vicious witches. The academy and coven

THE HORROR FILM PRIMER
WITCHCRAFT
MOVIES

are controlled by the mysterious Helena Markos, a.k.a. Mater Suspiriorum (Our Lady of Sighs), the embodiment of misery and sorrow, responsible for the despair and grief in the world. *Suspiria* was the first film of the "Three Mothers Trilogy," inspired by De Quincey's opium dreambook *Suspiria de Profundis*. Ferociously poetic and irrationally mesmerizing, the witches manifest themselves through Technicolor surrealism, conjuring a sensory overload that terminates logic and reason. Argento's direction seems like the random splatterings of a mad artistic genius, an ADD approach that jumps from one amazing set piece to another with little rhyme or reason. The pounding score by Goblin is just another spell cast by the witches in the film. Followed by *Inferno* and *The Mother of Tears*, *Suspiria* set a standard for witchcraft movies that still hasn't been bettered.

2.

The Lords of Salem (2013)—Rob Zombie

Salem, Massachusetts, will always be ground zero for witch horror, and Rob Zombie embraces the Puritan nightmares of curses and conspiracies in *The Lords of Salem*. The film offers up modern-day Salem as a sacrifice to those who were destroyed during the original witch trials, but these are not falsely accused victims—they are the real satanic deal. In a deliberate, ominous film that takes on a ritualistic aura and pace, Zombie invokes a ceremony of crones and drones; the power of evil exists in the fabric of the film itself The male characters are weak and ineffectual. The female characters are largely middle-aged, defiant, and intimidating. As head witch Margaret Morgan, Meg Foster transforms herself into the embodiment of darkness and the left-hand path. Zombie's direction is masterful, with brief surrealistic flashes of Kubrick, Russell, Polanski, Jodorowsky, and Argento, but these references are secondary to Zombie's own artistic interests and compositions. His use of color and sound are mesmerizing, especially the over-saturated Room 5, John 5's throbbing dream-weapon score, and the recurring use of John Cale's screeching viola, echoed in the hypnotic trance of The Lord's cacophonous album. Years from now, when The Lords return, their vengeance will not be exacted on the citizens of Salem, but on those who foolishly dismissed this uniquely powerful film.

3.

Horror Hotel (a.k.a. *The City of the Dead*, 1960) —John Llewellyn Moxey

Perhaps the most atmospheric horror film with the stupidest title (*Kill Baby Kill* is a close second), *Horror Hotel* is a shadowy, chiaroscuro ode to the denizens of the twilight realm. Directed by the underrated John Llewellyn Moxey and starring Christopher Lee, *Horror Hotel* focuses on the New England town of Whitewood, a strange village tenanted by Elizabeth Selywn, a reincarnated seventeenth-century witch and her minions. To keep her immortal status, a virgin must be sacrificed to the dark gods every year on Candlemass (the pickings must be getting slimmer all the time), and the chosen victim is a student who has come to the accursed municipality to research witchcraft's terrible legacy on the region. Shot in Shepperton Studios on a miniscule budget, *Horror Hotel* effectively uses foggy gloom, decrepit sets, and perpetual night to suggest a scaled version of Lovecraft's witch-haunted city of Arkham. The fate of one of the characters prefigures a major Hitchcock jolt from *Psycho* (though there is some question who did it first), and the American version had some dialogue excised because it would have offended our Puritan ears: "I have made my pact with thee O Lucifer! Hear me, hear me! I will do thy bidding for all eternity. For all eternity shall I practice the ritual of Black Mass. For all eternity shall I sacrifice unto thee. I give thee my soul, take me into thy service. O Lucifer, listen to thy servant, grant her this pact for all eternity and I with her, and if we fail thee but once, you may do with our souls what you will. Make this city an example of thy vengeance. Curse it, curse it for all eternity! Let me be the instrument of thy curse. Hear me O Lucifer, hear me!" Electric Wizard needs to sample this right quick.

4.

The Blood on Satan's Claw (1970)—Piers Haggard

Blood on Satan's Claw is the finest film produced by those weirdos at Tigon Film Productions. Even without the prestige of Hammer or the assembly-line-like release schedule of Amicus, Tigon released quite a few rough gems in its short existence. *Blood on Satan's Claw* (this has to be one of the most outré titles ever) is set in those glorious, open-minded days of seventeenth-century England as a supernatural awakening takes hold of the poor, ignorant peasants. Beginning with the discovery of a demonic skull in a field, the film offers spouting claws and thick, furry patches for those willing to join the coven. If that's not incentive enough, Angel (Linda Hayden), the leader of the lustful cult, is probably the sexiest, most seductive witch ever. Her tendency to go "sky clad" is reason enough to succumb to her provocatively evil charms. Using real countryside locations, director Piers Haggard invests the film with an authentically raw, rustic paranoia, and the score by Marc Wilkinson enhances the brooding tone with gusto.

5.

Haxan (a.k.a. *Witchcraft through the Ages*, 1922)
—Benjamin Christensen

Written and directed by great Dane Benjamin Christensen, *Häxan* is a silent film containing more deranged imagery and transgressive moments than ten modern horror films combined. Based on the infamous fifteenth-century Inquisitors' instruction book *Malleus Maleficarum* (*The Hammer of the Witches*), *Häxan* glorifies the sensual supernatural and condemns the witch-hunting hysteria as a tragic misinterpretation of mental illness and repression. The film is a strange hybrid of a documentary and theatrical re-creations broken up into four chapters that move through historical and dramatic depictions of witches and their persecutions and treatment. Part scholarly essay and part psycho-sexual freakout, the film was initially banned in the US for its scenes of extreme violence and perversion (including a blasphemous appearance by Satan played with relish by Christensen). An abridged version was unnecessarily released later; the only thing to recommend it is the narration by the twentieth century's greatest author, William S. Burroughs.

6.

Mystics in Bali (1981)—H. Tjut Djalil

Using the Indonesian mythology of the leyak and the penanggalan—cannibal witches and vampires with the unique ability to separate their heads and entrails from their bodies—*Mystics in Bali* is so out there that viewing it can cause one to hallucinate uncontrollably. The film centers on Cathy, a writer who falls prey to a black magic cult while researching a book on witchcraft. Baiting her with the promise of forbidden knowledge, a witch transforms Cathy into a vampiric creature that stalks its victims as a floating head and viscera. Balinese shamans are recruited to save poor Cathy and destroy the cult permanently. Even though it is extremely low budget and shot with a minimum of flair, the scenes of the flying head and guts attacking a woman between her legs has to be one of those 1,000 film moments you have to see before you die. The pantheon of exotic Balinese gods and monsters is a refreshing change from the usual Western spectral cast of characters. Operating on an entirely different wavelength, *Mystics in Bali* should be an integral part of an Indonesian tourism advertising campaign.

7.

Curse of the Crimson Altar (1968)—Vernon Sewell

Loosely based on Lovecraft's bonkers "The Dreams in the Witch House," *Curse of the Crimson Altar* brings together an inconceivably remarkable unholy trinity of Christopher Lee, Boris Karloff, and Barbara Steele in another freaky Tigon production. Searching for his missing brother, Robert (Mark Eden) discovers a witch cult centered on the grand dame Lavinia Morley (Barbara Steele), which is recruiting through psychedelic nightmares and hallucinations of ritual initiations and degenerate rites. On the surface it is a rather by-the-numbers witch film, but Barbara Steele's presence elevates it to an unearthly plain. Her queen of the witches' attire makes her look like she just stepped out of Kenneth Anger's pleasure dome after getting her body painted by Kandinsky. The mind boggles at the thought of Barbara Steele playing Lavinia Whately in a Mario Bava-directed version of "The Dunwich Horror."

8.

The Witch's Mirror (1962)—Chano Urueta

A Mexican fantasy film that incorporates elements of *Snow White*, *Rebecca*, *Eyes without a Face*, and *Suspicion*, *El Espejo de la Bruja* is a morality tale in which witchcraft plays the role of an equalizing force of justice. Starting out as a fairly routine story of murderous infidelity, the movie takes a left turn into the bizarre with a ghost, the devil, and a homicidal plastic surgeon. Surprisingly graphic for its time, the film's black-and-white quality adds startling clarity. Almost classically gorgeous in its composition, *The Witch's Mirror* has a lyrically fragile approach to criminal irrationality similar to Franju's archetypal film. Though not as frightening in its depiction of witchcraft as other films of its ilk, the supernatural occurrences staged by director Chano Urueta are impressive, especially the titular mirror and the haunting of the melancholy, cave-like mansion. Mexican folklore is especially rich in spiritism and the fantastic, and so maybe *The Witch's Mirror* belongs more in the category of magical realism than B movie horror.

9.

Viy (1967)—Konstantin Ershov/Georgi Kropachyor

Some good things came out of the Soviet Union: Tarkovsky, Eisenstein, Yakoff Smirnoff, and this

THE HORROR FILM PRIMER: WITCHCRAFT MOVIES

movie produced by the legendary Mosfilm. An adaption of a Nikolai Gogol story, *Viy* concerns a young priest who is required to spend three nights praying over a witch who he has accidently killed. Each session involves the witch rising from her coffin and attempting to use her dreadful powers and foul familiars to test his faith and destroy his humanity. Through these dark nights of the soul, the priest has only a protective circle to keep the terrors of hell at bay, personified by the mighty demon Viy. Directors Konstantin Ershov and Georgi Kropachyov craft an amazingly charming folk tale of a film with fairy-tale logic and an enchanted countryside filled with old world mysteries. The naive hero's quest from innocence to experience is a test of external and internal fortitude, starting with a wild ride on a broomstick and culminating in a cacophonous night where the devil unleashes all his underlings to break the will of the poor novice.

10.

Superstition (1982)—James W. Robertson

A hybridized slasher/witchcraft film, *Superstition* has lots of chilling moments of witch-derived mayhem. A witch who was drowned in the seventeenth century takes revenge on any trespassers that dare disrespect her execution site. A priest must unravel the secret of Black Pond and what lies beneath before the witch murders the new family that has moved into an accursed old house. The revivified witch is able to use modern technology such as a microwave oven and a circular saw in ingeniously destructive ways. This nasty video has graphic kills and an extended witch trial flashback, but the best scenes are the quick glimpses of the witch's contorted body and scaly hands. The effects and directing are quite effective, but the acting is sub-par, including one of the most inept police detectives in movie history. Rumor has it that Heather Locklear had a minor role in the film, but her scenes were edited out for time. It's a shame, because her thespian chops could only have raised the low bar of acting achievement, as manifested in this flawed but inventively gory movie.

11.

Witchcraft (1964)—Don Sharp

The Hammer film that should have been, *Witchcraft* is an unfairly neglected black-and-white thriller directed by second-tier British director Don Sharp (responsible for the oddity *Kiss of the Vampire*). Playing out like Romeo and Juliet crossed with *Black Sunday*, the film traces the feud between two families encompassing forbidden love, betrayal, financial chancery, and an exhumed witch determined to eradicate the descendants of the family that had her buried alive. Black magic is the means for one family to get revenge on the other, through setting up random fatal accidents. A car crash and a drowning are just the tip of the iceberg of the revenge that the returned witch Vanessa has in store for her hated rivals. Though a bit talky in parts, *Witchcraft* summons eerie scenes that are worthy of comparison with the Italian Gothics, such as necromantic rituals conducted in the family crypt.

12.

Pumpkinhead (1988)—Stan Winston

Though not ostensibly a witchcraft film, a witch plays a pivotal role in this contemporary creature feature. The directorial debut of Stan Winston, one of the elite special effects artists of all time, this impressive meditation on revenge stars character actor extraordinaire Lance Henriksen and the coolest monster introduced during the '80s. When a bunch of reckless yuppies carelessly cause the death of a country boy's son, an unstoppable force is released to punish those who have taken the man's pride and joy. As the demonic Pumpkinhead decimates the interlopers in appalling ways, the mourning Ed Harley begins to regret his rash desire for vengeance. The deaths of the irresponsible intruders are extremely frightening, but the lead-up to the creature's unleashing contains the most compelling moments in the film. In his frantic search for closure, Harley travels to a shack in the woods to request help from the witch Haggis, who is asked to bring the dead son back. Unable to do so, she agrees to summon Pumpkinhead to exact retribution. Her spell involves a pumpkin, a corpse, and blood from both father and son in a startlingly atmospheric sequence of steps toward oblivion. Florence Schauffler channels the EC Comics Old Witch in the most convincing portrayal of a necromancer ever.

13.

Mother of Tears (2007)—Dario Argento

Dario Argento is the Grand Sorcerer of witchcraft movies. His witch film mythos is spread out over the Three Mothers trilogy, a series of movies inspired by Thomas de Quincey's hallucinogenic "Levana and Our Ladies of Sorrow," in which the fury-like Three Sorrows are identified as Mater Lachrymarum (Mother of Tears), Mater Suspiriorum (Mother of Sighs), and Mater Tenebrarum (Mother of Shadows). The trilogy transforms these personifications of misery into three witches who rule the world and cause untold despair and destruction.

Starting with *Suspiria* (1977) and following with the frighteningly phantasmagorical *Inferno* (1980), horror obsessives waited twenty-seven long years for the trilogy to be concluded. Straining under the weight of almost three decades of expectations, *Mother of Tears* was finally released in 2007 and seemed to confirm all of the post-*Opera* Argento hating: the story was ridiculous, the acting monotone, and the directing bland—three cardinal sins that pre-1980s Dario had never committed but post-1980s Dario seemed to wallow in. And yet, the film has it kooky charms, and those charms seem to glow brighter with each subsequent viewing. The story, while ludicrous, has a surreal absurdity that fits perfectly with the rococo nonsense of *Suspiria* and *Inferno*, with plenty of witchcraft and bloody murders as Mater Lachrymarum inaugurates a black magic apocalypse on Rome. The notion that Asia Argento is the beneficiary of nepotism is put to rest through her charismatic performance. Lastly, though not reaching the dizzying camera absurdity of previous films, Argento's directorial style in *Mother of Tears* reflects an older, wiser craftsman who allows the story, rather than his technique, to carry the narrative weight. Whether the script is up to the challenge is a different argument, but the cool, mannered approach that Argento brings to the material makes it seem that much more real. *Mother of Tears* is certainly not Argento's best movie, nor is it even the best movie in the Three Mothers trilogy, but it gets the nod over the metaphysical insanity of *Inferno* because, even in the face of diminished influence, the fact that Argento is still trying to frighten and entertain is victory enough.

Honorable Mention

Witching & Bitching
Inferno
Necromancy
The Witches
The Devil's Own
Spider Labyrinth
Kill Baby Kill
The Witch's Cradle
Season of the Witch (a.k.a. *Jack's Wife*)

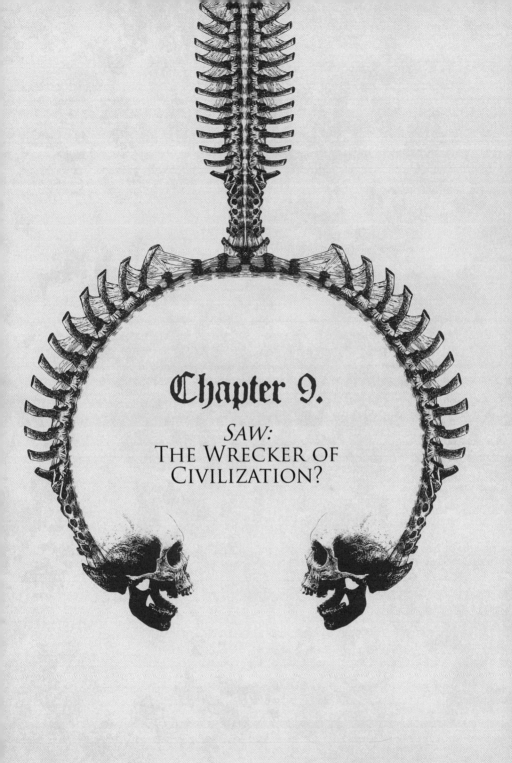

Chapter 9.

SAW:
THE WRECKER OF
CIVILIZATION?

irst, the facts. There are seventy-six deaths in the *Saw* film franchise, encompassing seven films released between 2004 and 2010. Some of the murders involve being cut with razor wire, burned alive by flammable jelly, shot in the head by four shotguns simultaneously, disemboweled by a scalpel, and bludgeoned with a toilet tank cover. All of these murders are featured in the first film, the tamest of the series. Actually, twenty-eight of the seventy-six deaths occur in the most recent installment *Saw 3-D*, where viewers can have the vicarious experience of having their eyes and mouth impaled by steel rods. Horror film followers know that this is not a new trend in portraying violence on the screen (be it movie, TV, or computer). The template for *Jigsaw's* gruesome traps and deadly puzzles can be traced to the 1970s as Bob Clark's *Black Christmas*, Mario Bava's *Twitch of the Death Nerve* (Sean Cunningham basically plagiarized this film in the form of *Friday the 13th I* and *II*), and, most famously, John Carpenter's epochal *Halloween*, which created the infamous "slasher film" genre. (We can thank Roger Ebert and Gene Siskel for popularizing that obnoxious term). Some horror films of the late '90s through today have earned the moniker of "torture porn," a term that

> There are seventy-six deaths in the *Saw* film franchise, encompassing seven films released between 2004 and 2010.

attempts to, quite unfairly, make the same unhealthy connection between fictional acts of brutality and real-life exploitation and degradation that the "slasher film" tried to make implicitly.

The horror genre has been the whipping boy for the end of civilization, a component of bread and circuses and the decline of the West since Mary Shelley had her titular character stealing God's thunder in 1818. A popular cliché, even among horror aficionados, is that the horror films of the '40s, '50s, and '60s were better, richer, more artistic films than the "garbage" of the last forty years. Claims that the classic films, the Universal horror cycle, Hammer Studios, and international art cinema such as *Kwaidan*, are more stylish, atmospheric, psychologically stimulating, and just plain scarier than the current crop of gore flicks slithering into America's theaters and living rooms seem to be taken as gospel. To be honest, my loyalties are more toward Boris Karloff, Vincent Price, Christopher Lee, and Peter Cushing than the interchangeable automatons that pass for actors and actresses infecting film today. Yet I also feel that the dismissal of contemporary horror cinema, by the general public and students of horror alike, is an example of glorifying the past while damning the present. Nostalgia is a wonderful feeling, but when it comes to evaluating art, the tendency to romanticize can obscure more than it reveals.

Horror films are as much a rite of growing up as dating, binge drinking, and stealing your parents' car. When people find out that I am a horror fan, they always feel the need to tell me (unsolicited, mind you) about a film or television show that scared the wits out of them when they were children. Whether it was *The Thing*, (the original and the John Carpenter remake), *The Exorcist*, *The Twilight Zone*, *The Texas Chainsaw Massacre*, *The X-Files*, *The Shining*, *Jaws*, or *Paranormal Activity*, an important ritual for all Americans is to confront one's fears by enduring some form of horror media. And to me that's the terrible but thrilling irony of the horror experience: we are constantly running to and from terror, scared to death but loving every minute of it, hands over face but fingers spread just enough so we can see everything. Of course, countless authors and psychologists have claimed that we face our repressed fears and desires through the surrogate dream/unconscious state of watching cinema. While I agree somewhat that horror engages our primal fears, I feel it presents modern contemporary dread in a much more meaningful and direct way. Whether it was the post-WWII trepidation over nuclear science and Communist machinations (*I Was a Teenage Frankenstein*, *Tarantula!*, and *Invasion of the Body Snatchers*), apprehension of counterculture social upheaval in the '60s (*Night of the Living Dead* and *Rosemary's Baby*), post-Vietnam/Watergate repulsion (*The Omen*, *Dawn of the Dead*, and *Deliverance*), even up to the current social, economic, and technological destabilization of the '00s (*Panic Button*, *Vanishing On 7th Street*, and *The Human Centipede*), horror has acted not only as a cultural barometer but also as a safety valve. Heck, even the remake of *The Amityville Horror* can be seen as a metaphor for the housing crash (or for the importance of having killer abs like Ryan Reynolds). If anything, the contemporary horror film makes a great case for thinning the rampant douche bag population infesting our culture.

Are the *Saw* films the cause of violence and inhumanity in our society or a reflection of it? Again, this attempt to find some causal connection between art and life has been going on since a Greek mother complained that her son jumped off the roof of their villa after seeing Aristophanes' latest play. And who's to say that the horror films of the 1940s–1960s wouldn't have been more violent and gory had there not been censorship bureaus like the Hayes Office, the Breen Office, or the MPAA? If Gordon Douglas had had no restrictions in creating *Them!*, would he have shown a giant ant slicing a man's torso in half with its pincers, blood and viscera spewing everywhere, rather than simply showing a bleached skeleton in the sand? In *The Black Cat*, would Edgar J. Ulmer have shown Bela Lugosi flaying Boris Karloff alive, skin peeling off as Bela slowly carves into the body of his hated rival, if the director had not had the long shadow of Joseph Breen over his shoulder? Would this explicitness have made more powerful films? I don't know.

These examples highlight the fact that horror and gore are in the eye of the beholder, and, for the vast majority of viewers, that eye doesn't like to be poked.

This is not to say that the years prior to the horror cinema of the 1970s were pristine. The notion that graphic film violence is a contemporary phenomenon is disavowed by watching any of the ultra-gory snuff driver's ed. films of the '50s and '60s, like *Highway of Agony*, *Mechanized Death*, and *The Last Prom*. These Technicolor bloodbaths were justified by their "educational" value as deterrents, and yet I would not be surprised if at least some of those Eisenhower teenyboppers weren't getting a thrill from seeing the road covered in body parts. Even the venerable Hammer Films was initially seen as a purveyor of the lowest, vilest swill when it released the one-two punch of *The Curse of Frankenstein* and *Horror of Dracula* in the late '50s. Today these films are cherished for being stately Gothic thrillers, but contemporaneous interviews with filmgoers reflected shocked indignation at the violence and explicitness of the films, especially since viewers could now see the vivid redness of the blood flowing down Dracula's fangs. These examples highlight the fact that horror and gore are in the eye of the beholder, and, for the vast majority of viewers, that eye doesn't like to be poked.

So, to misquote Simone de Beauvoir, must we burn the *Saw* films? Is there worth or significance in the ultra-violence of these perennial Halloween money makers? Do they have "redeeming social value," or are they the smut that the nomenclature of "torture porn" makes them out to be? Although it is easy to dismiss contemporary fright films as callous, brutal endurance tests for the dehumanized, apathetic, heartless rabble, perhaps the horror genre is more like Nietzsche's abyss: as we gaze at these films, the films gaze back at us, as if to say that we are more terrible than the fictional abominations projected onto the screen.

Chapter 10.

"We Blew It": The Death of the '60s on Film

I t's extremely difficult to say something new about the 1960s. Treated (with compelling reasons) like the Renaissance of the twentieth century, the myths, legends, and lore of this golden age have supplanted more objective, historical accounts of the era, but this is not necessarily a bad thing, nor does it make those more subjective perspectives invalid. In the post-WWII blooming of human consciousness rising out of the ashes of the old world like a tie-dyed phoenix, one cannot help being overwhelmed with the deluge of social, cultural, political, and artistic experiences and transformations. Truly, the '60s have to be celebrated for the dizzying array of alternate modes of being, understanding, and creating. Just as both history and fantasy are equally crucial and interchangeable in exploring the meaning of the '60s, a belief in the mind-body-spirit connection infused many aspects of culture, and so untangling the separate threads of what, who, how, and why becomes an exercise in futility. Pulling on any one strand threatens to unravel the whole tapestry.

In many ways, the '60s have become an albatross around the neck of any attempt at forming a healthy, sustainable underground that nurtures dissent. How could any movement match up to the utopian ideals of that tumultuous decade? Yet look closer at that Second Gilded Age, and the dulled edges and flecked surfaces start to show. Of course, punk rock helped to strip away the veneer, but there were already artists at the very heart of the '60s who, no longer blinded by the psychedelic lights, questioned the motives, consequences, and future of the flower children.

The late 1960s/early 1970s was a ferocious, drugged-out, sleazy period with little stability, an apocalyptic end time where hope and dreams gave way to darkness, doubt, and a feeling of the inevitable. The ubiquitous specter of the draft haunted the lives of young men who had to agonize daily over the realization that their lives were in the hands of monstrous bureaucrats eager to spill someone else's blood to reap financial rewards and feel the thrill of power. The curse of conscription would drive anyone to engage in desperate and irrational behaviors, gladly accepting any life preserver no matter how absurd, phantasmagorical, or self-serving. What would

> Truly, the '60s have to be celebrated for the dizzying array of alternate modes of being, understanding, and creating.

the new decade of the '70s bring? Would the counterculture, the Black Panthers, the Weathermen, woman's liberation, and the anti-war movement grow and conquer the forces of oppression, or would they destroy each other in a holocaustic orgy of self-interest?

This feeling of annihilation and upheaval was prophesied in George Romero's *Night of the Living Dead* (1968), as one way of life is challenged by hordes of devouring revolutionaries. Obviously, Richard Nixon's Gestapo-like domestic war on any sort of political, social, cultural, or artistic nonconformity didn't help the already paranoiac situation. Nor did the raised fists and flowers in rifles help international affairs as the Vietnam war machine revved up even higher, expanding its destructive agenda to murder the hearts and minds of Americans, Cambodians, Laotians, and Vietnamese. Because of its more immediate creation and distribution, music was in the forefront of commenting on this bewildering and potentially deadly era: the MC5's *High Time*, Neil Young's *On the Beach*, Funkadelic's *America Eats Its Young*, Marvin Gaye's *What's Going On*, and Sly Stone's *There's a Riot Going On* are only a few of the incredibly moving, angry, and thought-provoking musical explorations of this divisive time.

The first serious cinematic examinations of the '60s were Michelangelo Antonioni's *Blow Up* (1966) and Peter Watkins's *Privilege* (1967). That's not counting the hippie-ploitation films that preyed on generational prurience and fears, such as *Riot on the Sunset Strip* (1967), *The Love-Ins* (1967) and *The Big Cube* (1969), or comedies like the baffling *Skidoo* (1968) and *How to Commit Marriage* (1969) that used weird clothes and slogans as the butt of their jokes, laughter masking the terror of change. Although it is amazingly prescient, the fact that *Privilege* takes place in a future fascistic dystopia may have watered down the effect of its critique of counterculture's commodification. Antonioni's *Blow Up* strikes at the heart of '60s youth culture. Often held up as an artifact of Swinging London, the in-between phase where mods started going day-glo, Antonioni's film is hardly a celebration of the free love, psychedelic drug, and music scenes. One has only to witness the zombie-like masses at The Yardbirds's concert—the grasping sex, the hazy drug tedium that can't even feel excitement or outrage at a murder—to see quite clearly that Antonioni was not buying the bill of goods that the Love Generation was selling. Antonioni would turn his scathing eye once more toward the counterculture, this time in the US, for his critically maligned, much misunderstood masterpiece *Zabriskie Point* (1970). But the times had certainly changed. As the '60s turned into the even more troubled and schizophrenic '70s, ideologies got more radical and explosive or retreated into nostalgia and apathetic pleasure to forget all the failures and broken promises.

The experiment of the '60s (which really lasted until the Vietnam War's devastating end in 1975) has become, like any other cultural movement, lionized, memorialized, demonized, and emulated over time. Countless critics have commented ad nauseam on every aspect of the decade, and as the years pass, the era's significance seems to be receding in the rear view mirror of culture, occasionally propped up by academia or corporations desperate to sell product. Myopic hindsight has twisted an already bewildering historical period into so many knots that it seems pointless to try to untangle the memory, fact, fiction, truth, and projection.

Yet some filmmakers were trying to make sense of the quickly unfolding events of their culture. These films seem to offer a more authentic observation of what it was like to live, mature, and create during the late '60s/early '70s. Immediate and powerful, these films ruminate on the darker aspects of the United States during the '60s and certainly don't give the counterculture a free pass. As they were conceived in a troubled, unstable atmosphere, many of the films have a tentative and desperate tone, a feeling of cautious optimism buried under the collective weight of both idealism and brutal reality. Forced to act in the face of uncertainty, the protagonists are contradictory, hesitant, brooding, and volatile. They believe in nothing but want to believe in something so desperately that they end up taking on roles and obligations they are not equipped to deal with, leading to further isolation and disenfranchisement. Nothing can be counted on anymore: all institutions are repressive; big business is a den of Madison Avenue fascists; the government is run by shadowy, corrupt executioners; sex is entrapment; drugs are destructive escapism; even one's fellow hippies are selfish con men ready to use murder to get what they want—a flower in one hand and a knife in the other. Peace, love, and understanding masked a slew of pathologies that erupted at Altamont and 10050 Cielo Drive, only to be medicated later with disco, cocaine, and *Star Wars*.

Peter Fonda and Dennis Hopper's *Easy Rider* (1969) created the template for the downer, post-Woodstock counterculture film. Seeing both mainstream America and the hippie movement as conformist regimes looking to indoctrinate the individual, Fonda's character Wyatt (a.k.a. Captain America; ok, that's a bit heavy-handed) surveys both his own search for autonomy and the hippie quest to transform the moribund America of 1969. In rejecting the stifling mores and lifestyles of their parents, the hippies imprisoned themselves in a more colorful but equally constricting routine. Films like *Easy Rider* and Richard Sarafian's *Vanishing Point* (1971) equate freedom with mobility and speed, but both end in destructive crashes and can only offer an escape via oblivion. These obliterating denouements reflect the movement toward violence, despair, and all-consuming defenestration that became an accepted strategy regarding Nixon's mission to silence dissent and the suicidal escalation of the Vietnam War. Frustration, anger, and fear brought out the worst in a movement that had prided itself on not making the same mistakes. The Maysles Brothers' *Gimme Shelter* (1970) and Robert Hendrickson and Laurence Merrick's *Manson* (1973) are frightening in their unblinking verite documentation of the turn toward darkness and nihilism, when Thantos conquered Eros, and the Love Generation had to deal with its own murderous offspring. Films such as *I Drink Your Blood* (1970), *Beyond the Valley of the Dolls* (1970), *The Love Thrill Murders* (1971), *The Night God Screamed* (1971), *The Last House on the Left* (1972), and *Electra Glide in Blue* (1973) placed the unhinged elements of the counterculture front and center, expressing this new exercise of violence as a logical extension of a relativistic morality that freely gorged itself on sex and drugs, so why not murder?

Even more than sex and drugs, the aims and ethics of violence were a critical question for political groups trying to exact change but stymied by the unconstitutional and merciless repression of civil liberties. The crucial question of when violence is justified is addressed in *Medium Cool* (1969), *Getting Straight* (1970), *The Strawberry Statement* (1970), *Billy Jack* (1971), *Straw Dogs* (1971), *Rage* (1972), and even in the seemingly anti-hippie, pro-rugged individualism of *Dirty Harry* (1971). This uncertainty over the means and methods of change for the new decade is the central concept of Paul Williams's *The Revolutionary* (1970). Jon Voight's character "A" is a confused philosophy student struggling with the idealism of theory and the reality of practice, vacillating between peaceful understanding and last-resort destructiveness, but with no clear direction or goal.

There is no such ambiguity in Peter Watkins's *Punishment Park* (1971), a horrifically real-fake documentary in which the police state savagely represses any dissent by turning over political prisoners to a military tribunal that offers them two choices: ridiculously extended sentences in federal prisons or participation in a no-win game of manhunt in the desert, pursued by soldiers with real guns. *The Spook Who Sat by the Door* (1973) is perhaps the most interesting example of this type of film. An outwardly servile African-American CIA agent goes back to a Chicago ghetto and teaches black revolutionaries the guerilla methods that the government taught him in order to subvert and bring down the very ruling class that treated him as token but turned him into a weapon.

Violence and paranoia often go hand in hand, and so this period's counterculture film is suffused with mendacity, duplicity, and treachery. J. Edgar Hoover's mania for rooting out and extinguishing any deviation from the mainstream (clearly masking his own proclivities), the Pentagon Papers, and Nixon's *Götterdämmerung* of Watergate couldn't help but feed one's suspicions that the American

119

public was being duped, swindled, and made to look like fools. While these films came later in the counterculture cycle (often acting as elegies for the 1960s), they seem to be evidence that the crazy hippies were right: there was a massive, coordinated conspiracy between government, media, and big business to undermine any sort of political, social, economic, and institutional change in America. *The Parallax View* (1974), *The Conversation* (1974), *Network* (1976), *All the President's Men* (1976), *Blow Out* (1981), and *Cutter's Way* (1981) use various metaphors (whether it is television, the Vietnam War, the shadowy corners of government, noise, or the meaningless spectacle of campaigning politicians) to explore the control, dominance, manipulation, and propaganda used in terroristic ways against ordinary citizens. Though the war sputtered to an ignoble, numbing end in 1975, remnants of the Vietnam trauma still lingered, as New York City is just as horrifying as Da Nang for Vietnam vet Travis Bickle in Martin Scorsese's *Taxi Driver* (1976,

---

Even when the disillusioned reject the artificiality of modern American culture and return to the purity and simplicity of nature, there are significant problems.

Happy Bicentennial America!). Bickle's loner ideology—searching for something to believe in yet isolated, denied, disgusted, and infuriated—reflects not only the damaged late '70s American psyche but sets the stage for the reconstruction of American masculinity as the hard, machine-like action heroes of the '80s.

Even when the disillusioned reject the artificiality of modern American culture and return to the purity and simplicity of nature, there are significant problems. John Boorman's *Deliverance* (1972) puts to rest any notion that the '60s utopian ideal can be found in the loving bosom of Mother Nature, as the reality of the predatory cruelty of the strong victimizing the weak will make no exceptions for tree huggers. Dennis Hopper's *The Last Movie* (1971) suggests that any attempt by modern Westerners to glorify the very environment that we have raped and exploited is at best laughable and at worst even more destructive to ecosystems and indigenous peoples. A logical conclusion (well, logical to the Establishment) to the anti-Western civilization/anti-technology hippie ethos informs the post apocalypse of Boris Sagal's *The Omega Man* (1971), where the plague-ridden luddite survivors ban together under the name of "The Family," creating a Mansonian new world order as reflected in Charlie's song, "I am a Mechanical Man."

Immersing oneself in the ignorant bliss of youth provides only momentary happiness in counterculture films. *Wild in the Streets* (1968) and *Logan's Run* (1976) reveal the short-sightedness of a movement based on age and the idealization of a transitory developmental stage that is both celebrated and damned by its own innocence. Feminism is eyed suspiciously, but feminine rage is proven to be entirely justifiable by the protagonists of *Rosemary's Baby* (1968), *Let's Scare Jessica to Death* (1971), *The Stepford Wives* (1975), *Lemora: A Child's Tale of the Supernatural* (1975), *The Witch Who Came from the Sea* (1976), and *3 Women* (1977). Then again, the genre of women driven mad by a patriarchal society has been a staple of Hollywood long before anyone was burning bras. In Jeff Lieberman's *Blue Sunshine* (1978), one can't even retreat into the blissed-out memories of acid trips of years gone by with the threat of psychotic flashbacks inspiring murderous rampages. Interestingly, an equally devastating (at least metaphorically) side effect of the "blue sunshine" strain of LSD is losing one's hair, a horrifying reminder of the one enemy no amount of hippie idealism can combat. When the unifying symbol of youthful rebellion against conformity starts to thin and fall out, the stresses of middle age achieve what a million barbers dreamed of doing to the longhairs. Perhaps the only way to be happy is to emulate the titular character of *Joe* (1970) and enjoy all the new liberties that the counterculture ushered in, while scapegoating, abusing, and joyfully slaughtering those who struggled to get you those freedoms.

The most depressing "death of the '60s" film has to be Paul Schrader's *Hardcore* (1979). The story concerns a conservative, religious, successful businessman who searches for his runaway daughter in the hedonistic hippie-land of California, depicted as a nauseating hell of drugs, the sex industry, and snuff films. One expects a denunciation of the entire '60s social and cultural experiment, a noble enterprise that has devolved into porno ennui, cheap thrills, and senseless viciousness. A father that is the embodiment of the American Dream and the Good Christian has wallowed in the filth and inhumaneness of a licentious world spawned by the supposed triumph of the counterculture over traditional American values. He finally finds his indolent daughter, and her response to his demands that she come back to his safe, prosperous home reveals an important motive of the youth rebellion of the '60s: the daughter blames her father's inability to love anything but money, status, and obedience. She has found a family in pornography, prostitution, and drugs that offers her the attention that her cold, selfish father never even considered giving her outside of the material comforts his income bought. This pain over abandonment and deception fueled much of the insurgency against the post WWII imaginary wonderland that Cold War America erected around itself to distract from lynchings, spree killers, and the possibility of world annihilation. The death of the '60s has been mourned by both participants and observers for the last forty years, no more so than by those filmmakers who worked through their agony, anxiety, sorrow, and rage in the moment and put those awkward but beautiful personal expressions up on the screen.

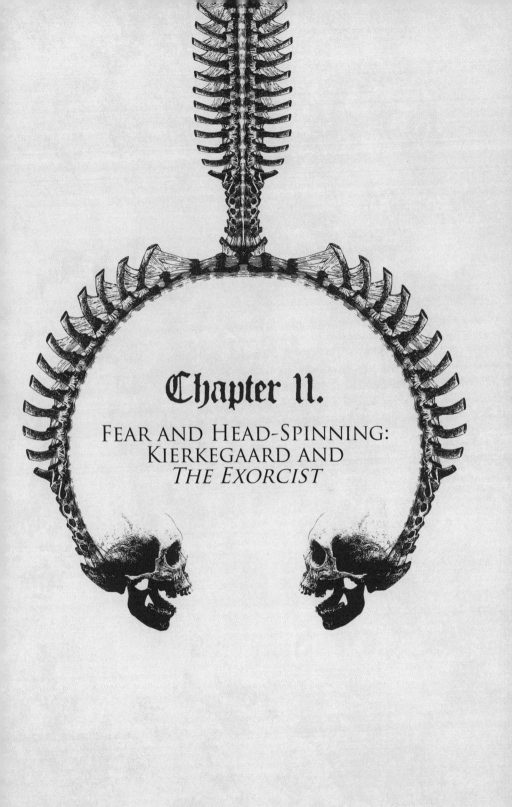

Chapter 11.

FEAR AND HEAD-SPINNING:
KIERKEGAARD AND
THE EXORCIST

hen *The Exorcist* was released on an unsuspecting America in December 1973 (Merry Christmas!), the press reported two distinctive reactions. The first reaction, shared by most movie critics and the public, was that *The Exorcist* was a Catholic film, a reactionary advertisement for orthodoxy that vilified science, technology, medicine, and psychology. Here was proof that the modern world was demonic. Churches reported record attendance in their pews, and requests for exorcisms were as plentiful as the new dollars in the collection basket. The counterculture chickens had come home to roost as the seeds of cultural and social licentiousness had blossomed into demonic children who rejected the traditional American values of God, family, and country. Hip critics accused the film of a return to medievalism and an attack on the democratic and scientific freedoms of the Enlightenment, where logic and reason highlighted the inherent goodness and equality of all humans. In the counterculturalbastion *Rolling Stone*, Jon Landau mercilessly crucified *The Exorcist*, calling it a "religious porn film." The other reaction was a bit more baffling. One would think that the Catholic church would have appreciated such propaganda, but after initially giving permission to aid the production of the film, the

> God's best friend Billy Graham stated (possibly apocryphally) that "there is a power of evil in that film, in the fabric of the film itself."

church's response to the finished product ran the gamut from ambivalence to condemnation to the belief that the film was blasphemous. God's best friend Billy Graham stated (possibly apocryphally) that "there is a power of evil in that film, in the fabric of the film itself."

How could there be such divergent opinions that would have one side seeing *The Exorcist* as a recruitment film and the other seeing it as a hatchet job? Could it be that *The Exorcist* is neither a Catholic film nor a sacrilegious atrocity? *The Exorcist* is a film that rejects both religious and scientific dogma and investigates the paradoxes of faith, and aligns most closely with the nineteenth-century Danish philosopher Soren Kierkegaard. And while it may fly in the face of William Friedkin's and Blatty's more traditionally pious intentions, looking at *The Exorcist* through a Kierkegaardian lens provides for a more satisfyingly existential experience.

To do a Kierkegaardian reading of *The Exorcist*, it might be helpful to quickly review his views of faith, anxiety, and despair. Kierkegaard believed that human beings cannot think their choices into life: we must live our beliefs. His critique of objectivity and reason was not only applied to the secular world but to religious orthodoxy and dogma as well. Passion and commitment had, in Kierkegaard's opinion, become abstract ideologies rather than lived experiences. Faith is a deep, strong restlessness that knows no certainty. It drives believers to reject the modern society of contemplation and boredom. It pushes them to choose, act, believe, and love in the face of the world's repulsion and uncertainty. Kierkegaard saw the bureaucracy of Christian democracy as taking away that freedom of choice, taking away the spontaneity of making a leap of faith into the unknown. The Church was creating nominal Christians, sheep that clung to the certainty and stability of dogma but were missing the exhilaration of risk that brought one closer to God.

And yet, Kierkegaard understood why someone would want to play it safe. His world view is one of angst, dread, and torment. Human beings are continually standing on a precipice before a dizzying abyss. The possibility of freedom, to make a choice and actually do something, is accompanied by feelings of alienation and anxiety, while the possibility of doing nothing, of hiding behind ideology and orthodoxy, seems safer and more reassuring. Though anxiety can paralyze, it can also be the avenue through which one is saved, because the repulsion we feel toward the world informs our choices and responsibilities. Anxiety can bring the recognition of true identity; it can be a spur that moves us from self-conscious, obsessive reflection to being in the world, a spontaneous immediacy that makes us feel alive. But feeling alive has its downside, too, as the despair of existence sets in and forces us to turn away from the world and our fellow human beings.

For Kierkegaard, the lowest form of this existential despair is "demonic despair," which is an understanding that one is in despair, understands what is causing the despair, and seeks a way to alleviate the despair, but no help seems forthcoming. We become hardened against any form of help or possibility of goodness in the world. We start to revel in the despair and refuse all forms of love, faith, and hope. Demonic despair prevents us from feeling passion, and Kierkegaard believed that passion and love had a divine source. It was through an acknowledgment and practice of passion, faith, love, and action that human beings could transcend the material repulsiveness of the world and achieve the highest form of existence: the religious stage. This stage could not be achieved through rites and rituals nor through obedience and conformity to an institution. Kierkegaard's concept of the individual working toward this stage of development is called the Knight of Faith, someone who has faith in God and can act independently. Knights of faith are always taking leaps of faith with their whole being. Knights of faith possess "elevation," always moving upward even when the world knocks them down. Examples of Kierkegaardian knights of faith are people like Abraham, Noah, and Jesus, willing to risk everything voluntarily, without certainty, for a God of love. Kierkegaard juxtaposes the Knight of Faith with the Knight of Infinite Resignation, a person who has given up in the face of despair, who takes no chances and will barely attempt what is humanly possible.

In the beginning of *The Exorcist*, we are presented with a Knight of Infinite Resignation: Father Damien Karras. Karras has lost his faith, his mother, his place in the world. He is a man torn between the spiritual and material, religious and scientific, and this anxiety leads him to hide from the suffering of the very people he should be helping, either as a priest or a doctor. Karras has rejected the world, seeing it as repulsive and vile, a place of no hope or goodness. Throughout the film, he is presented with horrible situations that he retreats from: a homeless man, the inmates of a psych ward in Bellevue, and finally his own sick mother. His inability to deal with his own lack of true faith and passion is seen in his fixation on physicality

---

Kierkegaard juxtaposes the Knight of Faith with the Knight of Infinite Resignation, a person who has given up in the face of despair, who takes no chances and will barely attempt what is humanly possible.

---

and on religious and scientific orthodoxy and routine: boxing, running, going through the motions of performing mass, initially dismissing Chris McNeil's pleadings for help by using both Catholic and psychological doctrine. It is only the guilt he feels when he witnesses Chris's emotional breakdown that forces him to act.

Karras's early meetings with Regan are limited to talk and tests: there's no action to engage with the repulsion of a possessed child. Regan represents the worst physical, psychological, and spiritual disgust: a festering, spewing, profane, ungodly, uncontrollable creature that Mother Teresa would pass on blessing. Even Regan's mother rejects her, claiming that that "thing" upstairs is not her daughter. Karras can't take a leap of faith and believe that Regan is demonically infested; he wants both scientific and religious "proof." The demon refuses to give him certainty, writhing after being sprinkled with tap water yet able to open drawers and speak languages preternaturally. Karras needs to be convinced of the reality that is right in front of his face. Even when he accepts the repugnant reality of Regan, he acts only through the system (echoing a line from *Crash Course*, the film Chris McNeil is making while enduring her daughter's possession). As a church representative, Father Merrin is the one who confronts the demon while Karras watches passively. Merrin, though courageous, is held back by his belief in dogma, using it as a parachute to soften the fall of the leap of faith. For Merrin, there is no personal anxiety or doubt in his encounter with the unknown. He counters Karras's view of the multiplicity and fragmentation of Regan's condition with certainty: "There is only one."

Time for a digression: I found *Exorcist: The Version You've Never Seen* (a suped up edition of *The Exorcist*), superfluous overall, with additions to a film that is already a masterpiece. Yet there is one revision that I think improves the film because it is an explicit statement of the Kierkegaardian ethos. In the "improved" cut of the film, Karras and Merrin have a brief discussion on the stairs between exorcism sessions with Regan (in the original film, their break is silent). Karras asks the key existential question of why this is happening to this little girl. Merrin's answer is right out of the great Dane's works: to make us despair, to make us think we are unworthy of love, to see the world as ugly with no hope. In other words, to sink us into demonic despair. And to keep this digression going, it's interesting to note the number of scenes that occur on stairs, as the film's movement is vertical: characters are constantly going up and down (which could be tied to Kierkegaard's concept of elevation, but I've already forced my round interpretation into a square hole).

In the end, even with all his rites, rituals, training, and canon, Merrin is killed: the demon defeats the sanctioned church official. It is only when Karras acts—when he seizes the repulsion and sacrifices himself by taking on Regan's repulsion, alienation, despair, and anxiety, spontaneously and with no certainty of success—that the St. Joseph's medal around his neck is broken. His last connection to orthodoxy is gone and he can make the leap of faith, literally jumping out the window. He has become a knight of faith because his sacrifice was done out of love. His risk results in death, but it is a death with true existential meaning. He leaps not as a priest or psychiatrist but as a fellow suffering human being. Regan is saved; Karras has made his choice independently of the church or science. He achieves his elevation by jumping and falling, because it is in the fall that we recognize how courageous the Knight of Faith is: "One need not look at them when they are up in the air but only the instant they touch or have touched the ground, then one recognizes them."

So to contradict myself, *The Exorcist* is a highly religious film, but it's also not a religious film. If you are looking for a validation of Catholic orthodoxy, you will not get that. But if you are looking for a film that illustrates the paradoxes of faith, that makes a compelling case for why we should never give in to repulsion, despair, or anxiety, why we should act, love, and take risks in an abhorrently chaotic world, then *The Exorcist* should fit the bill.

Chapter 12.

WE'LL TURN THE LIGHT OUT ON YA: *HALLOWEEN*, SEX, AND SUBURBIA

*I*n 1977, producer Irwin Yablans dreamed up the perfect horror film: a psycho kills babysitters on Halloween. It's such an obviously simple idea that he must have been kicking himself that he hadn't come up with it sooner. Sure, *Black Christmas* had sort of done the holiday killer thing, but that film was way too obtuse and sacrilegious to make any real money. Little did anyone suspect that Yablans's formula would become the seed of a seismic change in cinema, affecting all aspects of the filmmaking, marketing, and watching experiences. Unlike other aesthetic revolutions, this one did not start with the critics, cineastes, artisans, or art houses; it would be bankrolled by shady investors, fly-by-night production companies, grotty theaters, and filmmakers whose talents ran the gamut from genius to incompetence. Critics howled in disgust, blaming these films for every social, cultural, political, and artistic ill that was plaguing the late '70s/ early '80s. Though some were pure exploitation and wallowed in prurience, others were truly transgressive art, films that critiqued, explored, and broke down taboos and the boundaries of acceptable subject matter. In some ways, the slasher film was the

> ...and yet haven't women been typecast since the beginning of cinema as victims or villains?

bastard child of the counterculture films of the '60s and '70s, pushing back against the phony idealism and empty promises of the hippie love fest and the me, me, me pleasure-seeking of the Nixon-Ford-Carter years, kind of like the punk rock/industrial music movements that were launching their own contemporaneous attacks on the bloated phoniness of rock and pop.

Moral guardians took particular relish in reviling the slasher film for its portrayal of women, and yet haven't women been typecast since the beginning of cinema as victims or villains? Women are reified, blamed, and denigrated in all films (not just horror), while simultaneously expected to be objects of desire and virtue in almost all art. (This observation in no way excuses this depiction, but just shows the double standard used against horror). Largely because of the "final girl" who has to be masculine in her ability to fight back and survive but feminine in her hysteria and vulnerability, the slasher film is labeled misogynistic. Yet in all but the most clichéd examples, these films are more complex in their portrayal of gender than mainstream critics would admit. A perfect example is John Carpenter's iconic *Halloween*—possibly the film that kicked off the slasher craze and transformed Yablans's ballyhoo concept into art. Often held up

129

as the trendsetting puritanical warning against casual sex and uninhibited female indulgence, the co-writer/director explained on scifi.com: "It has been suggested that I was making some kind of moral statement. Believe me, I'm not. In *Halloween*, I viewed the characters as simply normal teenagers." What enhances this normality is the fact that the teenagers' dialogue was written by co-writer/ producer Debra Hill, one of the most unsung women of horror.

Though it is Carpenter's eye and Dean Cundey's camera that create the mood of impending doom, Hill's contributions to the *Halloween* script are what make the film so horrifying. Presented with well-rounded characters that are likeable and sympathetic, the viewer feels the violence visited on these regular people, and their deaths mean something. The believability of their dialogue and their balance of virtue and vice make for characterizations that bring gravity to the tragic events visited on them for no apparent reason. These normal people, much like us, are cut down by a cruel, malevolent universe. The past is inescapable; we exist in an unknowable world that has its own reasons for why things happen (of course, this existential terror would be totally undone by *Halloween II*). This force is personified in the Shape, Michael Myers, and it was Hill who realized that a white, emotionless mask could be evil: "The idea was to make him [Michael Myers] almost humorless, faceless —this sort of pale visage that could resemble a human or not" (Fangoria #15). If Carpenter's Dr. Loomis is Captain Ahab on a mad quest to right the wrongs of the past, then Hill's Michael Myers is Moby Dick, the symbol of inescapable fate and an uncontrollable, indestructible power that tramples the individual. The unfortunate victims of Michael Myers are not murdered because they have sex, smoke pot, or swear: they are just in the wrong place at the wrong time when fate lashes out. That kind of arbitrary terror seems much worse, as there is no amount of repentance or self-control that can save you from the indiscriminate horror of a cold, vindictive cosmos.

The true condemnation is not focused on the young women but on authority figures who refuse to admit they could be wrong. Their hubris and self-interest allows evil to triumph. Adults, administrators, police, teachers, and neighbors are all weak and ineffectual because they won't consider any ideas outside their own frame of reference. The one authority figure who is right is constantly dismissed and undermined by those in power. *Halloween* is a warning to young people that no one will protect you: parents, authority figures, and institutions are willing to sacrifice you to keep their self-image of perfection and certainty. The horror in *Halloween* stems from not paying attention to our surroundings because we have been taught to believe in the security of public and personal authority.

This solipsistic outlook is intrinsically part of the concept of suburbia, the setting of *Halloween*. The promise of the suburbs was safety and community, a place where one could count on not only one's biological family but a civic one as well. Rather than the savage isolation of a farm or the alienation of a city, the suburbs were imagined as a post-war capitalist utopia where families could engage in collective consumerism, yet erase the class barriers that feed crime and vice. Halloween is the first suburban horror film, as Michael Myers rends the veil of affluence, protection, and neighborly assistance to show how selfishness, abandonment, and ignorance lurk on the perfectly groomed lawns and in the two-car garages and split-levels of the 1970s/'80s middle-class. Indeed, one of the worst moments in Halloween is when Jamie Lee Curtis runs next door screaming for help and the neighbor turns on the porch light and then turns it off, leaving her to her fate, like Kitty Genovese but in a planned community rather than an urban jungle. Where are the parents, good Samaritans, and moral guardians when they are most needed? Prosperity, complacency, and egotism have blinded those who believe they have built an impenetrable wall around their fool's paradise to keep out destructive forces that would destabilize their perfectly ordered lives (though the groundskeeper of the Haddonfield cemetery notes that horrible murders occurred right there in the bosom of the suburban family home).

So why do the girls who have sex die in Halloween? Because sex leaves you vulnerable; it takes your attention away from the world around you and focuses it on a blissful moment that leaves you open to predators and forces that wait for an opening to strike. During sex, you let down your guard down physically, mentally, emotionally, and spiritually (if you're lucky). This allows you to be completely connected to another human being, but it could lead to manipulation and harm. It's crucial to remember that Bob, the male character that has sex in Halloween, is murdered, too. The slasher film acts like a contemporary Grimm fairy tale warning the young to be on guard for predators who lurk behind the guise of selflessness, and seems prescient given today's society of people looking down at their phones, pads, and pods rather than paying attention to the world around them. While the implications of fixating on high-tech accoutrements are scary on an individual level, the political significance of encouraging people to be so invested in technology that they literally bow their heads and ignore the environment might make the threat of a maniac in a Captain Kirk mask look like the least of our worries.

> It's crucial to remember that Bob, the male character that has sex in *Halloween*, is murdered, too.

131

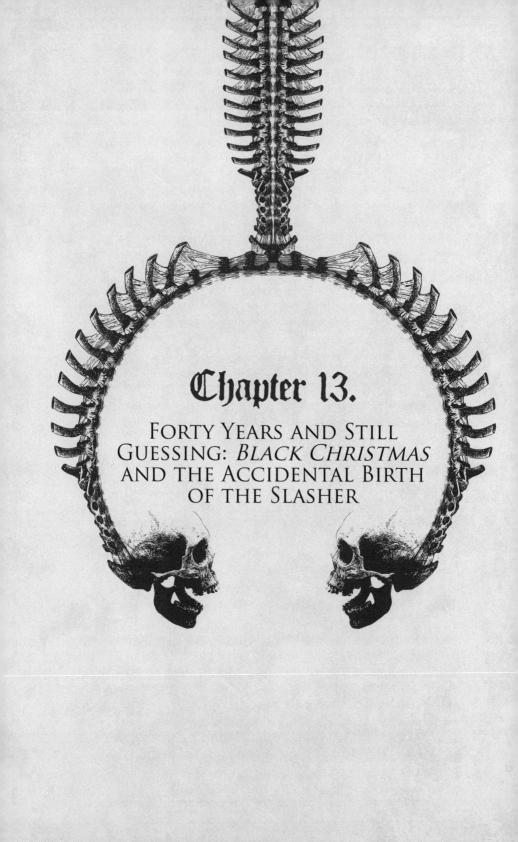

Chapter 13.

Forty Years and Still Guessing: *Black Christmas* and the Accidental Birth of the Slasher

lthough it is hard to believe given today's scorched-earth, capitalist-degraded charade called the holidays, there was a time when Christmas was sacred—a time of virtue. Not long ago, say in the early 1970s, celebrating Advent was a demonstration of meekness, generosity, and unconditional love. With political and social upheaval, war, inflation, and Watergate giving the American Dream a curb job, the one time of year North Americans could count on for a return to Rockwellian innocence was the multi-colored glow of Christmastime. So when a Canadian film titled *Black Christmas* was released in 1974, you could forgive people for thinking that the film was about trapped coal miners rescued by a holiday miracle. What unsuspecting viewers were actually subjected to was a nihilistic evisceration of peace, love, and goodwill toward men, especially toward women. Who was responsible for this travesty that portrayed the vicious murders of fresh-faced co-eds during their Christmas vacation by an obscene, psychotic killer who isn't even caught by the end of the film? From this lurid, low-budget yuletide shocker would spring one of the most reviled sub-genres of the already reviled horror genre, brought to you by the man who would later direct one of the

> From this lurid, low-budget yuletide shocker would spring one of the most reviled sub-genres of the already reviled horror genre…

most beloved holiday films ever: *A Christmas Story*. Revel in the fortieth anniversary of *Black Christmas*, a film that is still intriguing in its vagaries and shocking in its refusal to play by any rules, even the ones it supposedly created.

It all started with a script titled "Stop Me" authored by Roy Moore, supposedly based on seasonal murders in Quebec (this may be somewhat apocryphal as research has not turned up any Christmas killing spree in the early '70s in Quebec, but killers Ronald Glenn West and Henry Robert Williams were on the prowl in Toronto during this time period) and an earlier Moore script entitled *The Babysitter*, referring to the plethora of urban legends concerning a psychopath who telephones his teenage prey from inside the house. Moore shared the screenplay with Bob Clark, who was no stranger to horror, having directed creepy classics such as *Deathdream* (1972) and *Children Shouldn't Play with Dead Things* (1973). Clark made some significant revisions to the script, injecting much-needed humor and, most importantly, suggesting that the killer's identity and presence be vague.

The setting is a sorority house where the sisters are celebrating the impending holiday break. During the festivities, Jess Bradford (Olivia Hussey) answers the phone and hears the rantings of "the moaner," a psychotic who has been calling the house and whose ravings alternate between childish begging, perverted sexual taunts, and murderous threats. Unknown to the young ladies, a deranged prowler is living in their attic and may be the killer, creatively dispatching the co-eds with a plastic bag, a hook, and a glass unicorn, among other implements of death. But is the killer the caller? Is the caller the prowler? Is the killer the prowler? Are there multiple perpetrators? Nothing is as it seems, as all the characters have neuroses, emotional baggage, and issues that leave them vulnerable but cast suspicion on them as well. The authority figures (police, parents, adults) are revealed as incompetent and helpless in the face of the random attacks, failing to protect the young and preserve innocence as represented by the joyous season. The film's central symbol is the neglected corpse of a suffocated girl, plastic bag still over her fright-contorted face, placed in a rocking chair, holding a doll, and stashed in the attic above her unsuspecting friends. There is no satisfying denouement: the phone keeps ringing, the killer is still unknown, and no one is safe, even on Christmas.

The filming of *Black Christmas* began in early 1974 and was shot in forty days in Toronto with a budget of $620,000. Cinematographer Albert Dunk brought the viewer into the killer's perspective by mounting a camera on his back and creeping and crawling around the set, establishing a truly iconic POV that has been copied in just about every thriller since. Several major stars were approached, such as Bette Davis, Malcolm McDowell, Edmund O'Brien, and Gilda Radner, but the final cast of Olivia Hussey, Keir Dullea, Margot Kidder, Andrea Martin, Marian Waldman, and John Saxon could not have been better; they all brought a flawed, naturalistic realism to their roles. Carl Zittrer's underrated score is an ominous atonal lullaby played on a prepared piano and slowed unnaturally during the playback. To enhance the ambiguity of the caller's identity, Bob Clark, actor Nick Mancuso, and an unbilled actress blended their voices to create the demented voice of the phone calls.

Faced with this morbidly beautiful exercise in terror, American distributor Warner Brothers suggested a few changes that, as we can guess, would have been to the detriment of the film. They wanted a more conclusive ending with a definitive killer, wanted no part of the Christmas moniker, and were afraid that any title with "black" in it would be assumed to be a Blaxploitation flick. They suggested the not-so-bad title *Silent Night, Evil Night*. To Clark's credit, he stuck to his guns to keep his controversial ending but acquiesced to the title change for the initial release in the US. The film would undergo additional local retitlings depending on the market. The most interesting was the proposed TV edit called *Stranger in the House* that was cancelled with the decision that even a neutered version of *Black Christmas* was still too scary for '70s TV audiences (but was broadcast uncut on cable under that bland name).

Black Christmas was released on October 11, 1974, in Canada, and in the United States on December 20, 1974. As expected, this maverick film received largely negative reviews, but it won two Canadian Film Awards: "Best Sound Editing in a Feature" for Kenneth Heeley-Ray and "Best Performance by a Lead Actress" for Margot Kidder. Like many iconic films before it, *Black Christmas* would not immediately be acclaimed, but its status and influence would grow as perceptive viewers and future filmmakers attempted to unravel its mysterious web of violence. Along with Mario Bava's *Bay of Blood*,

---

Black Christmas is lauded as a foundational text for the slasher film genre, with a plethora of movies borrowing its holiday-focused milieu, dreary atmosphere, unconventional camera techniques, teenage victim pool, inventive kills, and psychologically damaged killer.

Black Christmas is lauded as a foundational text for the slasher film genre, with a plethora of movies borrowing its holiday-focused milieu, dreary atmosphere, unconventional camera techniques, teenage victim pool, inventive kills, and psychologically damaged killer. From *Halloween* (it is rumored that John Carpenter approached Clark about directing a sequel to *Black Christmas* early in his career) to *Scream*, *When a Stranger Calls*, *The House on Sorority Row*, and the entire *Silent Night, Deadly Night* series, to just name a handful of the hundreds of films made in its wake, *Black Christmas* was the innovator of many of the best aspects of the slasher film.

The films that followed in its creepy wake appropriated the surface accoutrements but neglected the deeper, more complex idiosyncrasies that make *Black Christmas* a masterpiece of homicidal misperception. The virginal girl is killed first and the promiscuous, drunk wise ass survives longer than most of the victims. An unwed pregnant woman is the heroine, and the initiatory trauma that created the killer is never revealed. What makes *Black Christmas* such a fascinating film is that none of the genre's conventions had been solidified or imitated yet. There is a strange awkwardness and disconcerting confusion over what exactly is happening in the film, what is the killer's motivation, and why the events are unfolding in this inexplicable way. We witness the events and are even privy to the killer's point of view, but feel as helpless as the victims, not knowing who to identify with or root for. Jason Voorhees, Michael Myers, and just about every unhinged slasher has a reason for existing, an agenda and philosophy that is expressed through death and dismemberment, often reflecting some childhood ordeal. Though their actions and reasoning may be deeply disturbed, they are understandable in that they make a terrible sort of vengeful sense: distracted sex-crazed teenagers allow a child in their care to drown, the victim becomes a killer that exacts revenge on all sex-crazed teenagers. Logically, this equation makes no sense, but emotionally one can kind of see how A+B=Z, especially if the precipitating catalyst began in childhood. *Black Christmas* does not allow us this avenue into the killer's motives; there can be no comprehension of or sympathy for the warped sensibilities that lead to such extreme violence.

Bob Clark's direction is uncomfortably claustrophobic, never allowing any sense of relief from the killer, especially as we know right from the beginning that there is an extremely unstable person hiding in the attic of the sorority house. The winter environment is bleak and foreboding, a reminder that no matter how happy the holidays are, they occur during the stillness, death, and despair of our seasonal cycle. The style switches from the warm, hazy, and impressionistic, reflecting the soft glow of Christmas lights, to the cold, austere Canadian darkness. The characters are multi-dimensional; none of the young women fall into the standard type of female character in a horror film. In particular, Olivia Hussey and Margot Kidder's characters are so believable because they are multi-faceted and complex: moral and bawdy, strong and vulnerable, innocent and experienced. Hussey had a big effect on Steve Martin, of all people. Supposedly he met Hussey and told her she was one of his favorite actresses, having seen *Black Christmas* twenty-seven times.

Bob Clark would go on to an impressive career, directing *Murder by Decree*, *Porky's*, *Porky's II*, *A Christmas Story*, *Rhinestone*, *Turk 182!*, *Loose Cannons*, and *Baby Genuises*. Unfortunately he passed away in 2007, but before that he returned to his influential creation by producing the Glen Morgan-directed remake *Black X-Mas* in 2006. Naturally, everything that the original did right, the remake does wrong. Its worst sin is its singular focus on the killer "Billy," giving him a fully explained, traumatic backstory and erasing any of the original's enigmatic, icy allure. It's either a tribute to Clark's original achievement or a commentary on the contemporary state of horror that a forty-year-old film can still shock, horrify, and inspire even in the face of "advances" in the genre. If you like horror that asks questions rather than provides answers, embrace the incomprehensibility and celebrate *Black Christmas*.

Chapter 14.

Confessions of a Battered Horror Fan: Dario Argento's *Dracula*

ghhhh. Do you have a friend that you feel the need to defend, for some masochistic reason, even in the face of irrefutable faults? Everyone else has pointed out, quite correctly, that this person's character flaws can be easily rectified, but you make excuses for him, coddle him, and protect him from criticisms that might actually be valid.

Like how Lester Bangs used to beg Lou Reed to torture him by throwing away his god-like talent on mediocre albums.

I am a Dario Argento enabler. I've never met the man but feel an extreme loyalty to him for changing not only the way I look at horror but the entire medium of cinema. Though it's unnecessary, I feel the need to list his absolute triumphs, films that elevated the genre and filmmaking to a higher level: *The Bird with the Crystal Plumage*, *Deep Red*, *Suspiria*, *Inferno*, *Tenebre*, and *Opera*. Most directors would kill to have one of these films in their oeuvre. He nurtured the talents of Michele Soavi, encouraged Goblin to do soundtracks, and is the father of an artistic dynamo named Asia. Even his lesser films are entertaining achievements. A girl that can communicate with insects? A razor-wielding chimp? C'mon, you're not going to see that in any J. J. Abrams or Joss Whedon flick. Yet around 1993, with the disappointing *Trauma*, fans started to doubt the maestro's formidable powers, and with each subsequent release bemoaned the decline of a once-great visionary. I think the films Argento made in the '90s and '00s are ripe for revaluation, as *The Black Cat*, *The Stendhal Syndrome*, *Sleepless*, and his two *Masters of Horror* episodes are underrated and represent a maturing directing style. I loved *The Mother of Tears*, which many fans attacked mercilessly because it wasn't *Suspiria* or *Inferno*, but that's like hating *Touch of Evil* for not being *Citizen Kane* or *The Magnificent Ambersons*. Granted, there have been some clinkers in Argento's career, but I don't believe they are entirely his fault. Reports of Adrien Brody's prima donna antics and the producers' chicanery pretty much sunk *Giallo* right out of the gate.

Which brings us to his latest film, another version of Bram Stoker's iconic character. Though Argento has often professed his love for Edgar Allan Poe and Gothic romanticism, when I first heard

> A girl that can communicate with insects? A razor-wielding chimp? C'mon, you're not going to see that in any J. J. Abrams or Joss Whedon flick.

about this project I didn't see it as a good fit. Argento's artistry comes from his ability to depict the intrusion of the irrational, nightmarish, and brutal into modern situations that should be protected by logic, law, science, or art. Detectives, doctors, scientists, police, musicians, and teachers follow certain rules and procedures. Schools, theaters, and museums are structured around rigidly acceptable forms of behavior. It is the incursion of the chaotic, represented by insanity or the supernatural, onto these rational characters and into these regulated settings that creates the horror in Argento's films. The period setting of Argento's *Dracula* takes that motif away from his artistic palette, and what we get is a contrived, clichéd depiction of some Transylvanian village where the viewer expects something supernatural to happen. Argento's screenplay doesn't even follow Stoker's narrative to London, the capital of decorum and repressive reason during the Victorian Age. It would have been the perfect environment in which to unleash the irrational.

That's just the tip of the iceberg in terms of what's wrong with this film. While Thomas Kretschmann as Dracula and Asia Argento as Lucy are hammy but fun in their roles, the rest of the acting is either bland or histrionic. What has happened to Rutger Hauer? I thought Anthony Hopkins was over the top as Van Helsing, but at least he did something with the role. Hauer alternates between narcolepsy and sleepwalking, with a few detours to nibble on the cheap scenery. The dubbing is atrocious, and that certainly doesn't help the performances. Argento's directing is quite American: flat and boring. If someone would have told me this film was a Sy-Fy production I wouldn't have batted an eye.

Some critics have condemned the gratititous nudity and gore during Dracula's attack on the town's leaders (which was the film's only interesting addition, as the town's leading citizens had been in collusion with Dracula to save themselves), and Dracula's CGI morphing into a praying mantis. But thank goodness these scenes were in the film, because something halfway interesting was being displayed on screen to break up the monotony.

If you want Dracula, don't start here. Watch Terrence Fisher's *Horror of Dracula* to truly experience the grandeur and darkness as well as the heroic and virtuous. Argento's entire film can't even measure up to the smallest moments from *Horror of Dracula*: the blood dripping down the stone eagle, Harker's realization of his vampiric infection, Van Helsing giving the little girl his coat and crucifix, and of course one of the most rousing climaxes in cinema history. Fischer's belief in the innate goodness of humanity, despite our weaknesses and ignorance, is perfectly realized by Peter Cushing's performance as Van Helsing: a man of science but open-minded, a thinker but ready for action, a man of compassion but a destroyer of the contagion of evil.

So, should we burn Argento? Are his days of unbridled creativity far behind him—ancient history given the short-term memories of the digital age? Horror fans should be wary of certainties and absolutes, because if there is one genre where anything can happen and the repressed can return in gloriously shocking fashion, it's horror. Still, after watching Argento's *Dracula*, I've decided that maybe enabling and blindly defending someone might not be the best way to help them.

Television

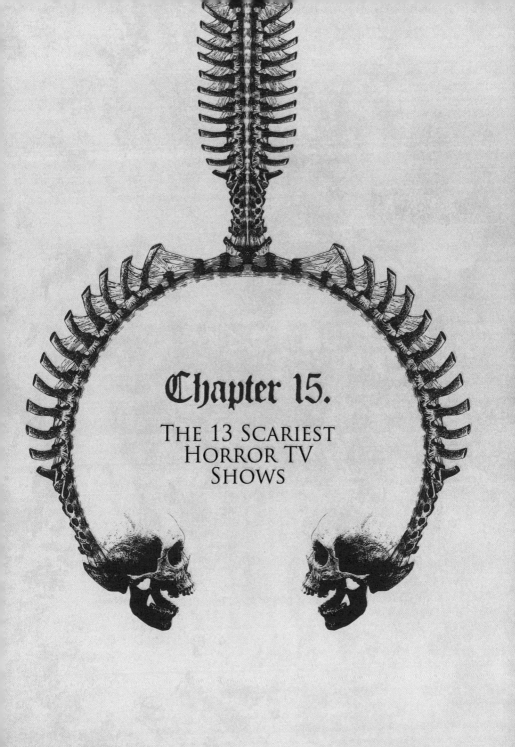

Chapter 15.

THE 13 SCARIEST HORROR TV SHOWS

elevision doesn't seem like the best medium for horror. The commercial breaks, shorter duration, censorship issues, limited filming techniques, and the fact that the viewing experience isn't as confined as a movie theater add up to conditions that aren't exactly conducive to creating prolonged terror. Though the concept of a truly scary horror TV show might seem like a hopeless oxymoron to hardcore horror fanatics, the idiot box has been essential for spreading the horror virus to generations of monster kids.

The first horror TV shows were filmed versions of radio programs such as *Suspense* and *Lights Out* or live teleplays as part of dramatic anthology shows. As the awkward first attempts at utilizing the new medium of television, these shows walk the line between mystery, thriller, and horror, often borrowing the ironic punishment ending of the infamous EC comics line. As the horror genre and television evolved throughout the 1950's, the contemporaneous interest in science fiction often mixed with the lingering effects of the Universal horror boom of the 1930s and '40s to inform television series such as *Tales of Tomorrow* and *Out There*, which would then blossom in the 1960s with such classic horror-suspense-sci-fi hybrid TV shows as *The Twilight Zone*, *The Outer Limits*, *One Step Beyond*, *Way Out*, and *Alfred Hitchcock Presents*. The first real horror TV series was *Thriller*, premiering in 1960. Though short lived, *Thriller* opened the floodgates for horror's sustained presence on television as networks and advertisers recognized the potential in attracting the demographic that was flocking to see horror films in theaters.

Horror TV series have spearheaded many changes in television's content, style, presentation, and viewer response. Horror's challenging subject matter and revolutionary approach inspires visionaries who are looking to push the boundaries of a medium that quickly became conservative and sophomoric, exchanging experimentation and substance for product placement and plagiarized repetition. The rebirth of television as an artistically meaningful platform in the

2000s, led by cable TV's imaginative programming and the major networks' attempts to compete, has included significantly transgressive elements of horror, whether they are the central premise of a series or simply add frisson to crime, drama, or historical shows. (But let's forget about the ghost/monster/Bigfoot-hunter type "reality" series that seeks to explain away all the majesty and mystery of the

---

Horror's challenging subject matter and revolutionary approach inspires visionaries who are looking to push the boundaries of a medium that quickly became conservative and sophomoric, exchanging experimentation and substance for product placement and plagiarized repetition.

---

supernatural through the pseudo-scientific bumblings of fools seeking the lowest form of celebrity. If it can measured, captured, or categorized, it ain't horror.) The saga of horror TV continues to be written as shows such as *True Detective*, *Hannibal*, *Sleepy Hollow*, *American Horror Story*, *Supernatural*, and *The Walking Dead* spread the gospel of the genre not only through television screens but now through laptops, tablets, and cell phones, which will affect both the viewing experience and the creation of future horror TV series. But as we go forward, the past still offers much enjoyment and many lessons to be shared in the warm, comforting glow of nostalgia. Here are thirteen television series that frightened, shocked, and entertained those of us who sat mesmerized, ruining our eyesight, in front of that giant radiation-spewing window into other worlds.

13.

Inhumanoids

The vast majority of '80s animation consisted of extended commercials to sell action figures and video games to young consumers dazzled by the influx of cool products during the Reagan years. Yet being a "toy property" didn't necessarily mean that a cartoon series couldn't be weird and intense, though that often did not bode well for ratings or product sales. Case in point: the Hasbro-owned and Toei-animated series *Inhumanoids*. The show details the battle between the Earth Corps, a combination science-military unit, and the Inhumanoids, a breed of enormous, subterranean, god-like creatures seeking to conquer the planet. Earth Corps gets assistance against these monstrosities from elemental and supernatural beings who are the Inhumanoids' primal arch-enemies. Combining the massive destructiveness of the kaiju with the Lovecraftian concept of the Great Old Ones, *Inhumanoids* are the most furiously evil Saturday (actually Sunday) morning cartoon creations ever. Add on a ruthless corporation looking to exploit the Inhumanoids for profit, a corrupt politician, and Cold War fears of mutual annihilation, and you have a much more mature and horrific animated series than, say, *The Snorks*.

The series began as short episodes for Sunday morning animated programming in an anthology called *Super Sunday*, but was then spun off into its own show, which ended after eight episodes. Those eight episodes featured some of the most graphically violent and disgusting scenes in children's animated programming, with limbs being cut off, facial disfigurations, and deaths in almost every episode. The best Inhumanoid was D'Compose, a gigantic, decaying monster with a hinged skeletal chest plate that was used as a jail to contain his human prey. Headquartered in his tomb-like realm of Skellweb, D'Compose could mutate people, rot materials, and resurrect the dead with his touch. In one episode, D'Compose uses the acid-destroyed corpse of a deceased character to create "Nightcrawler," an undead monster, and in another episode transforms teenage members of the Cult of Darkness into marauding zombie punks. The strangest episode is when D'Compse falls skull over heels in love with a resurrected dead woman. Unfortunately, the toy line failed and the show was cancelled, but not before gloriously scarring any child that happened to tune in after church on a Sunday morning.

12.

13 Demon Street

Is there a more tragic figure in horror history than Lon Chaney Jr.? Burdened with his father's legacy but not quite possessing his talent,

Chaney Jr. became a real-life Lawrence Talbot, cursed by the past and unable to create his own satisfying future. Chaney Jr. was able to eke out a living from his associations with horror cinema, but the toll it took on his mind, body, and soul are clearly evident to anyone who watches his later films. Occasionally, he would rise to the occasion and give a credible performance to display what could have been. Chaney Jr. introduced each episode of the Swedish horror TV series *13 Demon Street* with his trademark pathos. The series was created by *The Wolfman* writer Curt Siodmak, who provided a suitably expressionistic Universal horror feel to the series. Running only an appropriate thirteen episodes, *13 Demon Street* reconfigured horror stories and movie plots into morbid exercises in style. "The Photograph" modernizes M. R. James's classic "The Mezzotint," and "The Black Hand" uses the classic concept of the newly grafted-on appendage taking over the entire body and causing the recipient to commit grievous acts of revenge and murder. Two of the scariest episodes are "Green Are the Leaves," in which an on-air attempt to capture supernatural phenomenon live goes horribly awry (shades of *Ghostwatch*), and "The Book of Ghouls," where a failed schoolteacher uses an evil tome (written by Comte d'Erlette, perhaps?) to bring about his desires, with unexpected consequences. In an attempt to make money from the series, three episodes ("The Photograph," "The Girl in the Glacier," and "Condemned in Crystal") were chopped up and spliced together to create a movie called *The Devil's Messenger*, with Lon taking on the hosting role as Satan. And a sadder, more pitiful Lord of Darkness you could not find.

11.

Scooby Doo, Where Are You!

A friend once told me that he asked just two questions to evaluate other people: do you like The Beatles, and do you like *Scooby Doo*. A negative response to either question warranted an immediate dismissal of their qualifications to be a true member of the human race. Far be it from me to argue with such a foolproof system.

Scooby Doo has to be considered one of the most enduring and widespread gateway drugs to horror in the genre's history. With few interruptions, some configuration of the animated series has been beamed into homes around the world since 1969. Through the decades, countless children have been exposed to the classic horror elements: monsters, ghosts, witches, werewolves, haunted houses, castles, hotels, swamps, graveyards, ghost ships, and so on. Ninety-nine percent of these threats turn out to be masquerading con artists and criminals, and accepting that the Mystery Inc. amateur crime-solvers were tricked every single time demanded the greatest suspension of belief ever—at least until Agent Mulder in *X-Files*.

THE 13 SCARIEST HORROR TV SHOWS

Yes, the plots are identical, the jokes are inane, and Scooby's speech patterns are almost indecipherable, and yet kids love it. Some of the show's success comes from the great voice talents of Don Messick, Casey Kasem, and Frank Welker, but more so from the bizarre menagerie of villains that face the gang every week. Charlie the Funland Robot, the Ghost Clown, the Swamp Witch and the Zombie, the Space Kook, the Creeper, the Steam Demon, Dr. Coffin, the Specter, and the Snow Ghost (the ghost of a Yeti!) all combined iconic images of horror with early '70s hippie phantasmagoria. The monster that freaked me out was the Disc Demon, who resembled Gene Simmons in full makeup crossed with a glammed-up Ghost Rider. Though the more contemporary animated films seem to be more about humor than scares, *Scooby Doo* continues to make horror accessible to younger generations. If they really wanted to bring the horror back into *Scooby Doo*, they should get Jerry Reed to sing "Pretty Mary Sunlight" again. Kids wouldn't know what hit them.

10.

Ghost Story

Horror fanatics know that William Castle had an enormous influence on the popularity of horror cinema throughout the 1960s. Part Alfred Hitchcock, part P. T. Barnum, Castle never let a ballyhoo opportunity pass without giving it his all. Whether it was selling insurance policies to movie goers, shocking them in their seats, or sending skeletons flying at them as they watched, Castle knew that the theater-going experience was what closed the loop in terms of truly terrifying a viewer. When television proved to be an enemy that even the Tingler couldn't vanquish, Castle stopped trying to beat TV and joined it. *Ghost Story*, which he created and executive-produced, was a horror anthology series hosted by the erudite Winston Essex (Mr. French himself, Sebastian Cabot) from his haunted hotel. *Ghost Story* lasted only one season (and was retitled *Circle of Fear* to jump-start ratings), but it left a memorable impression thanks to acting performances by Helen Hayes, Patricia Neal, Gena Rowlands, Jason Robards, and Jodie Foster. *Ghost Story* also used some of the top talent in horror at the time with stories and teleplays from Richard Matheson, Robert Bloch, and Hammer Films's stalwart Jimmy Sangster. "The New House," directed by John Llewellyn Moxley, invokes the same atmospheric chills that Moxley's epic film *Horror Hotel* does, combining a haunted house with possession. Episodes like the eerie "The Concrete Captain" and "House of Evil," in which a deaf-mute girl with psychic powers is manipulated by her ruthless grandfather, successfully combine the visceral American strain of horror with the more staid, classical terror of British masters like Joseph Sheridan LeFanu and Arthur Machen. The Sangster-penned "Doorway to Death" is particularly menacing as the revenant of an ax-wielding child murderer seeks more victims beyond the grave. *Ghost Story* is proof that Castle's genius didn't stop at the movie theater and could have continued on in the living room.

9.

Werewolf

The Fox Network has consistently aired quality horror programming, none more so than *Werewolf*. One of the channel's earliest offerings, the series tells the tragic story of college student Eric Cord, who is bitten by his lycanthropic roommate (try explaining that to your RA) and embarks on a mission to destroy the progenitor of the werewolf line to cure himself of the curse. The original werewolf is crafty drifter Janos Skorzeny (named as an homage to the villain of the epochal horror TV film *The Night Stalker*), who hasn't lasted this long without extensive survival skills. Add bounty hunter Alamo Joe, who will not quit until Cord is killed, and you have a very tense situation. Making matters worse is Cord's discovery that Skorzeny isn't the originator and that an even more powerful, malevolent skin walker is the true answer to his salvation.

Werewolf began with a two-hour pilot episode and then ran for twenty-eight episodes before being cancelled. Similar to *The Incredible Hulk*, another shape-shifting series, each week Cord would wander across the country becoming entangled in random people's lives, finding out more about his dual existence as a werewolf, and always being one step behind Skorzeny and later Nicholas Remy (a reference to the real-life sixteenth-century witch hunter) in curing his affliction. The show revised the mythos of werewolves in a similar way that *True Blood* did for vampires: by making supernatural beings more realistic while possessing non-human abilities and suggesting that the presence of these monsters is embedded in historical events that have affected human progress. The transformation sequences were horrifying for 1980s TV, as the metamorphosis is signaled by a bleeding pentagram scar and then changes the afflicted into a feral amalgam of wolf, dog, and bear with razor sharp teeth and claws. Skorzeny's transformation is even more shocking as he peels back his human face to display his animalistic form. *Werewolf* is not available on DVD because of music rights issues, which is terribly ironic because the worse thing about the show was the dated, saxophone- driven soundtrack.

8.

The Omega Factor

The Brits have provided the world with some wonderful horror TV product, but their genre programming (outside of the superb institution *Doctor Who*) is notoriously short lived. It couldn't have helped that during the '70s, English horror and sci-fi TV fans had the notorious defender of morality, Mary Whitehouse, neutering any programming that even hinted at the macabre or transgressive. Outside lending her name to the great power electronics band, Whitehouse's influence had absolutely no positive effect on either raising the bar of television programming or protecting the young. If anything, the fact that she called an episode of *The Omega Factor* "thoroughly evil" only made viewers that more interested in the series. *The Omega Factor* focused on a top-secret government program called Department 7, a team of scientists and psychics who explore supernatural phenomenon. In the background is the shady think tank Omega: are they using Department 7 to control the world through the paranormal? On the good guys' side are psychic Tom Crane and Dr. Anne Reynolds (played by *Doctor Who's* warrior goddess Louise Jameson), and on the villainous side is the Crowley-esque Edward Drexel, who is responsible for Crane's wife's death. Mixing horror, sci-fi, and conspiracy theories, *The Omega Factor* plays out like a combination of *Scanners*, *The Prisoner*, and *The X-Files* with a touch of late '70s Cold War paranoia to boot. Shot on location in Scotland, the series lasted only ten episodes, but those episodes made the most of Edinburgh's Gothic architecture and brooding natural surroundings to enhance stories about haunted houses, ghostly Picts, and doomed dreamers, using those weird British TV special effects that make you feel like you have vertigo. The episode that got Ms. Whitehouse in such a tizzy was "Powers of Darkness," about a group of teenagers who fool with a Ouija board (haven't these kids seen *The Exorcist*?). They resurrect the spirit of a sixteenth-century witch who possesses one of the foolish girls, and Department 7 must save her soul from Lucifer. Perhaps Whitehouse objected to the truly terrifying scenes of the possessed girl performing a realistic satanic ritual using a dead bird on a desecrated church altar. According to those who worked on that episode, some paranormal occurrences accompanied the shooting of several scenes, with props moving on their own and clocks stopping. Maybe Mary was onto something after all.

7.

The Twilight Zone (1985–1989)

The original run of *The Twilight Zone* has reached iconic proportions in the American consciousness. Rod Serling's use of horror and science fiction to tell parables about the human condition (or at least what the human condition was imagined to be in the late 1950s/ early '60s) has taken its deserved place in the pop culture Hall of Fame, and no New Year's Day or July Fourth is complete without a *TZ* marathon. People might not have an opinion about climate change, but they will fight to the death to defend their favorite *Twilight Zone* episode. While the original series is rightly revered, the first revival of *The Twilight Zone* in 1985 deserves more attention. Brought back in hopes of benefitting from the release of *The Twilight Zone: The Movie*, the resurrected series ran for two full seasons and an abbreviated third season in syndication. The producers brought out the big guns: genre writers such as Harlan Ellison, George R. R. Martin, Ray Bradbury, Arthur C. Clarke, Robert McCammon Roger Zelazny, and Stephen King, and directors such as Wes Craven, William Friedkin, Peter Medak, Tommy Lee Wallace, Joe Dante, John Milius, and Jeannot Szwarc. New scripts and concepts were commissioned, with the ill-advised plan to remake classic episodes from the original series like "Night of the Meek." Unfortunately, this new *Twilight Zone* couldn't compete with the highbrow intellectualism of *Mr. Belvedere* and *Webster*, and so the gallant experiment in the return of quality genre programming died an ignoble death.

The series also had a black cloud over it when, early on, CBS Standards and Practices rejected Harlan Ellison's adaptation of Donald E. Westlake's story "Nackles" for *The Twilight Zone* Christmas episode. But before its end, the 1985 incarnation of *The Twilight Zone* brought two of the most frightening TV episodes to the screen. William Friedkin's version of Robert McCammon's "Nightcrawlers" is a nightmarish depiction of a Vietnam vet's post-traumatic stress disorder, which becomes a monstrous reality for those stuck in a diner with him. Even scarier is Bradford May's "Grandma," written and adapted by the dream team of Stephen King and Harlan Ellison, focusing on a young boy who suspects that his ailing grandmother has supernatural machinations to prolong her life. Rumor has it that the original ending of "Grandma" was too horrible for the censors. Let's just say it involved a spider and the boy's mouth and leave it at that.

THE 13 SCARIEST HORROR TV SHOWS

6.

Night Gallery

Rod Serling deserves much more credit as an artist. Sure, he is remembered as a personality and a television pioneer, but his writing, creativity, and conceptual talents are often neglected. Unfortunately, his artistic interests never seemed to jell with the corporatization of media, particularly the commercialization of the television medium. His stories just couldn't be made to sell fabric softener or reassure viewers that they could spend, spend, spend. His return to television in the early '70s was filled with trepidation, frustration, and network interference. It is a testament to his powers that *Night Gallery* was not a total disaster and that this anthology presented some of the best genre work television has ever seen. Hosted by Serling from a macabre art gallery (amazing paintings provided by Thomas J. Wright), *Night Gallery* presented both original stories and adaptations of classic works. *Night Gallery* is a pulp horror fan's dream with versions of stories by H. P. Lovecraft, Clark Ashton Smith, Algernon Blackwood, Seabury Quinn, Manly Wade Wellman, Richard Matheson, August Derleth, Fritz Leiber, and Robert Bloch.

The series began with a pilot TV movie of four stories (one of which was Steven Spielberg's debut as a director) and then settled in for a three-season run. Though Serling tried to keep the tone menacing and serious, the network demanded that he include "humorous" sketches and goofy asides to break up the horror. Despite the corporate meddling, *Night Gallery* has a litany of incredible episodes such as "Camera Obscura," "The Caterpillar," "Class of '99," "Cool Air," "The Doll," "Green Fingers, "Pickman's Model," "Silent Snow, Secret Snow," "The Girl with the Hungry Eyes," and "They're Tearing Down Tim Riley's Bar" (probably the closest story to an old school *Twilight Zone* tale). One of the strangest stories on *Night Gallery* (and one of the strangest things ever shown on network TV) has to be "The Tune in Dan's Café," a Borgesian recursive, surreal take on memory, loss, and regret. If you've ever wondered what an Alain Robbe-Grillet TV show would be like, check out "The Tune in Dan's Café."

5.

Kolchak: The Night Stalker

Having conquered the made-for-TV horror film with the one-two punch of *The Night Stalker* (1972) and *The Night Strangler* (1973), Darren McGavin reprised the role of intrepid news reporter/unlikely paranormal investigator Carl Kolchak for a weekly series. Lasting only one season, *Kolchak: The Night Stalker* is one of the few horror television series that had a strong supporting cast and humorous scenes that are actually funny. Perhaps that was the show's nail in the coffin, as it started to backpedal off the scares and McGavin wanted to emphasize the comedic elements of the ensemble cast. Before it ended, though, *Kolchak: The Night Stalker* provided plenty of monsters and supernatural mayhem for a dozen shows. Vampires, zombies, werewolves, witches, devil worship, Jack the Ripper, and a headless biker were just a few of Kokchak's memorable foes in his futile quest for the truth. The staff of the news agency Kolchak worked for was just as colorful as the creatures he ran up against— in particular, the heart-attack-waiting-to-happen editor Tony Vincenzo and the snobbish cultural critic Ron Updyke, a comic foil for Carl. When the chills and laughs came together, *Kolchak: The Night Stalker* could be extraordinarily entertaining. Episodes such as the *Blade Runner* prototype "Mr. R.I.N.G." and the Phil Silvers guest-starring "Horror in the Heights" (using Hindu folklore to startling effect) display Carl's cunning and vulnerability, essential characteristics of a genre hero. My introduction to the world of Kolchak and the horror genre itself was the episode "Bad Medicine," with Richard Kiel playing a demonic, shape-shifting Native American shaman living in an abandoned skyscraper. The 2005 reboot isn't even worth mentioning, but the three unproduced original show scripts floating around are definitely interesting for those obsessed with what if's.

4.

Thriller

One can make the argument that *Thriller* or *Boris Karloff's Thriller* is the first pure horror series on television. Other TV shows had used genre elements, but those shows had watered them down, mixed them with other genres, and dismissed truly supernatural explanations to create drama, suspense, and satisfying endings. *Thriller*'s raison d'être was to scare, not moralize, reassure, or educate. If a show's intent is to terrify, than having Boris Karloff host it is a no-brainer (Frankenstein pun intended). Karloff's elegant morbidity is in full flight on *Thriller*, and he appeared not only as the emcee but also acted in several stories for the anthology series. Adding to the macabre atmosphere are some stellar contributions from writer Robert Bloch, such as "The Grim Reaper," where William Shatner is confronted with a cursed painting of Death itself. (Between *Thriller* and *The Twilight Zone*, Shatner was routinely driven mad.) Ray Milland directed an adaptation of Bloch's oft-adapted "Yours Truly, Jack the Ripper" and produced a moody, atmospheric rendition of an undying murderous force. Another highlight is John

THE 13 SCARIEST HORROR TV SHOWS

Newland's creepy version of Robert E. Howard's "Pigeons from Hell," as two stranded travelers face pure evil in a deserted mansion. The story-telling in *Thriller* is rock solid, but it is the committed acting performances that raise the series to horror greatness. In addition to the master Karloff and the iconic Shatner, stars such as Leslie Nielsen, Rip Torn, Mary Tyler Moore, Hazel Court, Elizabeth Montgomery, Tom Poston, Ursula Andress, and John Carradine contribute to *Thriller*'s overall feeling of dread and despair.

Actress Ida Lupino directed "La Strega," one of the most hauntingly moving *Thrillers*, containing an absolute downer ending to cap off an already melancholic episode. *Thriller* ran for two seasons, but the *Gold Key* comic book based on the series was published for eighteen years after the show was cancelled.

3.

Twin Peaks

If anyone who saw *Eraserhead* in its initial release had prophesized that David Lynch would one day produce a widely popular television phenomenon, he or she would be spoken of in the same revered tones as Nostradamus. To create *Twin Peaks*, the TV series that became a cultural sensation, all Lynch had to do was sacrifice some of the graphic sex and violence of *Blue Velvet* while retaining the twisted, bizarro '50s Americana obsession with secret lives, murder mysteries, and illicit affairs. The labyrinthine saga of a bucolic Northwestern town and the mysterious murder of homecoming queen Laura Palmer, *Twin Peaks* was like nothing that had ever been seen on TV. At times campy and quirky, at others furiously dark and disturbing, *Twin Peaks* achieved the rare distinction of having both a cult and mainstream audience chomping at the bit for more catchphrases, coffee, cherry pie, and corpses wrapped in plastic. As the murder investigation progresses, the crime becomes more surreal and horrifying, especially when the culprit is revealed to be a malevolent other-dimensional being that can possess people and make them indulge in sick, venal indiscretions. The image of Bob (an improvised bit of Lynchian brilliance) conjures up all the clichés of the long-haired, denim-clad, homicidal creeper crouched at the foot of your bed, but it works on an almost subliminal level. The episodes where Bob materializes are unbearably intense and terrifying, but the episode where he kills Laura's doppelganger Madeline (shades of Hitchcock's *Vertigo*) is one of the most horribly brutal scenes ever seen in prime time.

Even after the catharsis of solving Laura Palmer's murder, *Twin Peaks* shifted into more shocking scenarios involving beings from the White Lodge and Black Lodge, inter-dimensional portals that spawn angels and demons who continue to torment and mystify the town denizens. Not even Special Agent Cooper—a paragon of purity and wholesomeness—is immune from the dreadful machinations of these supernatural entities. Though Lynch's episodes are wonderfully bizarre, it is the underrated Tim Hunter (director of *River's Edge* and episodes of *Hannibal*) who brought the fear to *Twin Peaks*. The series concluded on a devastatingly bleak note as our one hope for goodness in this strange world was brought over to the dark side.

2.

In Search of . . .

"This series presents information based in part on theory and conjecture. The producer's purpose is to suggest some possible explanations, but not necessarily the only ones, to the mysteries we will examine." So began every episode of *In Search of . . .*, a documentary-style series that explored the supernatural, extraterrestrial, the conspiratorial. Hosted by the serious Leonard Nimoy, the show provided actual footage and frighteningly real reenactments of monsters, aliens, ghosts, murderers, secret societies, cults, and vampires—any phenomena that might scare the living daylights out of kids watching it. Inspired by the wacky pseudo-science of von Daniken, the Warrens, and other so-called para-psychologists, the series' earnestness and objective, verite look made these enigmas and portents of a cataclysmic future absolute fact. Riding the wave of '70s occult/UFO chic, the series began with three one-hour specials: *In Search of Ancient Astronauts*, *In Search of Ancient Mysteries*, and *The Outer Space Connection*, all narrated by Rod Serling, the father of TV weird. The television series was developed with Serling in mind as the host, but his premature death left the chore to the reliable Nimoy. *In Search of . . .* could make the most benign subject matter (the secret life of plants?) seem terrifying, thanks to the use of a weird electronic score, the real-life awkwardness of the staged scenes, and Nimoy's objectively creepy narration. There are just too many horrific moments to catalog: Jack the Ripper stalking the streets of Whitechapel, the desolation of the lost Roanoke Colony, a Yeti attacking a Sherpa, voodoo trance rituals, Jim Jones's preaching, alien abductions, haunted castles, etc. My favorite episode is "The Amityville Horror," shown right before Halloween in 1979. This half-hour show contained more scares than the original *Amityville Horror* film and its remake combined (granted, the remake showed more abs). Demonic faces in a fireplace, the chair rocking itself, the doll with the glowing eyes, dancing Native American witch doctors, and piercing red gazes from outside a window are just a few of the hellish images this episode imprinted on my young mind. For years the show was a perennial syndication rerun and was revamped for a short-lived reboot in 2002, riding on *The X-Files* craze. Thank

THE 13 SCARIEST HORROR TV SHOWS

goodness the complete series is available on DVD, because while nostalgia can over-exaggerate the coolness of anything, the fact that viewing the show can still produce chills is evidence enough for me of its greatness.

1.

Dark Shadows

One of the earliest cult TV experiences, *Dark Shadows* still casts a gloomy spell over its fervent followers. The show started out as a dream that creator and TV horror god Dan Curtis had of a mysterious young woman on a train, speeding to a dark destiny. From this Gothic reverie came the first horror soap opera that originally aired each weekday just like any other soap opera, but this one was quite different. Well, initially it was just a darker version of your grandma's "stories," but it was when the writers decided to throw in supernatural elements like ghosts, curses, and a certain vampire that it became a monster hit. What makes *Dark Shadows* the perfect horror TV show is that it creates a self-contained world with its own mythos, history, rules, and logic. Nothing seems to exist outside the hermetically sealed reality of Collinsport, and even that reality is constantly rewritten and offshoots into alternative timelines and multiple character permutations. No other television series has the unique atmosphere and mood of *Dark Shadows*: the wonderful Robert Cobert score, the crashing waves of the title sequence, the ominous narration, the endlessly perplexing confines of Collinwood. Like Poe's "The Fall of the House of Usher," there is a psychic link between the Collins family and their abode.

Because of the sheer number of episodes produced (1,225), the characters were extremely well developed and complex, allowing for not only the growth of the characters (and alternate versions of those characters) but also for the viewer to really appreciate the talents of the actors and actresses. Jonathan Frid's reluctant vampire, Barnabas Collins, became an unlikely middle-aged heartthrob, but one viewing of his elegant Byronic performance and you will understand why teenage girls swooned.

Dark Shadows touched on all the right horror tropes and components (vampires, werewolves, unnaturally created beings, ghosts, zombies) but was at its best when portraying witchcraft and magic: the hand of Count Petofi, the head of Judah Zachery, Diablos and Nicolas Blair, and of course, Angelique Bouchard, the greatest witch to grace the television screen. Even the much-maligned Leviathan storyline was mind-bendingly awesome, as if Lovecraft wrote a soap opera. While some of the story lines and performances were overly melodramatic and took themselves way too seriously, that only added to the show's operatic grandeur. The 1990 revival series, while not approaching the stature of the original, was a noble experiment that could have grown into something special had it been given a chance. Tim Burton's film, on the other hand, was a massive disappointment, displaying only fleeting moments that capture that unique *Dark Shadows* feel.

Honorable Mention:

The X-Files
Millennium
Hammer House of Horror
American Gothic
Darkroom
Strange Paradise
Dead of Night
Supernatural
Hannibal
True Detective (first season)
Tales From the Crypt

157

THE 13 SCARIEST HORROR TV SHOWS

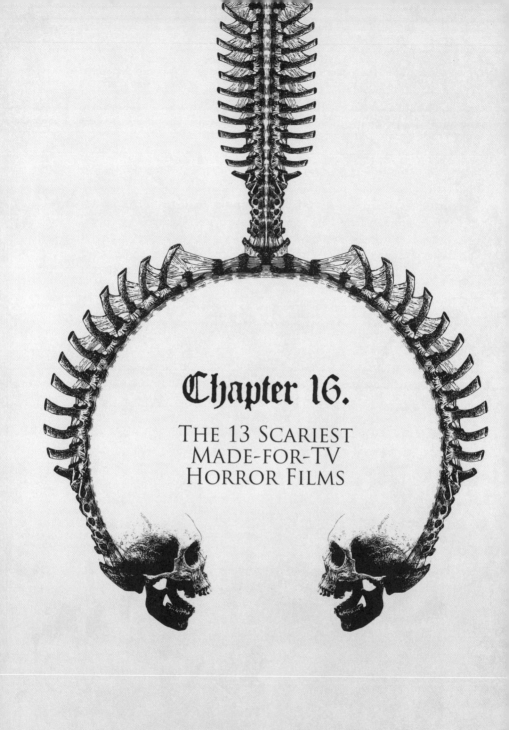

Chapter 16.

THE 13 SCARIEST
MADE-FOR-TV
HORROR FILMS

The phenomenon of the made-for-TV movie is a uniquely magical one. In our newfangled world of On-Demand, Hulu, Netflix, and thousands of cable channels, it might seem unbelievable that there was ever a shortage of programming for network TV. And yet, in those prehistoric days of the 1970s, the three big networks needed to compete with the increased violence and sex on display in theaters. The allure of free movies that you couldn't see in the theater but could be viewed in the comfort of your own home seemed like a desperate gimmick, but it produced an incredibly interesting and diverse number of films. Naturally, horror and the supernatural fit right into the melodramatic tone of these films that the whole family watched. Because of censorship restrictions, these TV films had to be more psychological, atmospheric, and spooky than disturbingly violent.

The smaller budgets and need for an almost weekly product ensured a healthy amount of creativity and downright bizarre subjects and scenarios. How about a movie about a plane possessed by Celtic sacrificial stones starring William Shatner as a drunken ex-priest? Weird enough for you? You got to see movie stars before they were stars, or formerly famous actors and actresses slumming it to pay

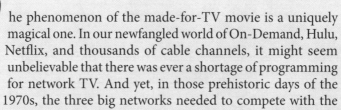

How about a movie about a plane possessed by Celtic sacrificial stones starring William Shatner as a drunken ex-priest? Weird enough for you?

the bills. Some of the films acted as pilots for TV series. Some of these TV movies were even released theatrically in Europe with extra footage to pad out the length or add spice to get those cultured Europeans in the seats. The heyday of the TV movie lasted from 1969–1976, but made-for-TV movies were still being made until the '90s. Cable and the VCR killed their network profitability. Though the old-school TV movie is only a fond memory (many are available on YouTube), if you were a young horror fan in the 1970s and early '80s, you were probably psychologically scarred by a strange encounter with made-for-TV horror films.

13.

A Ghost Story for Christmas (1971–1978, 2005)
—Various (mostly Lawrence Gordon Clark)

The US certainly doesn't have a stranglehold on the creepy made-for-TV movie format. The BBC's annual *A Ghost Story for Christmas* films frightened British children on Christmas vacation from 1971 to 1978 and were brought back in 2005. Before the reign of Halloween, Christmas was the time of hauntings and spirits (as evidenced in Dickens's *A Christmas Carol*), and the BBC revived the tradition of telling ghost stories on Christmas Eve. Each year a different story would be adapted into a short film for the series. The first five were based on the stories of M. R. James (the greatest ghost story writer ever), with a Dickens adaptation and two original films rounding out the annual holiday sequence. Although all the films are unnerving, three are particularly unsettling. James's "A Warning to the Curious" concerns a ghostly guardian of an ancient crown foolishly disturbed by an amateur archeologist. "Lost Hearts" is the epitome of Jamesian terror as bloodlust and savagery lurk behind the smiling face of a jolly, avuncular figure looking to sacrifice his young cousin so he can live forever. His past victims try to warn the young boy, appearing as ghoulish revenants dancing to hurdy-gurdy music even though their hearts have been ripped out. Last, but certainly not least, is the original film "Stigma," an Arthur Machen/ Nigel Kneale-esque story of the removal of an ancient stone circle and the revenge of a witch who was ritually sacrificed there. The use of natural locations adds immeasurably to the eeriness of these films, specifically England's desolate, brooding coastlines and plains. The British seem to have no qualms about scaring children, as these Christmas airings and the equally chilling BBC kid's movie *Ghost in the Water* clearly demonstrate.

12.

Jenifer (2005)—Dario Argento

Okay, maybe I'm cheating a bit because this premiered on cable, but c'mon: Argento, Jones, and Wrightson. Is that a combination made in the infernal depths, or what? Made for the uber-cool *Masters of Horror* series, *Jenifer* is a short movie based on the horrifying black-and-white comic book story that originally appeared in the epochal magazine *Creepy*. Written by the witty Bruce Jones and drawn by the czar of horror comic book artists Bernie Wrightson, *Jenifer* is a blood-soaked, sex-crazed tragedy about vulnerability, seduction, and destruction. A cop rescues a deformed woman from being murdered, which sets into motion a string of events that perpetuate a cycle of viciousness. This ironic tale of lust and brutality seems tailor-made for the Mad Maestro, Dario Argento. Although *Jenifer* is not a return to the Technicolor insanity of his peak period, Argento lets the story tell itself, utilizing his more mature style that horror fans seem to hate. And yet for this TV film, it works perfectly as the intensity of the violence, lust, and obsession slowly builds to a frenzy of hunger and cannibalism, with bodies violated and devoured because of the blindness of love. Carrie Fleming's performance as the titular character is grotesque and sympathetic at the same time. All *Jenifer* needs is a score by Goblin, and it would be hailed as an Argento masterwork.

11.

The Devil's Daughter (1973)—Jeannot Szwarc

The seismic effect of *Rosemary's Baby* and *The Exorcist* created a Me-Generation Mephistophelian obsession with Satan during the early '70s. A whole sub-genre of made-for-TV films focus on decadent dealings with Lucifer: *Satan's School for Girls, The Possessed, Look What's Happened to Rosemary's Baby, Good Against Evil, The Devil and Miss Sarah, Conspiracy of Terror*. Though all three major networks produced made-for-TV satanic films, ABC was the elite standard for gonzo Saturday night demonic horror. An example is this diabolic melodrama about an arranged marriage to Satan and the birth and maturation of his future wife, destined to be Miss Lucifer. Who knew that Satan needed to be set up on blind dates? The film succeeds in equating upper-class opulence, dissolute ennui, and self-indulgent supernaturalism. Riding the occult chic wave, *The Devil's Daughter* contains a rogue's gallery of '70s "stars": Joseph Cotton, Shelly Winters, Abe Vigoda, and William Holden. Even Barnabas Collins himself, Jonathan Frid, makes an appearance. Expertly directed by the underrated Jeannot Szwarc (*Jaws 2, Supergirl* . . . maybe I'm not making a case for him by using these examples), this shocker mixes satanism and Dr. Spock for the Love Generation.

10.

Gargoyles (1972)   Bill L. Norton

Filmed on location in Carlsbad Caverns, New Mexico, *Gargoyles* has an incredible air of authenticity, a verisimilitude that makes the viewer wonder if there really might be an unknown species of half human/half dragon living in the ancient caves of the Southwest. Father and daughter archeologists stumble upon the skeleton of a gargoyle and before they can get it to the Museum of Unnatural History, they are stalked

THE 13 SCARIEST MADE-FOR-TV HORROR FILMS

by a group of creatures looking to keep their existence a secret. Director Bill L. Norton (son of made-for-TV horror legend William F. Norton) provides quite a few uncanny moments, such as the attack on a roadside attraction exhibiting the skeleton, the voices of the gargoyles (kind of like a Dalek on quaaludes), and the movement of the gargoyles—a sort of half-speed lumbering grace. The cast—including such '70s stalwarts as Bernie Casey, Grayson Hall (the always-a-vampire-bridesmaid-never-a-vampire-bride Dr. Julia Hoffmann from *Dark Shadows*), and a young Scott Glenn—is great, but the film would go down in cinematic history as the first makeup credit for Stan "the Wizard" Winston. I always wondered if Alan Hewetson and Maelo Cintron's Skwald comic series *The Human Gargoyles* influenced or was influenced by this made-for-TV monstershow.

9.

The Norliss Tapes (1973)—Dan Curtis

Directed by the god of '70s TV horror Dan Curtis and written by William F. Nolan (no slouch himself with writing credits for *Darkroom*, *The Turn of the Screw*, *Trilogy of Terror*, and *Burnt Offerings*), *The Norliss Tapes* tried to mine the same fertile territory as the Kolchak movies and TV series. Reporter David Norliss has disappeared, leaving only the tapes of his investigation into voodoo and reanimated corpses. His publisher listens to the tapes and tries to piece together what happened to the missing reporter. This episode was the pilot for a TV series that never happened, and the fact that Norliss is an absentee protagonist might have made a very interesting premise for a weekly thriller. Rather than pine for what could have been, we should just revel in the horrible riches of this film: blue-skinned zombies with super strength; an Egyptian scarab ring that invokes Osiris, the god of eternal life; and a Corvette Stingray. The cast is amazing, including such cult actors as Roy Thinnes, Angie Dickinson, Claude Akins, and Vonetta McGee. Although not quite up to the gold standard of Kolchak, David Norliss could have made a compelling investigator into the supernatural. And just imagine a Kolchak/Norliss crossover!

8.

John Carpenter's Cigarette Burns (2005)—John Carpenter

Master of horror John Carpenter is no stranger to the made-for-TV genre, with such TV films as *Someone's Watching Me!*, *Elvis*, and *Body Bags* under his belt. His first contribution to the *Masters of Horror* series, *Cigarette Burns* (his second was the polemical *Pro-Life*), is a cineaste's dream and nightmare come true. In-debt theater owner Kirby (*Walking Dead* hunk Norman Reedus) is hired by a cinephile (the debonair Udo Kier) to find the only existing print of a mysterious movie, *La Fin Absolue du Monde* (*The Absolute End of the World*). Rumor has it that the film was so transgressive and blasphemous that it caused a crazed homicidal riot during its premiere, after which all prints were supposedly destroyed. The search for this possibly apocryphal work of art brings disaster, not only to the film's viewers but to all who drift into its horrific orbit. Carpenter's metaphors of the theater as cathedral and film as gospel result in some of the most beautiful and profane imagery to appear in one of his films. The fragments of *La Fin Absolue du Monde* that tease the viewer are enough evidence that if anyone created a film that could make angels weep and demons scream, it would be John Carpenter.

7.

Snowbeast (1977)—Herb Wallerstein

Bigfoot was one of the best pop culture crazes of the 1970s. This ultimate misunderstood loner appeared on just about every '70s TV show, from *In Search Of . . .,* to *The Six Million Dollar Man*, to *Bigfoot and Wild Boy*, where he starred in his own show. (My childhood dream was for *Starsky and Hutch* to add Sasquatch as a partner). Our noble wood ape helped ease the pain of the oil crisis, whipping inflation, and the sinking of the Edmund Fitzgerald. The made-for-TV movie think-tank could not let this phenomenon go un-dramatized, and so *Snowbeast* was unleashed on a Yeti-obsessed public in 1977. The title character is an enraged Abominable Snowman preying on a ski resort in the Rocky Mountains (shot on location, hoping to mimic the authenticity of the infamous Ray Patterson footage). Ski hunks and snow bunnies are being slaughtered during the winter carnival, and it's up to two of the manliest men in made-for-TV history, Clint Walker and Bo Svenson, to stop the beast and get back to the lodge to sip cocoa and cognac in the hot tub. Competently directed by Herb Wallerstein (who earned his pop-culture-directing chops on *I Dream of Jeannie*, *Star Trek*, and *The Brady Bunch*) and written by Joseph Stefano, co-author of a little known chiller called *Psycho*, *Snowbeast* gives its Bigfoot-craving audience plenty of furry action and black diamond thrills.

THE 13 SCARIEST MADE-FOR-TV HORROR FILMS

6.

The Night Stalker/The Night Strangler
(1972/73)—John Llewllyn Moxey/Dan Curtis

The highest-rated ABC TV movie ever, *The Night Stalker* spawned a second film, two TV series, and a diehard cult following that continues even now with comic books and novels. Based on a novel by Jeff Rice, reporter Carl Kolchak (played perfectly by Darren McGavin) tracks a serial killer in Las Vegas, who is revealed to be a vampire. Directed by John Llewllyn Moxey (responsible for *Horror Hotel*, one of the most atmospheric horror films ever), adapted by Richard Matheson (perhaps the best horror writer of the 1960s), and produced by Dan Curtis, *The Night Stalker* contributed to the reinvention of the vampire that began with the Count Yorga films. Janos Skorzeny is cold, calculating, and refined, a thoroughly modern vampire, and there are no traces of castles, villagers, and widow's peaks. McGavin's performance as Kolchak achieves that special balance of comedy and bravery, jaded and believing—the perfect hero for the Watergate era.

The success of *The Night Stalker* inspired a second TV movie, *The Night Strangler*, in 1973, and the sequel was equally scary. This time, Kolchak searches for another killer of women, but this killer is strangling his victims to attain an elixir that will keep his ghastly cycle of life extended. Again scripted by Matheson but this time directed by Curtis, *The Night Strangler* was also an audience grabber. It was expected to lead to a third Kolchak film about UFOs, androids, and replacing humans, but ABC decided to turn the Kolchak premise into a TV series. *Kolchak: The Night Stalker* (which makes Carl sound like he's a vampire) wasn't as popular as the films, and this underappreciated series lasted only one season. With this ignoble end, it would seem that Kolchak would be consigned to the obituaries, but a young Chris Carter was watching, and the concept of a paranormal investigator searching for the truth in the face of skepticism would inspire *The X-Files*.

5.

Ghostwatch (1992)—Lesley Manning

The made-for-TV equivalent of Orson Welles's *War of the World*'s panic, *Ghostwatch* was a fake reality television special broadcast on the BBC in 1992. Shown "live" on Halloween, British audiences believed that they were seeing an actual documentary of a haunted house investigation in London. It seems an extremely malicious poltergeist nicknamed Pipes (it has a tendency to knock on the house's plumbing pipes) is terrifying a family, especially the children. Pipes's motives become even more sinister when it is revealed that it is the spirit of a child killer. If that's not bad enough, Pipes uses the broadcast to infect the BBC, taking control of the studio and projecting its malevolence across the country, culminating in the possession of real-life talk show host Michael Parkinson. Written by Stephen Volk (who also scripted Ken Russell's film *Gothic*) and directed by Lesley Manning, *Ghostwatch* is uncannily authentic, using interviews and live footage in such a believable way that many viewers reported psychological effects from watching the film, including a suicide blamed on its powerful presentation. The fleeting, subliminal glimpses of Pipes as a disfigured, androgynous, blurry figure wearing a cloak are especially disturbing. The fact that the filmmakers got Michael Parkinson, one of the great English broadcasters and journalists, to play along only increased the believability. Imagine if Tom Brokaw or Dan Rather appeared on the evening news and started shaking, eyes rolling back, and speaking with a demonic voice. You'd freak out, too. The BBC banned *Ghostwatch* for a decade before agreeing to rebroadcast it.

4.

Dark Night of the Scarecrow (1981)—Frank De Felitta

Why did it take so long for horror filmmakers to seize on the scary potential of the scarecrow? *Dark Night of the Scarecrow* plows the fertile environment of a bigoted Southern community to tell a tale of prejudice, injustice, and supernatural revenge. Gentle giant Bubba (Larry Drake channeling Lenny from *Of Mice and Men*) is wrongly accused of attacking a little girl, and the town bullies form a vigilante posse to go after the poor half-wit. In their fervor to exact punishment, the lynch mob kills Bubba (disguised as a scarecrow to evade their fury) and is later acquitted for murder. Soon a wraithlike scarecrow appears, taking a ghostly vengeance on the exonerated killers. This rural morality play seeps with atmosphere and menace as the golden fields play silent witness to the spectral scales of justice. The look of the film is striking, resembling what *Days of Heaven* would have looked like had it been shot by Dean Cundey. Directed by novelist Frank De Felitta (author of reincarnation thriller *Audrey Rose*), the figure of the scarecrow is absolutely frightening, the dark eye holes in the sack-covered head seeming to stare into the murky recesses of the soul.

THE 13 SCARIEST
MADE-FOR-TV
HORROR FILMS

3.

Crowhaven Farm (1970)—Walter Grauman

Inheriting a pre-Revolutionary War homestead in New England may sound like the bee's knees, but when it happens to be the witch-infested Crowhaven Farm, you'd better think twice about signing the deed (in blood). Ben and Maggie Porter move to the eponymous property to strengthen a shaky marriage, but are soon confronted with the dread of the past manifesting itself in the resurgence of an ancient coven of witches. It seems that marital problems are not just a modern concern, as the history of Crowhaven Farm involved joining in a witch's sabbath and sending a spouse's soul to Satan to effectively arrange a divorce. Kind of like *Dark Shadows* meets *The Crucible*, *Crowhaven Farm* incorporates witch trials, revenants, demonic pregnancies, and the repetition of ancestral evil on the current populace. Though filmed in California, director Walter Grauman conjures up a definite New England feel, as the farmhouse resembles what I imagine the cannibal's house looks like in Lovecraft's "The Picture in the House." Featuring such B-movie thespians as Hope Lange, John Carradine, and William Smith, the film casts an eerie spell over the viewer as we are confronted with characters with no hope except to give in to the ensnaring influence of the past.

2.

Salem's Lot (1979)—Tobe Hooper

The dream team of Stephen King and Tobe Hooper came together for this superlative adaptation of King's novel. *Salem's Lot* aired over two nights in 1979 and terrified viewers young and old (particularly kids allowed to stay up and watch it). Starring David Soul (Hutch!) and James Mason, one of the greatest actors in the English-speaking world, the plot concerns a writer returning to his home town to face some inner demons and discovers that vampirism is infecting the citizens of Salem's Lot. There are so many horrific set pieces, scenes, and images that it's hard to keep track: the Marsten House, Straker killing Ralphie Glick as an offering to his vampire master, Danny Glick popping out of his coffin, Barlow's slaughter of Mark Petrie's parents and the local priest, and the iconic sequence where Danny floats outside Mark's window asking him to open the latch. Hooper proves how versatile a director he is by completely changing his usual approach, moving away from his frenetic *Chainsaw* style and appropriating a more deliberate Jacques Tourneur/Val Lewton pace. The film builds slowly and methodically, so that when moments of unexpected violence explode on the screen, it is truly terrifying. Reggie Nalder, as the Nosferatu-like Barlow, is a hissing, feral, verminous creature far away from King's more humanistic vampire in the original novel. The soundtrack by Harry Sukman (who also scored John Carpenter's made-for-TV movie *Someone Is Watching Me!*) helps to build on the latent menace festering at the heart of a small town. *Salem's Lot* was recut, losing some scenes and gaining new ones for its theatrical release in Europe, but it is the original two-part adaptation that fully expresses all the modern Gothic fright of King's masterwork.

1.

Don't be Afraid of the Dark (1973)—John Newland

Because of their need to appeal to the whole family, made-for-TV movies often had female protagonists as both victims and perpetrators. Domestic issues were used as expressions of horror so that everyone, from adults to children, could identify with the exaggerated threats to relationships, identity, and the family unit. As horror is a safety valve allowing social anxieties and fears to be revealed and dealt with in an acceptable way, issues of gender equality, repression, and dominance played out in many late '60s/early '70s horror films. *Rosemary's Baby* was a touchstone for exploring feminist concerns in the horror film, and *Don't Be Afraid of the Dark* pushes those themes of victimization and subjugation into even more disquieting areas. The film focuses on Sally Farnham, a housewife (but not a mother) seemingly confined in a new home where she feels uncomfortable and has nothing to do. Attempting to exert her authority over this domestic scenario, she unwittingly unleashes a group of miniature creatures from within a sealed fireplace that she had been warned to stay away from. The creatures want to possess her and take her down into the dark hole from which they emerged (Freud would have had a field day with this movie). Of course, nobody believes Sally's accounts of being harassed, attacked, and psychologically tortured by the creatures. In the end, the masculine monsters trap her in the house permanently, where she will be wife and mother to them forever. This film has such an air of creepy oppression that it is almost a relief when Sally is finally engulfed. The creatures are hideous little nuisances with a propensity to whisper in an unnerving way. Just hiss "Saa–lly, Saa–lly" to any horror fan who grew up in the '70s and watch them shudder involuntarily. Kim Darby gives a haunting performance as the female protagonist, and John Newland creates a suffocating atmosphere of dread and sorrow. Do I even have to say that the theatrical remake released in 2010 is a total waste of time?

THE 13 SCARIEST MADE-FOR-TV HORROR FILMS

Honorable Mention

Spectre
Robin Redbreast
A Cold Night's Death
The House That Would Not Die
The Werewolf of Woodstock
The Day After
Helter Skelter
Schalken the Painter
Innsmouth wo Oou Kage

Literature and Comic Books

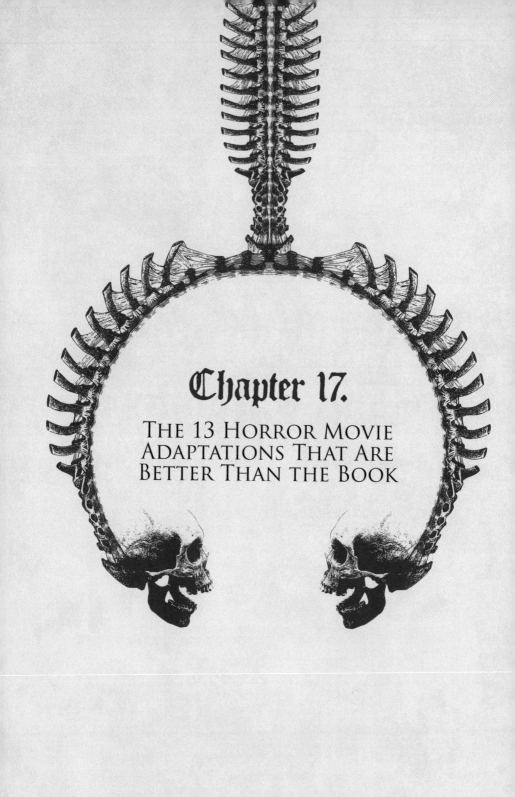

Chapter 17.

THE 13 HORROR MOVIE ADAPTATIONS THAT ARE BETTER THAN THE BOOK

One of the oldest maxims in the civilized world (I believe it was first mentioned in Plato's *Republic*) is that the book is always better than the movie. Never mind that this comparison is as logical as judging the value of music by how accurately it reflects the relationships that inspired it, but it has become an accepted truism that transcends time, space, genre, and box office results. How could a movie ever re-create the depth and richness of the novel—the expressive quality of prose and the interpretive complexity of literature? Behind this lauding of the solitary reading practice over the mass communal viewing experience is an assumption that exposes both the classism and elitism that infuses the arts—the ever-present highbrow/lowbrow split between upper-class academic literati and low-class moving-picture gawkers. Supposedly, readers don't need someone to visualize characters, settings, relationships, symbols, or plot for them; the power of their own elevated intellect and imagination can conjure up much more satisfying and artistic projections than some all flash/no substance director. This notion that just because people can read, their mind can challenge or even surpass the bold creative visions of artists like Fellini, Bergman, Tarkovsky, or Bunuel suggests that many readers are living in a fool's library.

Granted, the gaping maw of the film industry is constantly trolling for any and all product to consume, digest, and spit out to a starving audience, but occasionally a director will not only be able to boil down and refine the essence of a book, but also expand on and enhance the raw material, transforming leaden prose to golden images. Just because someone is an author doesn't mean that he or she can hack it as a visual artist. Have you ever seen a film that was directed by an author, adapted from his/her own work? Take a gander at *Maximum Overdrive* or *Tough Guys Don't Dance* and tell me with a straight face that the skills transfer. Let's face it, most books are boring: over-explained, clichéd, pretentious, smug, self-referential, and irrelevant. Their worst trait is that, even more so than the movie business, they offer little that is original or different, and they run their few innovations into the ground almost immediately with mimicry. The aesthetics of film have left literature in the dust, especially when it comes to effects, montage, editing, and juxtaposition of image, sound, and dialogue (authors Joyce, Woolf, Burroughs,

How could a movie ever re-create the depth and richness of the novel—the expressive quality of prose and the interpretive complexity of literature? Behind this lauding of the solitary reading practice over the mass communal viewing experience is an assumption that exposes both the classism and elitism that infuses the arts—the ever-present highbrow/lowbrow split between upper-class academic literati and low-class moving-picture gawkers.

Acker, and Genet are exempted from this grossly generalized criticism). Cinematography and performance have novels beat by a long shot.

Horror novels and short stories have been and continue to be extremely popular sources for films, and some of the first film adaptations in the history of cinema have drawn from fanatastique literature, in particular the works of Georges Méliès. While the majority of written works that have been adapted do have certain advantages over their cinematic interpretations, there are some films that have exceeded and improved on their sources. Here are thirteen horror films that bettered their literary progenitors.

13.

Lifeforce (1985)—Tobe Hooper

Why Colin Wilson was ever taken seriously is a mystery to me. His vastly over-rated book, *The Outsider*, is basically a rip-off of Freud and Camus, and any claims he makes to being a philosopher are laughable in the face of real thinkers like Sartre, Heidegger, or even Dr. Phil. If you think being prolific is laudable, then you may be impressed with Wilson's oeuvre, but if that's one's measure of greatness, than the Octomom is a notable woman. Wilson has spewed out books on a number of subjects (true crime, the supernatural, the occult, unsolved mysteries), all filtered through his enormous ego and sexist, half-baked Nietzchean theories. Even his novels are infected with this need to lecture and convince the reader that he is a deep thinker. His 1976 novel *The Space Vampires* has an interesting plot, but it is unfortunately ruined by his intellectual insecurities: cosmic inter-dimensional vampires are discovered in space, transported back to Earth, and prey on the life energies of human beings. The notion of energy vampires that drain life force and can possess human bodies is quite creative, but the action gets bogged down in boring 1960s treatises about sexuality, vampirism, the criminal type, bio-energy transferals, and the soul. In an extreme act of hubris, Wilson borrows ideas from much superior authors Clark Ashton Smith and M. R. James as if to give legitimacy to his own.

Thankfully, horror maven Tobe Hooper seized the energy vampire concept, culled the pretentious Psych 101 pontificating, added fantastic special effects, and created the gonzoid 1985 masterwork *Lifeforce*. The legendary Dan O'Bannon worked his magic on the screenplay, which kept the novel's basic structure but pushed the preposterous concept of space vampires unleashed on London so over the top that, after a while, you don't even notice the naked energy suckers parading through the film. The acting performances run the gamut from emotionless (Mathilda May) to frantic (Patrick Stewart) to wild (Steve Railsback). *Lifeforce* has some of the most freakishly dazzling special effects ever committed to film: the umbrella-like spaceship inside Halley's comet, the space vampire's original bat creature forms, the sapped corpses trying to gasp one last breath before exploding into dust, and most impressive of all, the draining of vitality from London as bolts of lightning and columns of light streak through a devastated city. (I'm always reminded of the apocalyptic issue #15 of Alan Moore's *Miracleman*

THE 13 HORROR MOVIE ADAPTATIONS THAT ARE BETTER THAN THE BOOK

whenever I watch these scenes.) The climax in St. Paul's Cathedral achieves what Wilson's novel can't: the melding of Thantos and Eros in an explosion of chakras that transcends space and time. Of course, Wilson trashed Hooper's film, but what else could he do when shown what a real artist can produce?

12.

The Keep (1983)—Michael Mann

The occult interests of the Nazi regime are a font of sinister inspiration for the horror genre. Doubling the real-life evil of the Nazis with black magic and Faustian bargains with malevolent forces might seem politically dubious, but this Machiavellian relationship does have some historical validity. F. Paul Wilson's bestselling novel *The Keep* focuses on a regiment of Nazis (both front line soldiers and overconfident SS officers) tasked with occupying an ancient Romanian fortress. Their intrusion awakens a powerful being named Molasar who seeks to be released from his prison. Desperate to control the supernatural entity, the Nazis force a Jewish historian to unlock the secrets of the fortress. Molasar is even more ruthless than the Nazis in achieving his ends, and a mysterious man arrives to prevent the corrupt creature from conquering the world. Filled with Joseph Campbell archetypes, Christian symbolism, and folk mythology, *The Keep* is a metaphysical exploration of good and evil that starts with the historical depravity of the Nazis but moves upward to the universal spiritual questions of ethical choice and moral responsibility. While satisfying for speculative fiction, it doesn't quite cut it for a horror novel, and that's where Michael Mann's 1983 film adaptation comes in. Mann keeps the skeleton of Wilson's plot but drapes it with splendiferously gaudy accouterments. Mann's film is a Wagnerian opera crossed with the more perverse, euro-Gothic Universal films like *The Black Cat* and *Dracula's Daughter*. Wilson's subtleties are erased by the larger-than-life cinematic presentation and the aggressive acting of Gabriel Byrne, Jurgen Prochnow, and Ian McKellen. Mann's depiction of the epic struggle between light and darkness overpowers any attempts at logic, reason, or explanation. This is a film the viewer feels rather than contemplates: scenes bypass the conscious mind and dig deep into the primordial part of the brain. Everything about the film is pushed to the limit: colors, sound, music, and images batter the viewer into submission. (Tangerine Dream's score is unearthly, one doesn't know whether to be in awe of or disgusted by Molasar). Wilson hated what Mann did to his novel, but cineastes should thank the flashy director for taking an interesting book and turning it into a once-in-a-lifetime kind of film.

11.

The Lair of the White Worm (1988)—Ken Russell

Bram Stoker's *Dracula* is one of those iconic books that everyone has heard of but not many people read anymore. Stoker's prose is laborious to plow through, often taking twenty words to say something that should have taken five. Stoker suffers from the Victorian writer's ubiquitous habit of taking forever to say nothing. Stoker's final novel, *The Lair of the White Worm*, is a prime example of this tendency, so much so that when it was republished, over a hundred pages were excised and forty chapters were cut down to a still-excessive twenty eight. Nonetheless, the core of the novel is intriguing: predatory people squabbling over an estate go to extreme lengths including mesmerism, murder, and a gargantuan snake monster to secure the inheritance. Arabella March is a ruthless woman willing to sacrifice anyone in her way, usually by throwing them down a pit into the creature's lair, to rise into a higher social class and gain a title through marriage to the heir. Stoker's novel ingeniously connects the monstrous woman with the monstrous worm, but soon the story goes off into strange tangents about hypnotism and giant kites used to scare off hawks.

Leave it to the irrepressible Ken Russell to throw out almost all of Stoker's meandering plot and social commentary, creating a film that gives us what we want: the giant snake! The legend of the "d'Ampton worm" is proven to be real and the monstrous dragon-like being is actively worshipped and cared for by an immortal priestess who can transform into a snake woman. Russell's adaptation pits Christian morality against pagan sensuality, and if you are a fan of Russell's you know which side wins. Amanda Donohoe's performance as the slinky Lady Sylvia Marsh is seductive and serpentine, especially when she lovingly spits venom on a crucifix. Russell brings his flamboyant style to the proceedings and one is never sure whether to laugh at or look away from the grotesqueries (is any director better at dream sequences?). The beauty of Ken Russell is that no matter what he is adapting, whether the story is based on music, biography, science fiction, literature, or history, the originals become his own through the power of his unique vision.

THE 13 HORROR MOVIE ADAPTATIONS THAT ARE BETTER THAN THE BOOK

10.

The Dead Zone (1983)—David Cronenberg

The literary value of Stephen King is hotly debated. His popularity and the genre he writes in certainly don't help to convince academics and literary critics of his artistic worth, but are those prejudices the only reason why King has been left out of the American literature canon? Is King merely a very good but not a great writer? Do his talents transcend the medium that he creates in and break through to the divine? King's aesthetic and intellectual shortcomings often become more pronounced when he is adapted by a superior artist. His novel *The Dead Zone* is the story of Johnny Smith, who spent five years in a coma after a car crash. On awakening, Smith finds that he can see a person's inner life and future. This talent becomes a curse as Johnny can't relate to other human beings because some are fearful of his power, while others try to use him. After shaking hands with a sociopathic politician, he is burdened with the knowledge of a hopeless future unless he acts to stave off world annihilation. King's novel does an adequate job of relating the lonesome burden of Johnny Smith's ESP, an ability many of us dream of having without thinking through the consequences of being able to see everyone's future but one's own. Here is where the depth and gravity of an actor's performance can make us truly empathize with a character, more so than a writer's description.

In David Cronenberg's adaptation of *The Dead Zone*, Christopher Walken's Johnny Smith is one of the most heart-wrenching portrayals of an outsider ever committed to film, and occurred well before Walken became a parody of himself. (Surely, the only other performance that rivals Walken's pathos is Lon Chaney Jr.'s in *The Wolf Man*.) Walken's mannerisms, gait, and haunted eyes say more about the angst and despair of someone who is different than any author's words could. The world has passed Johnny by and he can never have the simple life he had hoped for. Walken's scenes with his former girlfriend, Sarah (played brilliantly by the underrated Brooke Adams), are almost too painful to watch as Johnny is still in love with a woman who has moved on after five years. Cronenberg's depictions of Johnny's visions are frighteningly real. Whether they are of a fire threatening a child, a serial killer stalking his prey, a boy falling through an icy pond, or the launching of a nuclear attack by a crazed president, Johnny's "gift" results in horrible shocks that are destroying him. The scenes involving the Castle Rock Killer are particularly chilling in that not only does Johnny identify the killer but also uncovers the killer's mother's complacency in the crimes. The killer's act of scissor seppuku is unbearably ritualized. Because of Walken's performance, the ending is vastly superior to King's novel, as Johnny makes a heroic sacrifice that ends his future but preserves the world's. Cronenberg allows Johnny one final moment of happiness in the arms of his lost love, like a true tragic hero. Now isn't that literature?

9.

The Midnight Meat Train (2008)—Ryuhei Kitamura

Clive Barker's influence on horror cannot be overestimated. His books, art, movies, and personality helped move the genre out of the late '80s doldrums and into a more experimental and carnal demesne ruled by the Liverpudlian. His *Books of Blood* series hit horror fiction like a barbed wire-wrapped fist. Stories about a demon that could tie his genitals in a knot, cities that create immense warring giants out of their inhabitants, sensory deprivation experiments that drive people to insanity, and a primordial phallic monster that can be stopped only by a feminine fertility talisman earned Barker praise from Stephen King himself. Barker would adapt his own story, "The Hellbound Heart," into the iconic film *Hellraiser*, but another cinematic adaptation of one of his stories actually improves upon the original. Barker's short story "The Midnight Meat Train" is the tale of Leon Kaufman, who has the bad luck of falling asleep on a New York subway. He is taken to a mysterious location where he encounters Mahogany, a killer who slaughters people on the train to feed subterranean creatures that must be appeased for the sake of the city. Barker's story is streamlined in its brutality and mythos, not offering much of an explanation for this urban ritual of blood sacrifice.

While leaving things enigmatic often works in horror, Ryuhei Kitamura's cinematic adaptation of the story offers us more information that, far from reassuring the viewer, intensifies the monstrousness of the conspiracy to keep the meat train going. Bradley Cooper (pre-*The Hangover*) plays Leon, a timid photographer who investigates the disappearances of subway passengers and runs into the "Subway Butcher," an immensely powerful man who slaughters his victims with a cold, focused sense of purpose. The murders are unceasingly harsh as the victims are carved up, dressed out, and their carcasses hung on hooks inside the subway cars. Leon suspects that the same man is responsible for crimes stretching back 100 years. Dismissed by the police, the photographer starts to convince his friends that this is not your average serial killer, and when they gain access to the Subway Butcher's decrepit apartment, the film kicks into a higher realm of weirdness than Barker's original text as we glimpse the personal life of this sociopathic monster.

THE 13 HORROR MOVIE ADAPTATIONS THAT ARE BETTER THAN THE BOOK

In the short story, Mahoney is just a faceless pawn of the underground lords of New York City, but in the film Mahoney is a brutality personified ogre in a suit and tie that goes about his unpleasant occupation in an efficient and business-like manner. Vinny Jones's performance is a case study in cruelty and physical intimidation. He is a viciously callous operative who lets nothing come between him and his work. And yet it is questionable whether those broad shoulders can hold up under the enormous task imposed upon him. The final confrontation between Mahoney and Leon is a bit anti-climactic, but it leads to an encounter with the hidden masters in an underground cave littered with bones, skulls, and bodies in various states of decomposition. From the charnel recesses emerge the ancient dwellers in the darkness, who demand that a new butcher take the place of the deceased Mahoney. Guess who must take over the job? The sense of inescapable fatalism and acceptance at the heart of *The Midnight Meat Train* is far less poignant in the original story, and yet Barker must be given kudos for allowing Kitamura to go in his own direction for the cinematic version, as Barker's Midnight Picture Show company produced this stellar adaptation.

8.

The Masque of the Red Death (1964)—Roger Corman

One cannot out-goth Edgar Allan Poe, and any film that tries to be more dark, decadent, poetic, or insane than Poe's original stories is fighting a losing battle. Roger Corman's famed Poe adaptations for AIP often used camp, humor, and melodrama to bring something different to these short slices of death (not always successfully). But Corman's *The Masque of the Red Death* used existential pathos and a vivid color scheme to do something no one has ever achieved: a Poe adaptation better than its source.

The short story is a nasty little conte cruel concerning the vile Prince Prospero and his celebration in the face of a plague called the Red Death. Prospero's masquerade ball is an act of indifference, but the festivities cannot stave off the inevitable appearance of the Grim Reaper. Poe's love-hate relationship with mortality, sickness, and irony is in full evidence here, and his use of different colors to represent psychological and emotional states creates a mood of inevitable doom. The only way to further enhance this dread is to actually show the ghastly hues and shades, and that's where Corman's 1964 adaptation succeeds brilliantly. The film keeps the essential aspects of Poe's story, but the great Charles Beaumont adds references from other Poe stories (such as "Hop Frog") to the screenplay to deepen the tale's tragic aspects. Vincent Price owns the role of the debauched Prospero, a satanist who delights in his ability to decide the fate of his subjects and his power to corrupt and humiliate the innocent. Yet his control is shown to be an illusion in the face of Death, where even Satan is revealed to be a human construct used by terrified people in the same way that the pious project their fears of impermanence onto God. Prospero's castle is a prison, not a refuge, a fool's paradise in which Death easily gains access no matter how tightly its borders are guarded. An atmosphere of existential trepidation permeates the film, particularly those scenes involving the shrouded wraiths who act as solemn harbingers of a fate no one can bargain with.

Corman's film is heavily influenced by Ingmar Bergman's iconic *The Seventh Seal*, as an expressionistic medieval setting suggests that though history has progressed, questions of being and nothingness still haven't been adequately confronted. Nicolas Roeg was the cinematographer (before becoming one of the most innovative directors of the '70s), and his use of color is mesmerizing: the white, yellow, golden, blue, and violet phantoms, the satanic black and purple room, and the browns and grays of the peasant's village suggest exterior and interior states of existence. Finally, it is the majestic Red Death dealing out tarot cards, at the beginning to an old woman and at the end to a young child, who reminds us that "Sic transit gloria mundi." I think Poe would have agreed.

7.

The Birds (1963)—Alfred Hitchcock

The works of Daphne du Maurier, though not highly appreciated in literary circles, have been transformed into some of the greatest films of all time. Maybe it's her straightforward style and tendency to not over-explain things in her prose that allows for such creative interpretations of her stories. The great Alfred Hitchcock thought so: he adapted *Jamaica Inn*, and his version of her novel *Rebecca* was the only Hitchcock film to win an Oscar. Hitchcock would return to du Maurier for his classic 1963 thriller *The Birds*, where the master of suspense would add an uncomfortable layer of personal angst and interpersonal failure to the Fortian tale of nature turned antagonist. Du Maurier's "The Birds" is a novella set in England that uses marauding sea gulls as a metaphor for British worries over aerial attacks that they cannot stop (the story was published only seven years after Nazi bombings leveled many British cities). There is also a Cold War aspect to this fear, as England must have

THE 13 HORROR MOVIE ADAPTATIONS THAT ARE BETTER THAN THE BOOK

felt particularly vulnerable reconstructing the country with the threat of the Soviet Union looming from the east. The protagonist is a disabled WWII veteran who slowly realizes that birds are becoming more aggressive and tries to figure out the reason for their increasingly brazen attacks. As a national emergency is declared, the realization that nature can't be stopped concludes the story with a grim awareness of humanity's helplessness. The genius of du Maurier's story is that she uses a ubiquitous sight as a threat and never explains why the birds turn on human beings.

While the novella makes political and worldwide statements, Hitchcock's film turns inward to explore the chaos and risk of emotional attachments. It takes place in Bodega Bay, California, and introduces us to a cast of characters who are suffering from some sort of relationship anxiety, whether it is the fear of starting a new romance or the panic over losing a closeness they've come to depend on. Love, sorrow, sexual attraction, and familial obligations intermingle, creating a tense but understated Freudian web. It is when characters make themselve vulnerable emotionally, opening up about their feelings, needs, desires, mistakes, and regrets, that the birds savagely attack. Confessions are made even more uncertain and perilous by the threat of the anarchic birds waiting to swoop down on the weak, exposed characters. Even children aren't spared the horrid consequences of honest demonstrative expression. Du Maurier's birds are a metaphor for specific, topical fears; Hitchcock's birds are a metaphor for all fears. The end of Hitchcock's film suggests the only way to live with the constant menace of the birds hanging over us is to proceed with caution and never let ourselves be so susceptible that our sentiments lead us to become victims.

6.

The Innocents (1961)—Jack Clayton

Henry James's *The Turn of the Screw* is one of the most adapted ghost stories ever. Fuelling these movie versions is the question of the main character's reliability: are the ghosts she believes are terrorizing her young charges real or projections of her hysterical mind? While many readers seem perplexed by the so-called ambiguity of the text (though much evidence shows that James saw the hauntings as real and not a figment of the governess's imagination), the lack of a definitive answer allows for variations on the story. The novella focuses on a young governess who is hired by an uninterested guardian to watch over the two children he inherited when their parents died. The governess soon suspects that all is not right with her charges, Miles and Flora.

Her suspicions turn to the supernatural when she learns of the unhealthy attachment the children had to the sadistic groundskeeper, Peter Quint, and the masochistic former governess, Miss Jessel. Are these deceased lovers still abusing the children after death? James's novella is the epitome of the psycho-sexual Victorian Gothic story, with fear, yearning, attraction and abhorrence projected onto the irrational paranormal, and yet by intimating that the ghosts are a real threat to the children and governess, some of the truly interesting perversities and destructive denials are left undeveloped.

Leave it to Truman Capote to twist the story into a glorious Freudian pretzel that tips its thematic cards with the title *The Innocents*. (I imagine Tennessee Williams could have done wonders with this adaptation, too.) Capote's screenplay places the blame for the attacks squarely on the repressed, deranged mind of the new governess, Miss Giddens (an extraordinary performance by Deborah Kerr). Clearly, Capote sees Miss Giddens as desiring the dominating, savage ravisher Quint, while settling for young Miles as her object of desire and disgust. Her passive-aggressive treatment of Flora, seen as a rival for Miles's attentions, becomes more and more menacing, driving the poor little girl to hysteria. Director Jack Clayton's devastating climax provides terrifying images such as the emaciated wraith of Miss Jessel standing in the reeds and Quint's leering visage in the window. Unsung horror craftsman/master cinematographer Freddie Francis's use of deep focus and stark lighting provide a stunningly haunting mood and stifling atmosphere, alleviated only by the beauty and sensuality of nature. The film has one of the most unbearably agonizing denouements in the history of cinema, as Giddens slowly torments Miles to death: the obsessive quest for purity drives her to destroy the very innocence she was striving to protect.

5.

The Thing (1982)—John Carpenter

John W. Campbell's "Who Goes There?" is such a cool sci-fi yarn that it has been adapted twice. First appearing in *Astounding Science-Fiction* in 1938, the story is pure pulp nirvana: isolated scientists in Antarctica unwittingly thaw a frozen alien that can perfectly replicate the identity of any human being. As the scientists begin to turn on each other, trying to figure out who is an extraterrestrial imitation, the "thing" exploits this distrust and suspicion to stay hidden, preying on the men and biding its time to escape to civilization. Christian Nyby was the first to adapt Campbell's work in 1951 with *The Thing from Another World*. Though fondly remembered by baby boomers, it was significantly inferior to the personality-duplicating original. In the opening sequence, replacing the otherworldly protoplasmic replicator with a blood-sucking vegetable erases some of the disturbing ambiguity that the original story thrives on.

One of the baby boomers scarred for life by this early horror/sci-fi hybrid film was horror champion John Carpenter, whose first major studio movie was a more faithful version of Campbell's work. Following the source loosely, Carpenter's *The Thing* is routinely cited as one of the greatest horror films ever made. It represents the confluence of several crucial factors in creating a classic: a genius director, an intelligent script, an amazing ensemble of actors, a threatening setting, a terrifying antagonist, and probably the most incredibly real special effects ever to grace a fantastique film, courtesy of FX wizard Rob Bottin. The unnatural transformations of the body that Bottin achieves in the film are legendary and still look mind-blowingly authentic. While most monsters and aliens in horror and sci-fi films resemble the human frame, the Thing's configurations look truly extra-terrestrial. Carpenter's film is not merely a copy of the original (though that would be apt), as his revisions modernize Campbell's themes by bringing them in line with postmodern theories of the fluidity of identity and the lack of a coherent self. Carpenter even improves on Campbell's ending: where the novella allows the scientists to triumph over the space invader, Carpenter's film cannot give the viewer a satisfactory conclusion. Perhaps the uncertain ending was a major reason the film didn't catch on immediately but has grown exponentially to achieve god-head status. Avoid the 2011 prequel like a shape-shifting alien from a blood test.

4.

Jaws (1975)—Steven Spielberg

It's hard to understand how the *Jaws* phenomenon grew from such a mediocre source. Peter Benchley's 1974 novel offers the reader a cool great white shark, but little else. Benchley seems to think that we are interested in the back stories and psychological motivations of the characters (Hooper has an affair with Brody's wife?), anti-climactic scenes that have no suspense (the deputy finds the shark's tooth in Ben Gardner's boat?), and information about the inner workings of the town of Amity (the mayor is in cahoots with the Mafia?), when all we want is the shark, the shark, and the shark. It gets even worse when Brody, Hooper, and Quint finally pursue the shark, as they safely return to port every night rather than being stuck out in the hostile waters. The novel's boredom culminates in the big anti-climax as Brody faces off against the shark and the shark just . . . dies. No shooting the scuba tank, no "Smile, you son of a bitch," no explosion; the shark just stops. An adaptation by Ed Wood could have improved on the source novel, but luckily a young Steven Spielberg, who, despite his successes, still felt he had to make remarkable films to achieve movie greatness, enriched every aspect of Benchley's work. The triumvirate of Roy Scheider, Richard Dreyfuss, and Robert Shaw join the other iconic movie triad from *The Treasure of the Sierra Madre* as the epitome of the American id, ego, and superego. Spielberg takes a page from the Hitchcock playbook by giving us incremental glimpses of the impressive mechanical shark, so by the time we get to see the leviathan's enormity, it has achieved mythic status. The epic stature of the hunt, the realization of how unknown the sea really is, and the feelings of total terror and exhilaration as the climax detonates attest to Spielberg's craftsmanship. Although the film is both critically and popularly lauded, one wonders if it would have been as successful without John Williams's jaunty, Academy-Award-winning soundtrack—a score that (with the possible exception of Morricone's *The Good, the Bad, and the Ugly* soundtrack) is the most recognizable film music ever heard. Nonetheless, Spielberg's *Jaws* is one of the highest grossing movies of all time. This blockbuster, along with *Star Wars*, was the epitome of '70s maverick cinema.

3.

Psycho (1980)—Alfred Hitchcock

Author Robert Bloch is hard to figure out. His early Lovecraftian stories are quite chilling and unsettling but, little by little, satire and dark humor started to creep into his works until he seemed to become a comedian who used repulsive imagery. Yet, every so often, the truly evil muse that fuelled Bloch's initial pulp thrillers reared its magnificently ugly head, and the author responded with a horror classic. Inspired by the legendary crimes of Ed Gein, Bloch wrote a sick novel entitled *Psycho* that pushes the Oedipus complex into an even weirder, more twisted rapport. Poor Norman Bates is a middle-aged loser, stuck in a dead-end job running a run-down motel and beholden to a shrewish harpy of a mother. When Norman is tempted by a pretty, fugitive guest, momma runs amok and murders her rival for Norman's affections. The search for the missing woman leads to the unraveling of Norman and Mrs. Bates's unhealthily intimate relationship. The novel is a sleazy Freudian nightmare alluding to all sorts of aberrant sexuality, repressed cravings, and the enticement of death. Bloch's style mimics the dawning genre of true crime literary journalism pioneered by

THE 13 HORROR MOVIE ADAPTATIONS THAT ARE BETTER THAN THE BOOK

Capote's *In Cold Blood*, and his objective tone deflates some of the lurid shocks that could have been pushed even further into the taboo. Demolishing the limits of good taste was a challenge that Alfred Hitchcock rose to admirably, and his adaptation of Bloch's novel ushered in a decade that would tear up and burn the accepted rules for cinema.

Hitchcock's *Psycho* is a masterpiece that builds on Bloch's tale but makes a few significant improvements that elevate the film into all-time greatness. Hitchcock's Norman Bates is a young, handsome, angst-ridden figure who elicits both sympathy and admiration, much different than Bloch's older pathetic slob. Anthony Perkin's energetic yet twitchy performance enlivens one of the most psychologically tortured characters in cinema. While everyone rightly praises the wondrously choreographed shower attack, the falling-backward murder on the stairs, and the final, revolting reveal of Mrs. Bates by swinging light fixture, it is Hitchcock's little touches that make the film truly horrifying: the stuffed birds perched in the Bates Motel lobby, the painting *Susanna and Her Elders* that covers Norman's peep hole, the increasingly devolved décor on each floor of the Bates house, the record of Beethoven's Third Symphony ("Eroica") on the gramophone, the little-boy sheets on Norman's bed, the crossed bronze hands on Mrs. Bates's dresser. These subtle hints of Norman's psychosis are much more satisfying than the dopey psychiatrist's diagnosis at the end of the film (which is also in the novel). Hitchcock's *Psycho* changed what could be included in a film, which meant that bras, showering, desiccated corpses, and flushing toilets were now fair game. Add Bernard Herrmann's shrieking, stabbing score, and you have one of the finest films ever made. How could Robert Bloch compete with that?

2.

The Shining (1980)—Stanley Kubrick

Stephen King's well-documented dismay with Stanley Kubrick's adaptation of *The Shining* always sounded like sour grapes to me. Basically, King hated every revision Kubrick made, from casting Jack Nicholson as Jack Torrance to Kubrick's more intellectual take on the ghostly emanations that corrupt Jack. Perhaps King realized that Kubrick had transformed a somewhat clichéd horror melodrama into a frighteningly brilliant exploration of colonization, capitalism, and patriarchal control, using the supernatural as a metaphor for the irrationality of racism, misogyny, and oppressive violence. King's novel stops at the familial level of fear, while Kubrick expands the scope of terror, connecting the micro level of one man's abuse of his family to the macro level of US Western expansion that uses economic exploitation, class hierarchy, and the extermination of "inferior" races to achieve dominion.

The novel is the story of the Torrances and how their lives change when they move into the Overlook Hotel, a secluded, haunted abode that has a violent and tragic past. Jack's son Danny has the ability to see the past and future through his psychic "shining," and the hotel's evil spirits want to possess Danny and his powerful gift. The ghosts prey upon Jack's insecurities, writer's block, and alcoholism to recruit him to their side and eliminate Danny so that his spirit will be trapped in the Overlook forever. The novel uses stock horror tropes such as inanimate objects coming to life (topiary animals threaten Danny), the devouring father, and the climactic destruction of the offending structure. Kubrick's film improves on the novel by adding a significant subtext to the trials of the Torrance family. Kubrick's version of their domestic problems replicates the terrorist strategies of American imperialism. Hatred, fear, selfishness, weakness, reward, and an obsession with doing one's "protective" duty as an excuse to exercise masculine authority are motives behind Jack's tyranny, the Overlook's manipulation of Jack, and the historical westward expansion and colonization.

Kubrick's Jack Torrance doesn't need a slow descent into violent psychosis; he's already sexist, racist, angry, anxious, and arrogant, a middle-class shlub ripe for the revenants of the ruling class to use and abuse. Kubrick's epic vision turns the Overlook into a representative of America itself: gold ballrooms and servant's quarters, inhabited by "all the best people," attended by caretakers, an edifice built on the blood of Native Americans and decorated in imagery from a conquered and decimated culture. So many scenes from the film have taken a prominent place in the pop culture lexicon: the gliding steadicam shots of Danny's rides through the hallways, the vision of the strange little English girls, "Here's Johnny," Danny's talking finger, "All Work and No Play Make Jack a Dull Boy," "Redrum," the maddening shrub maze, and the closing photo of Jack living it up in 1921 (on July Fourth, of course). Ultimately, King's frustrations reflect the resentment authors feel when a superior talent turns their entertaining tale into a work of art.

THE 13 HORROR MOVIE ADAPTATIONS THAT ARE BETTER THAN THE BOOK

1.

The Exorcist (1973)—William Friedkin

People who claim that William Peter Blatty's novel *The Exorcist* is scary may be responding more to the concept than the actual writing. Blatty's account of the demon-possessed, twelve-year-old Regan MacNeil and her flawed guardians' attempts to save her mind, body, and soul sounds impressive until you crawl through his hackneyed, histrionic, half-baked theological and social pontifications. Based on a "true" story of an exorcism performed in 1949, Blatty's lapsed-Catholic guilt and idolization of the Jesuits, as well as his insistence on writing in a Hollywood hacky-schticky style, are not only eye rollingly annoying but make a poor vehicle for discussing important themes of faith, love, and sacrifice.

In adapting the novel, iconic director William Friedkin got rid of almost all the bad dialogue, tired characterizations, and transparent red herrings, producing not only one of the greatest horror films, but one of the greatest films in any genre. (Blatty interfered throughout the scripting, filming, and editing process.) Friedkin's dedication to the film bordered on the sadistic, torturing his impressive cast in order to get the responses he thought would be authentic when confronted with the essence of evil. Friedkin's film is no commercial for Christianity, as it blatantly shows the failures of both secular science and institutionalized religion. The officially sanctioned exorcist fails, and only when Father Karras's St. Joseph medal is broken is he freed to make a truly selfless sacrifice. If anything, Friedkin's film exposes an existentialist sort of spirituality, a belief system that rejects dogma, ritual, and certainty and embraces doubt, fear, and action. Karras's leap of faith results in his fall, but also his elevation; he is the only character who successfully faces both the inner and outer repulsion of this absurd situation.

Friedkin's directing is masterful and assured, moving effortlessly from documentary realism to supernatural terror overload, but one must also acknowledge the makeup magic of cinematic artiste Dick Smith, who convincingly transforms cherubic innocence into demonic abjection. *The Exorcist* was a cultural sensation, making tons of money and affecting its viewers on physical, psychological, and metaphysical levels. The film was nominated for ten Academy Awards (including the first nomination of a horror movie for Best Picture), but won only two (Best Sound Mixing and Best Adapted Screenplay, which, ironically, Friedkin had to share with Blatty). Still considered one of the scariest films of all time, *The Exorcist* is a magnificent example of the kind of artistic masterpieces that the horror film genre could generate and inspire. When was the last time someone said that about the book?

Honorable Mention

Rosemary's Baby (*Rosemary's Baby* by Ira Levin)
Dead Ringers (*Twins* by Bari Wood and Jack Geasland)
Ghost Story (*Ghost Story* by Peter Straub)
The Body Snatcher ("The Body Snatcher"
by Robert Louis Stevenson)
Island of Lost Souls (*The Island of Dr. Moreau* by H. G. Wells)
Matango ("The Voice in the Night" by William Hope Hodgson)
They Live ("Eight O'Clock in the Morning" by Ray Nelson)
Nightbreed (*Cabal* by Clive Barker)
Black Sabbath ("The Family of the Vourdalak" by Aleksey Tolstoi)

THE 13 HORROR MOVIE ADAPTATIONS THAT ARE BETTER THAN THE BOOK

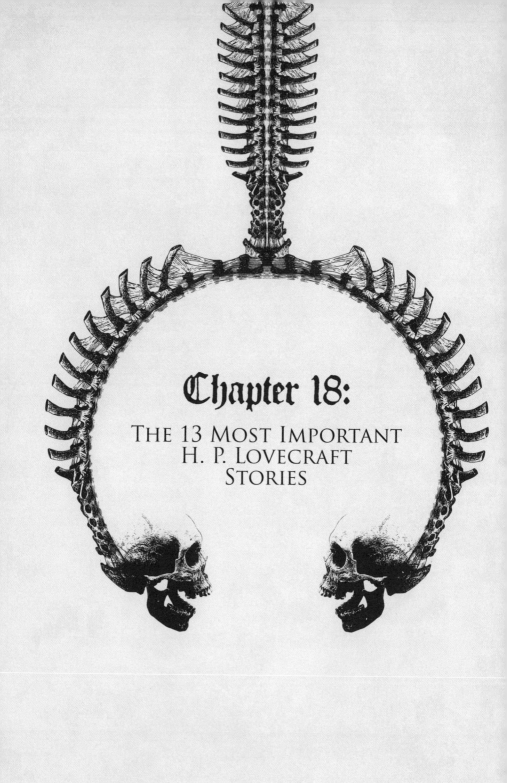

Chapter 18:

The 13 Most Important
H. P. Lovecraft
Stories

he iconic H. P. Lovecraft. What other author's shadow looms so large over our cultural landscape? While the canon of literature needs to be constantly resuscitated by mandated curriculum, public TV, and movie producers frantic for more product, Lovecraft's influence continues to grow without the help of academics or Hollywood. Perhaps the obscurity and critical dismissal he experienced during his lifetime ensured his fruitful afterlife, as his works were allowed to be discovered organically rather than being forced down our throats in school (à la Poe) or overexposed in film and mass media (à la King). The vultures of academia, advertising, and big business have not yet picked apart the healthy body of Lovecraft's works, but how much longer can they be kept at bay? The Great Old Ones have nothing on graduate students, media bloggers, and corporations looking for the next big thing to exploit.

What is it about this antiquarian pulp writer who died almost 80 years ago? Some say his philosophy of materialist pessimism imbues his stories with a prophetic vision of existentialism, neo-pragmatism, and speculative realism that haunts our essentially meaningless existence. Others appreciate the frighteningly innovative scaffolding his stories provide for their own writing (though only Ramsey Campbell and Thomas Ligotti have equaled the old gent from Providence). Whether it's his philosophy or aesthetics, Lovecraft's immense imagination is the glue that holds it all together. Lovecraft's horrors highlight the ancient influences on modern anxieties. It doesn't really matter whether his creatures are gods, aliens, or indigenous beings. Do we care what ants think of us? Lovecraft's tales suggest that nothing—not history, nature, the universe, even our own biology—is stable or predictable; the absurdity of human existence lies in our own arrogance and need to place ourselves at the center of everything. We are all "fumbling at the latch," clumsily, thoughtlessly, and conceitedly throwing open the door to knowledge that will lead to our annihilation.

> We are all "fumbling at the latch," clumsily, thoughtlessly, and conceitedly throwing open the door to knowledge that will lead to our annihilation.

The decay of Lovecraft's beloved New England heritage is a microcosm for his sense of the global breakdown of old world supremacy, his creatures and extraterrestrials mirroring the ascendancy of Fanon's "wretched of the earth." His works will continue to terrify because, like Kafka's, they express a dawning ontological awareness that all intelligent people must confront at some time in their lives. And there is a giant octopus dragon that sleeps on the bottom of the ocean waiting to take over the world, too. In honor of his remarkable cultural and artistic achievements, here are the thirteen best works by H. P. Lovecraft:

13.

"Dagon"

One of Lovecraft's earliest mature tales, "Dagon" was written in 1917. Playing off Germany's desperate ploy of unrestricted submarine warfare during WWI, "Dagon" is told from the perspective of a terrified, drug-addicted sailor whose ship was captured by the Germans in a remote part of the Pacific Ocean. Escaping in a lifeboat, the sailor is set adrift in an unchartered area of the vast sea, finally coming ashore on a unknown island that he conjectures has been thrust up from the depths by some geological upheaval. After spending days exploring this decrepit atoll, he finds a titanic monolith covered by hieroglyphics that use marine creatures as symbols. Out of the water emerges a gigantic anthropomorphic sea creature that seems to be worshipping the monolith. Driven mad by his secret viewing of this primal ceremony, he somehow gets back to his lifeboat and is rescued. His return to society offers no solace as he obsesses about the possibility that these undersea monsters will rise up and destroy humanity.

Heavily influenced by Poe and Coleridge, "Dagon" can be seen as an early run-through of many of the themes that would come to fruition in the epochal "The Call of Cthulhu": a sea creature emerging from the depths, a land mass that appears from nowhere in the ocean, a sailor driven mad by his knowledge of a race that can overthrow civilization. Most important, "Dagon" introduces a key Lovecraftian idea: what we believe the natural order to be has to be rewritten, and human beings are no longer at the top of the evolutionary chain. This world-shaking knowledge destabilizes the foundations that we use to structure our lives and questions our significance in the universe. Perhaps reflecting anxieties about the outcome of WWI and the configuration of the post-war world, "Dagon" is the start of Lovecraft's "thrill of repulsion": characters that are simultaneously exhilarated and annihilated by their experiences with the unknown.

12.

"The Picture in the House"

Like Nathaniel Hawthorne, Lovecraft was a master of New England horror. His use of the geography, culture, history, and folklore informs most his stories. Lovecraft clearly loved the region; he felt an almost

THE 13 MOST IMPORTANT H. P. LOVECRAFT STORIES

metaphysical bond, and yet he also saw the underlying fear, ignorance, and malevolence that caused death, terror, and misery in the upper six states. "The Picture in the House," written in 1920, opens with a brilliantly written explanation of why New England is much scarier than any of the stock horror settings such as mausoleums, castles, keeps, and lost cities. To prove his point, the narrator illustrates New England's "perfection of the hideous" by relating a story of being caught in a storm while exploring the backwoods of the Miskatonic Valley, looking for a shortcut to the city of Arkham. He takes refuge in a dilapidated colonial house where he meets an old man who speaks with an antiquated New England dialect. The hoary Yankee gets more and more excited discussing the attractions of cannibalism and its supposed life-extending properties. The narrator begins to think that perhaps this cannibal theorist may be practicing what he preaches. Marred only by a cop-out ending, "The Picture in the House" begins Lovecraft's ingenious creation of a fictional geographical expanse (Miskatonic Valley) and its infamous city of Arkham (only referred to and not visited yet). By constructing his own imaginary place in the midst of real places, people, and events, Lovecraft achieves an amazing verisimilitude that allows him to suspend disbelief and yet keep his settings believable. For Lovecraft, there is a fine line between being an antiquarian and an abomination: one respects the limits and boundaries of time, while the other disrupts and makes a mockery of history's linear progress.

11.

"The Mound"

If Lovecraft were alive today, he would be making money tentacle over fist from publishing, merchandising, and adaptation rights. Unfortunately, he was a man before his time (though he felt he was born much too late) and lived a life of borderline poverty, clinging to familial glories last seen in turn-of-the-century Providence. To supplement his meager wages from his own writings, Lovecraft toiled as a ghost writer, revising the works of others who desperately wanted to publish. Forever the gentleman and Samaritan, he would extensively rewrite these often sophomoric stories, doing much more work than he was paid for so that these fledgling authors could get published. Though these revisions are generally not up to the grand standards of his own creations, a few manage to entertain on a higher level. "The Mound" is a novella written between 1929 and 1930 based on a story idea by Zealia Bishop. Lovecraft used Bishop's premise of an Indian ghost haunting a mysterious mound in the Southwest to dry-run some of his social critiques that would later inform *At the Mountains of Madness* (1931) and "The Shadow out of Time" (1934–35). Though his political analysis would become more expansive and in-depth in those two later works, "The

Mound" is more visceral and shocking. The mound is really an entrance to an underground world of the K'n-yan, a highly advanced immortal race of all-powerful beings (kind of like the Vril-ya) discovered by Zamacona, a wayward Spanish conquistador. Though appearing to be the perfect species, the K'n-yan are revealed to be a decadent, sadistic, selfish society that can feel things only through subjugation, torture, and licentiousness. Can Zamacona return to the surface world and warn his fellow humans about these monstrous demi-gods? "The Mound" mixes its cultural insights with some truly bizarre grotesqueries and doesn't unnecessarily prolong the climax like its two later (and better known) conceptual progeny.

10.

"Herbert West: Re-Animator"

Though Lovecraft would probably be horrified, "Herbert West: Re-Animator" is one of his most recognized works, thanks to the wondrously gonzoid film and stage adaptations directed and produced by Stuart Gordon—one of the most Lovecraftian filmmakers ever. "Herbert West: Re-Animator" was a serialized story written in 1921 and 1922 that appeared in six issues of the amateur publication *Home Brew*. A parody of Frankenstein, the story arc follows the Grand Guignol-esque misadventures of Dr. Herbert West and his quest to prove to the world that the human body is just a machine that needs to be jump-started to return to a semblance of existence after it conks out. His experiments result in his test subjects becoming raging, disfigured berserkers with a taste for human flesh and revenge. Banding together to form a reanimated legion of rejected guinea pigs, the resurrected chickens come home to roost for the murderous doctor. Lovecraft thought the story was beneath his usual aesthetic sensibilities and felt that the serialized format of having a "cliffhanger" ruined the totality of effect he tried to employ in his stories. But that's exactly what makes the picaresque stories so incredibly mind-blowing: the need to top the previous insanity of the last part drives Lovecraft to dizzying heights of absurdity and gruesomeness. When a story ends with a revived brain-dead boxer chewing on a baby's arm, you would be a masochist if you didn't want to see how the author could out-gore himself with the next installment. If that wasn't enough, "Herbert West: Re-Animator" contains the first mention of one of the most hallowed fictional institutions of learning: Miskatonic University.

9.

"The Hound"

Lovecraft's knack for parody was so dead-on that many readers and critics mistook his mastery of irony for his true writing style. "The Hound," written in 1922, sees Lovecraft point his satirical pen at the Decadents, a Poe-influenced cultural and literary movement of the late 1800s that elevated artifice, perversity, and elegant degeneration. Decadent authors such as Charles Baudelaire, J. K. Huysmans, and Oscar Wilde focused on pleasure, debasement, and oblivion as responses to an industrialized, Victorian bourgeois conformity. Lovecraft recognized that the inherent ghastliness of Decadent characters would make them good protagonists for a horror story, and so "The Hound" is narrated by a true Decadent. It seems that two Decadents can shake their crushing ennui only by robbing graves and decorating their shared bachelor pad with their ill-gotten gains (tombstones, skulls, bodies). These are not merely smash and grab jobs, but have a crucial aesthetic component that turns the necrophilic fantasies into works of art. After disrespecting the final resting place of an infamous necromancer, they take his jade ghoul amulet imprinted with the image of a winged hound. Soon the two flowers of evil hear the baying of a hound that seems to be getting closer no matter how far they travel from the defiled grave. Lovecraft emulates the Decadent flair for Gothic camp through over-exaggeration, excessive verbiage, and opulent descriptions, not only to give his tale an authentic narrative voice but also to critique this aesthetic form. Lovecraft believed that a weird tale needed to be based on realism and scientific fact to make the violation of reality seem truly uncanny. The Decadents' rejection of logic, reason, and propriety, so far from Lovecraft's own creative philosophy, would have been ripe for spoof and ridicule. "The Hound" is also important because it contains the first mention of a little-known book called *The Necronomicon*.

8.

"Pickman's Model"

Another satire on aesthetics, "Pickman's Model" was written in 1926. Its adaptation became one of the best episodes of Rod Serling's *Night Gallery* in 1972. One of Lovecraft's most idiosyncratic tales, the story is told through a monologue, as if the narrator were speaking directly to the reader. Lovecraft's style is idiomatic and informal, as if the narrator has just walked into one of Gatsby's Jazz-Age bashes with a cigarette in one hand and a flask of hootch in the other. Lovecraft-haters love to harp on his supposedly purple, archaic, adjective-abusing prose, yet here he shows that he could easily have aped the then-current "modern" fiction voice if he so chose.

The story relates the life and works of Richard Upton Pickman, a painter of the terrible and the grotesque, an artist whose shocking realism has led him to be ostracized from the local arts community, perhaps with good reason. "Pickman's Model" can be read as both a criticism of modernism (the imagined listener to the narrator's tale is named Eliot, perhaps alluding to T. S.) and a treatise on Lovecraft's own beliefs about art and the horror genre. The narrator name-drops such giants of the macabre as Fuseli, Dore, and Goya, explaining that what makes their works (Pickman's included) so frightening is the graphic authenticity reflecting instinct, tradition, and the sublime—traits the modernists sought to deconstruct and abolish in their quest for the "new." These primal, biological, and historical connections to fear are what make their creations so threatening to the viewer: their realism is based on a deeper existential level that hits us right in the aboriginal parts of the brain.

7.

"The Haunter of the Dark"

This was Lovecraft's last story, written in 1935 only two years before his untimely death. After the glacially paced "At the Mountains of Madness" and "The Shadow out of Time," "The Haunter in the Dark" was a welcome return to a more rousing quality of horror. A sequel to Robert Bloch's inferior "The Shadow from the Steeple," Lovecraft's tale revolves around Robert Blake, a horror author who, while investigating an abandoned church in Providence, runs afoul of The Shining Trapezohedron and its guardian, the Haunter of the Dark. Eschewing the more philosophical and cosmic concerns of his previous two works, "The Haunter in the Dark" gives us good, old-fashioned occult thrills and Lovecraftian esoterica like The Necronomicon, the Starry Wisdom cult, Yuggoth, Nephren Ka, Yog-Sothoth, and an avatar of Nyarlathotep. The Shining Trapezohedron is every stoner's dream; by gazing into the alien crystal, one can see across time and space into other worlds and dimensions. However, use of this extraterrestrial lava lamp summons its protector, who demands a ghastly price for this knowledge. On the surface, the payback seems to be only physical dissimulation, and yet Blake's final words allude to Roderick Usher, suggesting that the Haunter's real fee is absorption of the soul and identity. This final work stands as a fitting testament to Lovecraft's genius.

THE 13 MOST IMPORTANT
H. P. LOVECRAFT
STORIES

6.

"The Dunwich Horror"

Lovecraft was not known for constructing well-developed characters. Often used as cyphers or frames from which to hang his horrific speculations, his characters are merely fodder to be stepped on by an indifferent universe. The main character of the much-loved "The Dunwich Horror" may be Lovecraft's most interesting and well-developed fictive personality. Written in 1928, "The Dunwich Horror" relates the story of the Whately family, a degenerate clan in the desolate town of Dunwich, Massachusetts. The reader is witness to the birth of Wilbur Whateley, a deformed being who grows abnormally fast and is raised by his grandfather, Wizard Whately, schooled in the dark arcane arts. After his grandfather dies, Wilbur is left to care for the farmhouse and his family, and eventually finds a copy of *The Necronomicon*. His search for this dreaded tome takes him to Miskatonic University, initiating a series of events that brings about the Dunwich horror. Whateley is the ultimate outsider: over eight feet tall, he looks like a goat, dogs hate him, and he is shunned by his community. His father is absent; he is saddled with an insane mother and other familial obligations that increase exponentially. In the end, he is destroyed by the pressure of trying to satisfy his grandfather's expectations. Much more than Dr. Armitage, the "good guy" of the story, Wilbur is a tragic hero, a complex character who elicits fear and sympathy from the reader. Heavily influenced by the psycho-sexual-magickal work of Arthur Machen, "The Dunwich Horror" reflects a certain prurience in Lovecraft's writing. The coupling and sexuality suggested in the story are presented as elements of loathing and disgust, and yet there seems to be a definite pleasure in lingering over the abhorrence. It is one of Lovecraft's most geographically evocative stories, blending fictional and real elements of the New England landscape and lore (The Devil's Hopyard, the Moodus noises, Wilbraham Mountain) to construct a forebodingly lovely setting to prepare for "clearing off the earth."

5.

"The Whisperer in the Darkness"

One of the myriad reasons why Lovecraft is still so significant and readable is that he blurred the boundaries between fantastique genres. Not content with the strictures of horror and recognizing the potential of the terrifying new world as revealed through science fiction, Lovecraft merged futuristic scientific realism with eldritch Gothic sensibilities to create a thoroughly dismal portrait of the present. His best example of this crossbreeding is "The Whisperer in Darkness" written in 1930. Many Lovecraftians (and Lovecraft himself) would point to "The Colour out of Space" as the finest specimen of this peculiar genus, but "The Whisperer in the Darkness" prefigured the head-in-a-canister motif that was prominently featured in *Futurama*, thereby trumping everything. Narrated by Miskatonic University professor Albert Wilmarth, strange creatures are reportedly running rampant in the Vermont backwoods and nobody will take the warnings of resident Henry Akely seriously. After a convincing correspondence between the two men (including physical evidence to validate the sightings), Wilmarth journeys to Akely's besieged home, only to find a changed man and shocking revelations about the motives and travel procedures of the otherworldly Mi-Go.

Finding dread in non-terrestrial objectives and intentions, Lovecraft rejects the supernatural as the only form of terror and anxiety and uses the amoral, cold rationality of an advanced organism to extinguish any notion of humanity's superiority. By refusing to obey the natural laws that limit us weak human beings, are the Mi-Go really evil or just victims of our ignorance, fear, and jealousy? Even more frightening are the human henchmen that help the creatures. What are their motives in betraying their own race? Lovecraft's creation of an isolated, oppressively sinister feeling amid Vermont's rustic splendor is particularly impressive. I would love to have heard the droning soundtrack of the Mi-Go rituals as captured on record by Akely. I imagine it would sound like Throbbing Gristle's first album.

4.

"The Festival"

Even Lovecraft's harshest critics have to recognize his amazing ability to invoke an eerie atmosphere. The best example of this is "The Festival," written in 1923 and considered one of the earliest entrees into the Cthulhu mythos—what some see as his greatest achievement and others see as an albatross. "The Festival" was inspired by a trip to the colonial village of Marblehead, Massachusetts, that powerfully influenced his imagination. The tale's narrator is summoned to his hometown of Kingsport, Massachusetts (based on Marblehead), to participate in an ancestral pagan festival. Following his relatives into an underground cavern beneath an ancient church, the narrator witnesses unholy rites and primordial creatures that drive him to the brink of madness. This is Lovecraft's finest invocation of the deep-rooted beauty and evil of New England. The descriptions of Kingsport are especially melancholic and redolent of both reverence and malevolence.

THE 13 MOST IMPORTANT H. P. LOVECRAFT STORIES

197

The narrator sets the mood: "Beside the road at its crest a still higher summit rose, bleak and windswept, and I saw that it was a burying-ground where black gravestones stuck ghoulishly through the snow like the decayed fingernails of a gigantic corpse. The printless road was very lonely, and sometimes I thought I heard a distant horrible creaking as of a gibbet in the wind. They had hanged four kinsmen of mine for witchcraft in 1692, but I did not know just where." Short and sweet, "The Festival" distills all that's splendid about the adjective "Lovecraftian." Plus, it's a Christmas story!

3.

"The Call of Cthulhu"

Arguably the most important short story in the horror genre, "The Call of Cthulhu" started a phenomenon that, slowly but insistently, has emerged as an essential component of the twenty-first-century horror landscape. For such a dominant work, its structure is highly unconventional and complex: fragmentary, displaced, and seemingly arbitrary. It starts with one of Lovecraft's most quoted dissections of humanity's tentative mastery of the planet and our inescapable step into the abyss. Divided into three chapters, the narrative begins with the discovery of notes written by the narrator's deceased great uncle. The notes fixate on the great uncle's dealings with Henry Wilcox, an art student whose intense nightmares of an ancient sunken city and ominous chanting of the words Cthulhu and R'lyeh inspire him to sculpt an image of a strange creature that resembles a hybridized octopus, dragon, and human. The artist's dreams coincide with a global pandemic of insanity and Fortean occurrences that end after a frenzied outpouring of mass psychosis.

The second chapter continues the investigation of these bizarre events through the relation of a past experience with the chanted, seemingly nonsensical words. American Archaeological Society members are stunned by an artifact confiscated by a police inspector involved in the arrest of murderous cult members in the Louisiana swamps. Under interrogation, one of the prisoners divulges that there is a secret worldwide network of believers who worship the Great Old Ones, aliens/monsters/gods from the cosmos that arrived on earth billions of years ago and still command the super-antediluvian cult from hidden locations. These beings are in a state of suspended animation and are awaiting a certain cosmic convergence to release them. Cthulhu is the greatest Great Old One of them all, and he sleeps in his sunken Pacific city R'lyeh waiting for human assistance to reign once more.

The final chapter finds the narrator attempting to link these pieces of the narrative with the story of a sailor that inadvertently encountered the Great Old One, and the consequences of that meeting for him, his crewmates, and the rest of humankind. "The

Call of Cthulhu" brings together many contemporary fears and anxieties: chance, accident, upheaval, conspiracy, instability, hopelessness, and inevitability. Nothing can be depended on anymore; humanity can find no solace in religion, science, history, culture, or philosophy. All the institutions that give our lives meaning are shown to be houses of cards, falling domino-like in the face of forces that we have no control over. This sentiment is what makes Lovecraft the prophet of twenty-first-century existence.

2.

The Case of Charles Dexter Ward

Lovecraft wrote only three novels; his best is *The Case of Charles Dexter Ward*, later adapted as two great films. Written in 1927 but unpublished during the author's lifetime, *The Case of Charles Dexter Ward* is one of Lovecraft's most personal works. Taking place in his hometown of Providence, the novel focuses on Charles Dexter Ward's attempts to come to terms with his familial past and the region's history that has informed that past. Ward discovers a purposely obscured ancestor named Joseph Curwen, an ageless necromancer who was seemingly destroyed by an outraged and frightened community of his fellow Rhode Islanders. Finding diaries, papers, and public versions of events, Ward's research validates Curwen as a historical figure and later, through Curwen's forward-looking machinations, as an actual resurrected fiend.

The intertwining of Ward, Curwen, and Providence reflects Lovecraft's relationships to his own ancestors, his love for Providence, and his obsession with antiquities, ostensibly a safe haven from the disquietude of the present. This escape into the past, at first exciting, later disastrous, is a trap that Curwen uses to return to life, parasitically latching on and draining the present of its potential and its future. Lovecraft's brilliant weaving of actual personages, geography, classical writings, and happenings with his own fictional creations breaks down the rhetorical boundaries between History and history, suggesting that there is no truly objective narrative of people, places, and things. All these accounts are filtered through subjectivities that require multiple interpretations and perspectives, but even then there is no guarantee of truth. Ward's insistence on an unambiguous truth leads to his destruction as Curwen preys upon the young man's enthusiasm, idealism, and hubris. Rich with detail and supernatural authenticity, *The Case of Charles Dexter Ward* begins the epic ruminations on time and history that culminated in the later *At the Mountains of Madness* and "The Shadow out of Time." But unlike those works, *The Case of Charles Dexter Ward* never drags or is predictable; it surprises, terrifies, and makes you wonder, like the best horror novels.

THE 13 MOST IMPORTANT H. P. LOVECRAFT STORIES

1.

"The Shadow over Innsmouth"

The pinnacle of Lovecraft's oeuvre, "The Shadow over Innsmouth" brings together many of Lovecraft's key themes in an exciting, horrifying, and ambitious work. Composed in 1931, "The Shadow over Innsmouth" oozes with a rotting atmosphere and despondent tone. It is a tale of one expiring way of life and the awakening of another. Displaying Lovecraft's anxiety about heredity, the story describes the narrator's journey to research his genealogy and the detour it takes through the putrefying seaside town of Innsmouth. Innsmouth history is haunted by misfortune, miscegenation, and misery connected to a Faustian bargain that backfires on its inhabitants and accelerates the downward financial, cultural, and genetic spiral. The town and its denizens are striking in their repugnance, reflecting each other's de-evolution and breakdown. Yet from destruction and decay often springs new and better hybridized forms of life. The layered images of nautical customs and sea creatures create a nauseatingly claustrophobic environment, and the labyrinthine design of the town entraps like the coils of hidden DNA strands. What takes the story to the rarified status of a classic are the elements of self-doubt, self-realization, and self-discovery that originate in outward repulsion and end with internal acceptance and empowerment. The "Innsmouth look" starts as a curse, but becomes a sign of superiority and higher existence. This concept is not truly understood until the highly satisfying conclusion—a twist that makes subsequent re-readings entirely different experiences. Stuart Gordon's 2001 film *Dagon* borrows much from "The Shadow over Innsmouth," which should make sense since he tried to adapt it in 1991 (Bernie Wrightson did some unbelievable character designs); however, the project was unrealized. Here's hoping that some Lovecraftian director can bring this fish tale to the big screen soon in a form that celebrates the art and thought of the great master.

Honorable Mention

"Nyarlathotep"
"The Music of Erich Zann"
"The Rats in the Walls"
"The Colour Out of Space"
"History of the Necronomicon"
At the Mountains of Madness
"The Thing on the Doorstep"
Supernatural Horror in Literature
"Hallowe'en in a Suburb"
"The Diary of Alonzo Typer" with William Lumley
"Two Black Bottles" with Wilfred Blanch Talman
"The Loved Dead" with C. M. Eddy Jr. (There is some debate over whether Lovecraft had any hand in revising this story, but it deserves to be read regardless. This character study is so morbidly obsessed that it makes *Nekromantic* look like a Hallmark movie.)

THE 13 MOST IMPORTANT
H. P. LOVECRAFT
STORIES

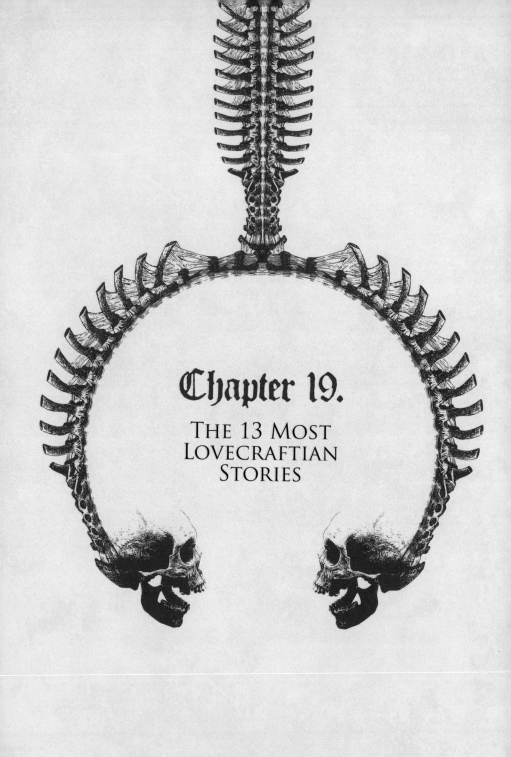

Chapter 19.

THE 13 MOST LOVECRAFTIAN STORIES

s H. P. Lovecraft was the most influential horror writer of the twentieth and twenty-first centuries, it may behoove horror fanatics to ask the simple question: what does it mean to describe something as Lovecraftian? Connected to this question is the related inquiry: what exactly is the Cthulhu Mythos? Is it enough just to infuse a story, movie, comic book, or game with tentacles, unpronounceable creature names, and an unholy grimoire? Is it enough to cram Lovecraft's creations into a loosely plotted narrative and then add a few of one's own monstrous gods to the already overstuffed pantheon? These stereotypical approaches to Lovecraft have turned an obscure pulp writer into a million-dollar cottage industry, but have prevented the Old Gent from Providence from being taken seriously as an artist and thinker. He didn't come up with the concept of an ordered, categorical classification of his imaginary beings; this was the work of author and editor August Derleth, perpetuator of the Lovecraft legacy, but an often misinformed disciple who did both harm and good to the Lovecraft brand.

The Cthulhu Mythos is a collective fictional cosmos through which writers use Lovecraft folklore as metaphoric symbols for his thematic and philosophical con-0cerns. While Lovecraft was alive, he encouraged his fellow pulp writers to engage in a communal sharing of character, creature, and object names to give a certain resonance and authenticity to their stories. Much like other mythologies (and the twenty-first-century version of mythology, fan fic), the nature of the references could diverge wildly, though the names were

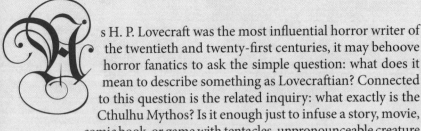

> Is it enough just to infuse a story, movie, comic book, or game with tentacles, unpronounceable creature names, and an unholy grimoire?

basically the same. This allowed authors to adapt and revise these creations to fit their storytelling motives. Writers such as Clark Ashton Smith, Robert E. Howard, Robert Bloch, Frank Belknap Long, Henry Kuttner, and Fritz Leiber borrowed, changed, and invented ideas that fell roughly in line with Lovecraft's own employment of these concepts.

Unfortunately, with Lovecraft's death, Derleth imposed an inflexible organization on these mythos, lording over the supposed schemata like Zeus on Olympus, decreeing what was and was not to be included in the mythos gospel. This misunderstanding confuses the true definition of Lovecraftian. To be Lovecraftian is to project a cosmic outlook that informs one's aesthetic, ontological, and epistemological beliefs. It is an outlook that accepts humankind's insignificance in a cold, mechanical universe. It is an outlook that recognizes that individuality is meaningless and that nothing can be counted on—not science, religion, history, nature, language, or existence. Everything we know is wrong. Thank Yog Sothoth we can't experience the true face of reality; even the façade is enough to drive us mad. Ignorance is not only bliss, it's a necessity to keep up the lie that humans are an intelligent species at the top of the evolutionary chain, made in God's perfect image. Lovecraft's legacy lives because he was so far ahead in his imaginative and existential attitude that we have only begun to really understand the consequences of his work. Here are thirteen stories that truly deserve the appellation Lovecraftian.

13.

"Jerusalem's Lot"—Stephen King

The only writer to challenge Lovecraft's status as the greatest horror author ever (at least in terms of product sold), Stephen King paid homage to H. P. early in his unbelievably prolific career. "Jerusalem's Lot" is a short story told through a series of letters and diary entries relating the experiences of Charles Boone and his return to his ancestral home. Discovering a nearby abandoned village named Jerusalem's Lot, Charles finds a desecrated church, a family curse, and the dreaded tome *De Vermis Mysteriis*, which awakens the undead and a whole lot worse. King's story references Lovecraft's "The Rats in the Walls" and "The Dunwich Horror," as well as the early work of Robert Bloch. But it shines on its own as a pulpy throwback that piles on the eldritch horrors in a rapid-fire manner. King's later deep descriptions are already in evidence in this early tale, and this story begins King's own mythos as it acts as a prequel to *Salem's Lot* and pops up in other future works such as "One for the Road" and *Wolves of the Calla*. How fitting that King's exceptional career would begin with a Lovecraftian story, almost as if the torch of horror fiction was being passed.

12.

The Lurker at the Threshold —August Derleth and H. P. Lovecraft

Often dismissed as a bait-and-switch posthumous "collaboration" between Derleth and Lovecraft, *The Lurker at the Threshold* is a short novel incorporating two fragments that Lovecraft sketched out in his "commonplace book," with tacky embellishments by Derleth. Lovecraft's fictional essay "Of Evil Sorceries Done in New England" forms the foundation of *The Lurker at the Threshold*, a novel that follows the Billington family across 300 years of black magic, Great Old One worship, forbidden inheritances, and unnatural continuations. Though somewhat tainted by Derleth's goody-good take on Lovecraft's hopelessness, there is still enough Lovecraftian menace to reward readers. Because of this textual presence, *The Lurker in the Threshold* is light on the Derlethian Cthulhu-meets-Catholicism and heavy on creepy New England atmosphere with a sinister Narragansett medicine man, colonial warlocks, Puritan preachers, and that hallowed

THE 13 MOST LOVECRAFTIAN STORIES

institution of learning, Miskatonic University. Though these "jointly" written works are justifiably criticized, *The Lurker at the Threshold* is an engaging and eerie addition to the mythos, and if it wasn't for Derleth and his dedicated need to spread the message of Lovecraft, we might not have it to enjoy. Then again, we wouldn't have Derleth's imitative sleep-inducing fiction, either.

11.

"The Courtyard"—Alan Moore

It should come as no surprise that author/occultist/comic book revolutionary Alan Moore is a Lovecraft acolyte. (I first heard of Cthulhu in a *Swamp Thing* reference.) Moore's iconoclastic effect on the comic book medium can be compared to Lovecraft's seismic impact on horror fiction. Moore's short story was published in D. M. Mitchell's transgressive anthology *The Starry Wisdom: A Tribute to H. P. Lovecraft* in 1995. "The Courtyard" is a future noir take on the mythos with a federal agent investigating ritual murders in a world steeped in Lovecraft references. Sex, drugs, and rock 'n' roll are filtered through Lovecraft's creations and Moore's uncanny ability to weave seemingly unrelated minutia into a complex tapestry of meaning. The story is a magickal sigil with allusions to "The Horror at Red Hook," Clark Ashton Smith, "The Dunwich Horror," Arthur Machen, "The Cats of Ulthar," Robert W. Chambers, "The Dream Quest of Unknown Kadath," "The Music of Erich Zann," "Pickman's Model," and "The Shadow over Innsmouth," and probably a bunch more that are way too obscure for me. This may sound like the very definition of a sloppy Cthulhu Mythos mélange, but Moore works his wizardry to create a believable Cornell-Woolrich-meets-Kenneth-Grant Lovecraftian homage. Musician Antony Johnson adapted "The Courtyard" into a comic book mini-series, and *Neonomicon*, a comic book sequel to "The Courtyard" scripted by Moore, was released in 2010.

10.

"The Death Watch"—Hugh B. Cave

Prolific is not a strong enough adjective to describe Hugh B. Cave. In a career lasting more than seventy (!) years, Cave published more than 1,000 short stories and forty novels in every literary genre. His offerings to the horror genre began with his contributions to weird menace and shudder pulps in the 1930s. With this type of pedigree, Cave would surely have come across Lovecraft, and he melded the Cthulhu Mythos with a Southern Gothic/voodoo feel in "The Death Watch." Set in the Florida swamps, this murky, feverish nightmare focuses on a group of people vigilantly waiting for the return of a dead man. Portentous messages, occult books, and a strange Seminole named Yago figure into this tale of regret and unnatural longing. The Lovecraftian elements don't stop at the mention of Nyarlathotep and the Lake of Hali; Cave's bleak, forlorn mood recalls the tragic hopelessness of "The Thing on the Doorstep" and "The Colour out of Space." Whereas mythos tales are usually outrageously outré, "The Death Watch" is almost meditative in its sorrow and trepidation. Cave's works are in serious need of reappraisal from fans and critics alike.

9.

"The Howler in the Dark"—Richard L. Tierney

A first-generation Lovecraftian weaned on Arkham Houses's initial hardcover publications of Lovecratft's works, Richard L. Tierney wrote his first Lovecraft-inspired novel in 1959 at age seventeen and has kept the pulp horror flame alive for over fifty years. Furthering his Lovecraft credentials, Tierney's weird poems appeared in *The Arkham Collector* and in his own collected volume from Arkham House. Tierney's biggest impact on Lovecraft studies came from his essay deconstructing Derleth's interpretation of the Cthulhu Mythos, in which he pointed out that Derleth's dualistic themes are at odds with Lovecraft's cosmic/existential philosophy. If that wasn't enough, Tierney has also written excellent Lovecraftian fiction like the mythos novel *The House of the Toad* and the brooding short story "The Howler in the Dark." The story focuses on the infamous Duncaster Abbey, a castle with a history of occult travesties and supernatural occurrences that has terrorized the surrounding countryside for centuries. This accursed keep has new eccentric owners, and there seems to be an increase in abnormal events since their arrival. Tierney's descriptions of the gray, windswept, rocky shore, jagged cliffs, and the ragged edifice of evil evoke a beautiful desolation often found in Lovecraft's style. These aesthetics of melancholic exquisiteness unite Lovecraft and Tierney in using fear and dread as ways to achieve the sublime. Tierney's mention of the "d'Erlettes of Averoigne" references August Derleth, Robert Bloch, and Clark Ashton Smith, further linking Tierney with his literary forbearers.

8.

"The Black Stone"—Robert E. Howard

Ultimate pulp writer Robert E. Howard is best known for his creation of a certain blue-eyed Cimmerian. Yet Howard wrote in pretty much every literary genre in the 1920–'30s before he blew his brains out. Howard's

THE 13 MOST LOVECRAFTIAN STORIES

intense correspondence with Lovecraft is fascinating reading as the two titans of the fantastique spar with, educate, and inspire each other. Howard wrote quite a few mythos stories, but his finest is "The Black Stone." The story introduces a key Cthulhu Mythos book: *Unaussprechlichen Kulten* (*Nameless Cults*) by Friedrich von Junzt, a work that is second only to *The Necronomicon* in being referenced by other authors. Imitating Lovecraft expertly, but still retaining elements of his own macho style, Howard's "The Black Stone" is an ancient monolith in the ominous town of Stregoicavar in Hungary. The narrator's reading of von Junzt leads him to the site, where he witnesses a human sacrifice to a giant toad. But was it only a dream inspired by the Black Stone's terrifying history? Howard uses many Lovecraftian tropes—an unholy continuity of malevolence, a narrator searching for validation of ancient lore, an artist driven mad by his own creations, the questioning of reality, and humanity's place in the universe—to provide a highly entertaining and influential tale. Though not quite as succinct as Alhazred's famed couplet, mad poet Justin Geoffrey's verse is decadently insightful: "They say foul things of Old Times still lurk/In dark forgotten corners of the world/And Gates still gape to loose, on certain nights/Shapes pent in Hell."

7.

"Black Static"—David Conway

The ubiquitous Cthulhu Mythos anthologies collect the good, the bad, and the derivative tales for easy perusal by rabid Lovecraft fanatics. Like the stories they contain, the anthologies can be well thought out and brilliantly executed, or they can be thrown-together claptrap with no attempt at thematic connection. One of the most bizarre, mind-shatteringly shocking collections of Lovecraftia is *The Starry Wisdom*. Editor D. M. Mitchell collected contributions that were not only explicitly Lovecraftian (Brian Lumley, Robert M. Price, John Coulthart's amazing graphic adaptation of "The Call of Cthulhu"), but also were implicitly connected with Lovecraft's aesthetics and philosophy (William S. Burroughs, J. G. Ballard, and Michael Gira of Swans' infamy). Among the notable contributors is David Conway, whose "Black Static" is one of the most outlandish takes on the mythos. The story describes what might happen if SETI's attempts at communicating with extraterrestrials resulted in contact with Lovecraftian beings (the Hyperbreed) and the mind-altering, body-morphing consequences of this cultural exchange. It seems that these extra-dimensional organisms have sleeper agents hidden all over the planet, just waiting for the signal to awaken and initiate total reality transformation. What makes the story Lovecraftian is Conway's use of the truly alien perspective of the entities to begin and conclude the narrative, a fluid yet impenetrable rush of information-thought-sensation-body-mind-metaphysical-data download. Whereas Lovecraft often alluded to non-Euclidian geometry, ultra-quantum physics, and non-human perceptions, Conway attempts to convey these experiences through a surrealistic/ scientific prose hybrid. Lovecraft probably would have hated it, but the story is a blissed out, experimental voyage into the void. What else would you expect from one of the founding members of My Bloody Valentine?

6.

"A Colder War"—Charles Stross

Which is scarier: the Great Old One's impending apocalypse or the mutual extermination politics of the Cold War? What if they were somehow combined into one mega-holocaust of annihilation? Charles Stross's "A Colder War" follows an alternative history in which the Pabodie Expedition (as detailed in *At the Mountains of Madness*) opens up the Cthulhu Mythos to international politics and an arms race that involves the use of alien super beings. The Soviet Union has constructed a doomsday weapon called Project Koschei, and the world's superpowers are scrambling to develop their own mythos-powered weapons of mass destruction. When Iraq plans on opening the gate to Yog-Sothoth to extinguish Israel and Iran, the resulting international war sets off a chain reaction that wakes the ultimate deterrent: Cthulhu. Narrated by a low-level CIA agent (entangled in an Iran-Contra-Shoggoth type mess), "A Colder War" vividly and authentically recasts all the important global historical events of the last seventy years through the lens of Lovecraft: WWII, the invasion of Afghanistan, the Middle East crisis, and Chernobyl are all affected by the governmental awareness of the mythos and its capability to influence the worldwide balance of power. Forget trying to bring *At the Mountains of Madness* to the big screen; "A Colder War" would be the ultimate war/sci-fi/horror film.

5.

"Black Man with a Horn"—T. E. D. Klein

The one-time heir apparent to the mantle of the new Lovecraft, T. E. D. (the E stands for Eibon) Klein's small body of work burned brightly but was ultimately short lived. His writing focused on the psychological aspects of Lovecraft and enhanced the Lovecraftian effect of the dawning realization of how profound and pervasive horror is in our lives. Klein's direct involvement in the mythos is "Black Man with a Horn," a novella originally published in the

THE 13 MOST LOVECRAFTIAN STORIES

Ramsey Campbell-edited anthology *New Tales of the Cthulhu Mythos*. The story is narrated by a horror author influenced by Lovecraft (yeah, I know. I usually hate when characters have an awareness of who Lovecraft is, too) who meets a paranoid missionary running away from something he encountered in Malaysia. The missionary is terrified that the Chaucha, a tribe of abominable natives, will find and eradicate him. Intrigued, the author researches the mysterious Chaucha and comes to the realization that the Chaucha are actually the Tcho-Tcho people, which Lovecraft mentioned in "The Shadow out of Time" and "The Horror in the Museum." The knowledge that this community is not a fictional construct alters the narrator's view of reality, and he suspects that he is being followed by the Shogoran, a black Tcho-Tcho deity with a horn-like attachment on its face. Though the fate of a person singled out by the Shogoran is terrible, the greater horror is the overturning of one's world view and the confidence one has in what is real and what is fiction. Klein's skeptical narrator (modeled on Lovecraft friend and horror writer Frank Belknap Long) starts to question everything and can find no solace in the escape that fiction usually provides for both author and reader. It's a real shame that Klein's frequent bouts with writer's block have so limited his output, because his distinctive voice is severely missing from contemporary Lovecraftian fiction. Maybe he can collaborate with Dario Argento again and write the screenplay for the sequel to *Trauma*.

4.

"Notebook Found in a Deserted House" —Robert Bloch

One of the most famous pulp writers, Robert Bloch's impressive career began alongside Lovecraft in *Weird Tales*, continuing with the novel *Psycho* and scripts for cult shows such as *Star Trek*, *Alfred Hitchcock Presents*, and *Thriller*. His stories have been adapted to film several times, and he wrote screenplays for William Castle and Amicus Productions. Bloch's early stories were self-described Lovecraft imitations, but they were well written and not too slavish toward his friend and mentor (Lovecraft based the protagonist of "The Haunter of the Dark" on Bloch). Bloch was most successful when he sublimated his Lovecraft influence to his own menacingly absurdist style. Case in point: "Notebook Found in a Deserted House," a mythos story that uses the narrator's own youthful ignorance and fear to not only induce sympathy but also terror for the narrator, as the reader comprehends the extent of the horror before the narrator does. The tale is the unedited text of Willie Osborne's notebook, a young boy who lives with his grandmother. The grandmother tells Willie about "them ones" who live in the ominous woods near their home. After his grandmother's death, Willie lives with his uncle and aunt, who try to protect him from the witch cult that worships in the forest surrounding their farm. When the aunt and uncle mysteriously disappear, an enigmatic cousin arrives to "help" Willie, and the true extent of the evil at work is revealed. Bloch's use of the boy's initial naiveté and his growing consciousness of the malevolence surrounding him has a powerful effect on the reader, making the boy's experiences all the more real and devastating. Because of Willie's limited knowledge, the clues left unanalyzed create a threat that is monstrous and cruel; Willie is an easy target, defenseless and innocent. The effect of Willie's inexperience is particularly haunting in his descriptions of Lovecraft's shoggoths, which Bloch transforms from their original protoplasmic fluidity into an unknowable perverse force. Bloch's fiction would get progressively less Lovecraftian and more darkly satirical (in my opinion, to its detriment), but he would give it one last shot with his novel *Strange Eons*, a work suffused with the spirit of H. P.

3.

"Sticks"—Karl Edward Wagner

"Sticks" doesn't directly address typical mythos tropes, but its overwhelming atmosphere of dread and eradication pushes it into Lovecraft territory. Wagner based his story on an anecdote told by fantastique artist Lee Brown Coye, in which Coye found a forsaken farmhouse filled with weird configurations of sticks. These witchy designs inspired Coye to incorporate the odd shapes into different aspects of his art. Coye never found a reason for the wooden sculptures nor who the sculptor was, and it is this anonymous aspect that Wagner uses for "Sticks." Following Coye's possibly apocryphal tale closely, the story relates how an artist, looking to go fishing in a remote area, discovers bizarre wood symbols that lead to an uninhabited house. Exploring the basement, the artist finds a sacrificial chamber, a stone slab, and a not-quite-dead sacrificial victim/guardian. Blocking the experience from his mind, the artist later incorporates the mysterious twig cryptograms into the illustrations for a book, but the cult responsible for the original images doesn't take kindly to this publicity and plagiarism. Referencing a striking image from *The Blair Witch Project*, Wagner's leitmotif of the mysterious lattices is never fully explained but gives the story a menacing tone. The symbols have some uncanny connection to a murderous supernatural cult with both living and undead members.

Wagner connects the artist's discovery of the unusual symbols with artists' tendency to channel their fear and anxiety into their work, but the

THE 13 MOST LOVECRAFTIAN STORIES

consequence of this transference is the loss of control over what is created and how an audience will interpret and use it. There are many unanswered questions, but not all of them are focused on the wood glyphs, as the protagonist is as inscrutable as the symbols he appropriates. The shock of the unknowable self and the unfathomable world around us is what makes "Sticks" so powerfully Lovecraftian.

2.

"The Tugging"—Ramsey Campbell

Ramsey Campbell's early stories are not merely the youthful Lovecraft pastiches he would have you believe they are. The stories in his initial two collections (*The Inhabitant of the Lake and Less Welcome Tenants* and, to a lesser extent, *Demons by Daylight*) do indulge in excessive but fun imitations, and Campbell's first substantial contribution to the mythos was their setting in Severn Valley, the UK equivalent to Arkham County in the States. Threatening locales such as Goatswood, Brichester, Severnford, and Temphill form an authentic, unpleasant backdrop for Campbell's tales of alien beings, supernatural incidences, and Great Old One manifestations. He even created his own wicked book called *The Revelations of Glaacki* that can sit on the shelf next to *The Necronomicon*. A place where decaying urban sprawl meets pagan rural atrocities, the Severn Valley was the ideal setting for a new mythos, best exemplified in the brilliantly disquieting roman à clef "The Franklyn Paragraphs." There are many exceptional Lovecraftian Campbell stories, but as his style matured, the Lovecraftian elements faded into the background and were replaced by a more personal, psychological, and emotional approach that would elevate him to greatness.

One of his later Lovecraftian tales is "The Tugging," a transitional story between the two styles that combines individual and global eschatology. A writer has been having disturbing dreams that leave him questioning his sanity and relationship with his parents. His search for the key to understanding himself leads to an old theater that was the secret observatory for a cult that watched the stars in anticipation of a great revelatory sign. His discovery of his grandfather's membership in the cult and the news of a rogue planet approaching earth are apocalyptically linked, leading to both self and world transformation. Campbell has occasionally wandered back to the Severn Valley, and here's hoping that he gets lost there again.

1.

"The Last Feast of the Harlequin"—Thomas Ligotti

The only horror writer who has attained the god-like genius of Lovecraft, Thomas Ligotti is the reincarnation of Kafka, Poe, and H. P. all rolled into one neurotic prophet of doom. Claiming an intensely intimate connection to Lovecraft, Ligotti arrived as a fully formed Lovecraftian from the very first story he published in 1989, and he has developed into the only horror author who has not only equaled H. P. but has taken the Lovecraftian into realms that Lovecraft's heirs never dreamed of. Ligotti's worldview is even more nihilistic than Lovecraft's. Where Lovecraft's view of the universe is a machine dispassionately grinding down everything in its path, at least the machine is there and can be counted on to keep grinding long after we have been turned into fertilizer. For Ligotti, the machine is a mass psychosis that hides the chaos, corruption, and state of collapse on which the universe constantly teeters. Ligotti's works (including his brilliant philosophic thesis *The Conspiracy against the Human Race*) navigate the black hole of existence and the deafening silence of the void, conveying an overwhelmingly despairing yet subtle mood. His horror resonates in the hole where our souls should be, providing the frame of mind for perhaps the most misanthropic character to appear on TV: Rustin Cohle of *True Detective*.

Ligotti's most overtly Lovecraftian story, written as an ode to the grand master, is "The Last Feast of the Harlequin." The story centers on the degenerate little town of Mirocaw and its annual winter festival of clowns that disguises an even darker ritual of transformation and abjection. Much like "The Festival," "The Shadow over Innsmouth," and "The Dunwich Horror," "The Last Feast of the Harlequin" methodically moves from myth, legend, and antiquarian research to terrifying reality, confrontation with the primal, and, finally, abysmal acceptance. Ligotti's motif of clowns is the metaphor for his transcendental pessimism: a distorted, unnatural face that masks even greater, squirming horrors beneath the facade. This atmosphere of weariness, futility, and misery pervades every page, spreading into the reader's deepest existential emptiness.

Ligotti's works come in fits and starts, whenever the sickness of creativity overtakes him, and so it is unclear whether he will continue writing. Thank goodness he is not content to limit his despairingly horrid vision to text. Ligotti has collaborated with the apocalyptic folk project Current 93 on several musical ventures, and his story "The Frolic" has been adapted into a short film. Often devotees of obscure artists hope that their work will someday be recognized by a larger audience. Perhaps it is better that Thomas Ligotti isn't well known. I don't think the masses could take it.

THE 13 MOST LOVECRAFTIAN STORIES

Honorable Mention

"Salt Air"— Mike Minnis
"Final Draft"—David Annandale
"And the Sea Gave Up the Dead"—Jason C. Eckhardt
"The Terror from the Depths"—Fritz Leiber
"Cold Print"—Ramsey Campbell
"Discovery of the Ghooric Zone"—Richard Lupoff
"Andromeda Among the Stones"—Caitlin R. Kiernan
The House of the Toad—Richard L. Tierney
"Vastation"—Laird Barron
"To Clear the Earth"—Will Murray
"Spawn of the Green Abyss"—C. Hall Thompson
"Black Kiss"—Robert Bloch with Henry Kuttner
Cthulhu 2000
Tales of the Cthulhu Mythos

Chapter 20:

THE 13 MOST GHASTLY HORROR COMIC ARTISTS

The scourge of humanity and the destroyer of youth? Not horror films. They were never the target of the Senate Subcommittee on Juvenile Delinquency, nor did horror filmmakers ever have to form a self-regulating association to prevent government censorship or anti-horror legislation. Rather, the cancer that threatened to infect 1950s America was horror comic books. Second only to the evils of Communism, horror comics were viewed as a corrupting influence on the post-WWII spirit of wholesomeness and prosperity. The future of the US was a gleaming science fiction dream of consumerism, leisure, and conformity brought about by a positivist fantasy of better living through technology. Horror comics were obsessed with death, cynicism, and doubt, and filled with extreme violence, sadism, and nihilism. The horror film had lost its teeth; it seemed old-fashioned and silly next to the real-life shocks of the

Acting like monthly missives from the depths of hell or the dark recesses of the psychotic mind, the accessibility of comic books for young people, who might not be able to see horror films but could sneak a few comics into the house, kept horror going during the lean years.

Holocaust and the atom bomb. Horror comics had more in common with film noir than with the neutered horror film of the late 1940s and early '50s. Viewed as more powerful than the film, horror comics bore the misplaced Cold War fear and paranoia, a phenomenon that would not return until the UK "video nasty" witch hunt of the early '80s (an era that saw a correlating spike in Cold War propaganda).

Horror comics were central to proselytizing for the genre before fanzines, magazines, websites, bulletin boards, conventions, and blogs. Acting like monthly missives from the depths of hell or the dark recesses of the psychotic mind, the accessibility of comic books for young people, who might not be able to see horror films but could sneak a few comics into the house, kept horror going during the lean years. Horror comics represent a significant contribution to not only the horror genre but to the history of the comic industry, a continuity that includes EC Comics, Warren Publishing, Skywald Publications, Eerie Publications, DC, Marvel, underground comix, and independent comics. The artwork was often outstanding, with artists able to let their imaginations run rampant in a genre that encourages the irrational and fantastic, even more so than with superheroes. These artists should not be confused with the Jim Lee, Joe Quesada, Todd McFarland, Rob Liefeld, Marc Silvestri abortions that pass for comic art. The best horror comic artists can stand shoulder to shoulder with the great illustrators of the bizarre and gruesome: Harry Clarke, Remedios Varo, Salvator Rosa, Alfred Kubin, Hieronymus Bosch, Gustav Dore, Goya, Francis Bacon, Otto Dix, Austin Osman Spare, Josef Vachal, H. R. Giger, Basil Gogos, Frank Frazetta, Ken Kelly, Boris Vallejo, and Jeff Jones. So here are the thirteen most ghastly horror comic artists ever. Gaze upon these mighty works and despair.

13.

Pablo Marcos

Born in Peru, Pablo Marcos first gained recognition in his home country in 1965 with his shockingly realistic illustrations that accompanied a story about the execution of a convicted rapist. His first work for US horror comics was "The Water World" in *Creepy* #39 (1971), a story concerning three astronauts stuck on a raft on a planet of water. Marcos also did work for the underappreciated Skywald Publications, drawing several stories for *Nightmare* and *Psycho*. He came into his own with his art for the Marvel line of black-and-white magazines such as *Dracula Lives*, *Monsters Unleashed*, and *Vampire Tales*. The pinnacle of his Marvel horror work was for *Tales of the Zombie*, where he drew the adventures of Simon Garth, doomed to walk the earth as a zombie. Though *Tales of the Zombie* only lasted ten issues, Marcos's Zombie was a brooding hulk of an automaton, silent but noble, much different than the usual rotting corpse. Marcos's expressive style resembles the haunted quality of classic black-and-white Universal films, but with a touch of the exotic. *Tales of the Zombie* #3's "When the Gods Crave Flesh," where Simon Garth has to help a film crew attempting to film a secret voodoo cult, is a perfect example of Marcos's take on the zombie, which is far removed from Romero and embraces its tropical roots.

12.

Junji Ito

Influenced by Kazuo Umezu, Hideshi Hino, and H. P. Lovecraft, horror manga artist Junji Ito has created three landmark horror series. *Tomie* concerns an immortal high school girl with a supernatural power to make anyone fall fanatically in love with her. She cruelly manipulates her admirers, driving them to murder, insanity, and suicide. Tomie's hair is sinisterly sentient, and she can regenerate and clone herself from her disembodied body parts. Tomie has inspired nine films: Later the subject of an anime film, *Gyo* is about an intelligent "death stench" that seems to be reanimating dead sea creatures to attack humans. Walking machines that propel the rotting creatures are made from metal from sunken battleships.

Ito's masterpiece is *Uzumaki*, a Lovecraftian tale of a town obsessed with spirals, adapted for film in 2000. *Uzumaki* brings together all of Ito's themes: body disgust, the breakdown of the individual and the corresponding social order, inexplicable natural processes, and the fathomless horrors of the compulsive mind. Ito's artwork is disarmingly stark yet brutally effective, illustrating a meaningless universe where his Kafkaesque characters are tortured for no discernible reason.

11.

Tom Sutton

One of the most prolific horror comic artists ever, Tom Sutton produced amazing work for Marvel, DC, Warren, Skywald, and Charlton Comics. Hating "fascist superheroes," Sutton started his career with "The Monster from One Billion BC" in *Eerie* #11 (1967) and was the first artist on *Vampirella* (1969). He drew for much of Marvel's horror line (*Werewolf by Night*, *Ghost Rider*, *Doctor Strange*, *Man-Thing*) and worked on DC's anthology series *House of Secrets* and *House of Mystery* (in particular providing art for the "I ... Vampire" serial). His best work was for Charlton, providing covers and interior art for *Ghost Manor*, *Midnight Tales*, *Monster Hunters*, and *The Many Ghosts of Dr. Graves*. Sutton's style was a surrealistic pop-art, exaggerated Goya nightmare, perfectly suited for his Cthulhu-inspired cover for *Baron Weirwulf's Haunted Library* #55. What else do you expect from a guy who used the pseudonym Dementia?

10.

Gene Colan

The master of Marvel horror, Gene Colan earned his stripes drawing *Daredevil* and *Howard the Duck* and co-creating the Captain America sidekick, the Falcon. Yet it was his stellar work on the epochal *Tomb of Dracula* and *Dr. Strange* that stunned and scared comic fans in the '70s. Working with master writer Marv Wolfman and inker Tom Palmer, who complemented him perfectly, Colan provided art for all seventy issues of *Tomb of Dracula*, giving Marvel its most enduring horror comic. Colan's expressionistic work is all shadows and moods, dream-like yet horribly visceral. Colan brought his dark, distinctive style to DC, where he began an acclaimed run on *Batman* and *Detective Comics*, as well as reteaming with his Dracula compatriot, Marv Wolfman, for a new series called *Night Force*. It lasted only fourteen issues, but it was a fun, supernatural team book led by the mysterious Baron Winters. Gene seemed to be psychically connected to the king of the vampires: he and Wolfman created a new *Tomb of Dracula* series (with the great Al Williamson) entitled *The Curse of Dracula*. Colan even had connections to some other beloved horror icons, co-creating Blade the Vampire Hunter, illustrating an adaptation of Clive Barker's "The Harrowers," and providing artwork for Rob Zombie's album *Hellbilly Deluxe*.

THE 13 MOST GHASTLY HORROR COMIC ARTISTS

9.

Hideshi Hino

The king of horror manga, Hideshi Hino used a terrible childhood to inform his ero guro meets Walt Disney approach to art. Born in China to Japanese parents, he was nearly killed escaping Manchuria at the end of WWII. His first published work was in 1967, and by 1971, his series "Hideshi Hino's Shocking Theater" established him as the Edward Gorey of Japan. Hino's cartoony, child-like style makes his subject matter (the malformed, the decaying, the unnatural) all the more disturbing. In particular, his work for Shojo manga (comic books for teenage girls) such as *Dead Little Girl* and *Ghost School* is sickeningly hideous but weirdly endearing. Not content to repulse only through the comics medium, Hino is also a filmmaker and scriptwriter. He has been deeply involved in the infamous *Guinea Pig* films (directing the truly demented *Mermaid in a Manhole* based on his own manga) and wrote the scripts for the six films based on his comics, collected under the umbrella title *Hideshi Hino's Theater of Horror*. Hino is another artistic link in the chain that joins such Japanese radicals as Edogawa Rampo, Koji Wakamatsu, and Yukio Mishima.

8.

Mike Ploog

Although Mike Ploog is an exceptional horror comic book artist, his best work was done for some of the most iconic fantastique films of the '80s. Ploog's work for Marvel on *Man-Thing*, *Monster of Frankenstein*, and *Werewolf by Night* set the standard for the new vanguard of comic artists in the '70s. Drawing from fine art, underground comix, and pulp illustrators, Ploog's style combined the detailed work of Will Eisner and Wally Wood with the over-the-top European innovators as showcased in *Heavy Metal*. He was the initial artist for *Ghost Rider*, and there is still some question of who created the demonic biker's distinctive flaming skull (Ploog, writer Gary Friedrich, and editor Roy Thomas have all claimed credit). Though Ploog's art for Marvel was wonderful, his work for movies (storyboards, pre-production and post-production work for *Ghostbusters*, Ralph Bakshi's *The Lord of the Rings*, *Hey Good Lookin'*, Michael Jackson's *Moonwalker*, *Superman II*, *Little Shop of Horrors*, *The Dark Crystal*, and *Labyrinth*) has been unreal. In particular, his conceptual designs for *Wizards* and John Carpenter's *The Thing* are a testament to an imagination fed, nurtured, and ripened in horror comics.

7.

Mike Mignola

Perhaps the most important figure in contemporary horror comics, Mike Mignola has carried the flame proudly into the twenty-first century. Mignola started work at Marvel on superhero comics *Daredevil*, *Power Man and Iron Fist*, *Alpha Flight*, *Incredible Hulk*, and *Rocket Raccoon*. When he went to work for DC, he created his first great horror-influenced works: *The Phantom Stranger* limited series with P. Craig Russell and the Batman/Lovecraft crossover *The Doom that Came to Gotham*. After a comic adaptation of Francis Ford Coppola's *Bram Stoker's Dracula*, Mignola began the legend that is Hellboy with *Hellboy: Seed of Destruction* (written by comics legend John Byrne) in 1994 for Dark Horse comics. From that demon germ grew the Hellboy Empire: a mythos that encompasses Nazi occultism, folk tales, government conspiracies, luchadores, and just about every monster and paranormal phenomenon that has ever been recorded. Mignola's vision has created such characters as Abe Sapien, Lobster Johnson, the BPRD, Sir Edward Grey, the Amazing Screw-on Head, and Lord Baltimore, to name a few. Mignola's distinctive style looks like Jack Kirby, if Kirby had been influenced by cubism and Salvador Dali.

Mignola began his partnership with famed director Guillermo del Toro when he worked as a concept artist on del Toro's *Blade II*. These kindred spirits collaborated on bringing Mignola's comic creations to the big screen with *Hellboy* in 2004 and *Hellboy II: The Golden Army* in 2008. Mignola has also supervised two Hellboy direct-to-video animated films: *Sword of Storms* (2006) and *Blood and Iron* (2007). Unfortunately, these extracurricular activities have curtailed Mignola's illustrating schedule, as he draws covers only for his Hellboy family of comics. Here's hoping he'll return to full-time illustrating sometime soon.

6.

Esteban Maroto

The Spanish invasion of artists from the Sellecioncs Illustarda studio centered in Madrid sent shock waves through the horror comic field in the 1970s. Along with the influx of Filipino artists, these foreign illustrators, usually with entirely different styles and sensibilities, caused American artists to raise their game. Esteban Maroto was foremost among these game-changing Spaniards. He began his career with the otherworldly sci-fi series "Cinco por Infinito," but it was with "Wolff," a

THE 13 MOST GHASTLY HORROR COMIC ARTISTS

psychedelic post-apocalyptic sword and sorcery epic, that people started to take note. Maroto displayed his horror chops with "The Viyi," a strip based on the same folklore that informed Mario Bava's Wunderlak episode of *Black Sabbath* and Giorgio Ferroni's *Night of the Devils*. He created fantastic imagery for Marvel's black and white mags: the slinky Satana in *Vampire Tales* and Red Sonja's metal bikini in *The Savage Sword of Conan*. His best work was for the Warren publications *Eerie*, *Creepy*, and *Vampirella*, where his serials *Dax the Warrior* and *Tomb of the Gods* ran. Maroto's work resembles Aubrey Beardsley on a DMT freak-out. Maroto teamed up with prolific comic scribe Roy Thomas to create *H. P. Lovecraft's The Call of Cuthulhu*, an adaptation of "The Nameless City," "The Festival," and "The Call of Cthulhu." Do I even need to say that this is a match made in R'lyeh?

5.

Stephen R. Bissette

One of the most enthusiastic and insightful thinkers in the history of the horror genre, Stephen R. Bissette should be appointed the United Nations Ambassador of Terror. A lifelong horror devotee, Bissette enrolled in the first class of the Joe Kubert Comic Art School, a curriculum that produced some of the best comic artists of the '80s, not to mention horror comic artisans Rick Veitch and Tom Yeates. Bissette brought an uninhibited counterculture aesthetic to his work for *Heavy Metal*, *Sgt. Rock*, *Epic Illustrated*, and *Bizarre Adventures*. However, it was his collaboration with Kubert School classmate John Totleben and a fresh-faced Brit writer named Alan Moore that would revolutionize horror comics (and comics in general). From 1983–87, their teamwork on *Swamp Thing* produced the premier work of horror in any genre during the 1980s. Tired of the grind of a monthly series and wanting to stretch his artistic vistas, Bissette formed Spiderbaby Grafix to edit and publish the influential transgressive horror comic anthology *Taboo* with John Totleben in 1988. *Taboo* ran for nine genre-challenging issues and introduced the world to *From Hell*, Alan Moore's greatest achievement. Bissette's finest work was displayed in his self-published series *Tyrant*, a paleo-perfect biography of a Tyrannosaurus Rex. His loose, frenetic illustrating style gives the reader the illusion of movement, especially important in a prehistoric world where speed and size can determine survival. Bissette's contributions to the horror genre go beyond comics to film criticism, fiction writing, and lecturing. Of specific interest is *Journey into Fear*, a series of lectures on the history of horror comics. He teaches comic art history, drawing, and film at the Center for Cartoon Studies in his home state of Vermont. Though not quite the Rare Book Room at Miskatonic University, the Stephen

R. Bissette Collection at Henderson State University in Arkansas houses his works and memorabilia.

4.

John Totleben

There must have been something dreadful in the water at the Joe Kubert School, because that hallowed institution produced some of the best horror comic artists ever. Case in point: John Totleben, the unholy child of EC Comics and Dürer. His first professional art appeared in *Heavy Metal* in 1979, but it was his work as an inker for Stephen Bissette's pencils on *Saga of the Swamp Thing* that brought him prominence. Though Moore is credited with revamping the Swamp Thing concept, Bissette and Totleben had established the postmodern horror aesthetic even before Moore joined the title. Undoubtedly one of the premier inkers in comics, Totleben also penciled and inked three issues of *Swamp Thing*, and they are among the most beautiful and terrifying comic art ever produced. His heavily detailed use of hatching and shading gives a depth to his art that is rare in comics. Just as amazing are his painted covers for *Swamp Thing*, with brushwork invoking Edvard Munch and Henry Fuseli. And yet the apotheosis of his art is the run he produced for Alan Moore's *Miracleman*. Illustrating the end of Moore's tenure on the title, Totleben's work runs the gamut from everyday verisimilitude to superhero god-like glory to alien weirdness. All the previous issues were just a warm-up for the infamous *Miracleman* #15, one of the most disturbing, mind-destroying comics ever produced. Totleben's devastating depiction of the Twilight of the Gods, obliterating London and killing thousands in the most twisted ways, can make you lose all hope in superheroes. Like something out of a Greek tragedy, this superbly talented artist was diagnosed with retinis pigmentosa, a degenerative eye disease. He's legally blind, but nothing can stop his frightful muse; he still makes exquisite renderings but, like anything worth waiting for, it takes time.

3.

John Coulthart

Winner of the Artist of the Year (2012) from the World Fantasy Awards, John Coulthart is a fantastique jack of all trades: an illustrator, author, and graphic designer who has produced numerous book covers, album covers, and posters. But it is his work on horror comics that has established him as one of the premier interpreters of the bizarre and disquieting. He first came to eminence with his

THE 13 MOST GHASTLY HORROR COMIC ARTISTS

monstrous artwork for Savoy Books's controversial *Lord Horror* series. If you can imagine Pasolini's *Salo* recast as a futuristic Orwellian holocaust, you might begin to approach the madness of *Lord Horror*. Coulthart's work on Lord Horror transformed London into an amalgam of *Metropolis* and Auschwitz. As one can infer, the guardians of decency and taste did not look favorably on *Lord Horror*, causing Savoy Books no end of legal and distribution problems. He has forged a bond with two of the greatest horror writers of the twentieth century: one psychically, the other in reality. Coulthart has produced several outstanding works based on the writings of H. P. Lovecraft, adapting "The Haunter of the Dark," "The Call of Cthulhu," and "The Dunwich Horror." He has also entered into a fruitful collaboration with Alan Moore, creating Great Old One tarot cards with the mage, and poster and cover art for Moore's spoken world albums. Coulthart's ability to move between realism, abstract expressionism, collage, painting, and fine pen and ink work results in artwork with an unpredictable, magickal quality that never loses its ability to shock. He is also a favorite with esoteric musicians, designing promotional art, album covers, and packaging for Cradle of Filth, Hawkwind, and Steven Severin. Coulthart's devotion to horror extends to film criticism as well; he contributed thirty film reviews and four essays to *Horror: The Definitive Guide to the Cinema of Fear*. Coulthart's best work is still before him, and horror fans should thank Cthulhu for that.

2.

Bernie Wrightson

The rightful heir to the EC tradition, Bernie Wrightson grew from a monster kid to a monster artist to a monster icon. A fateful meeting with Frank Frazetta at a comic book convention in 1967 inspired Wrightson to become a professional comic book artist. In 1968, he submitted his first comics work, which was published in DC's *House of Mystery* #179. He worked on the DC horror anthologies and Marvel horror anthologies like *Chamber of Darkness* and *Tower of Shadows*. Seeking to break free of the Comics Code, Wrightson contributed to the independent horror anthology *Web of Horror*, an experiment that lasted only three issues. His first significant contribution to the horror comic genre was his co-creation of *Swamp Thing* with writer Len Wein, drawing the first ten issues of the initial *Swamp Thing* series. In 1974, he left the majors to work for Warren horror magazines, perfecting his art through Poe and Lovecraft adaptations as well as his own creations like the Muck Monster and the Pepper Lake Monster. The zenith of his Warren work was "Jenifer," an atmospheric tale of love and death written by Bruce Jones. In 1975, he joined four of the most talented comic artists ever—Jeff

Jones, Michael Kaluta, and Barry Windsor-Smith—to form The Studio. They created this communal enterprise to help each other and to break free of the comic industry's narrow commercialism. For seven years, Wrightson worked on unbelievably detailed illustrations to accompany Mary Shelley's *Frankenstein*. His intricate style of pen, ink, and brushwork recalls the beauty of Franklin Booth, the dynamism of Hal Forester, and the gruesomeness of Jack Davis. Wrightson has also lent his immeasurable talents to the film industry, starting with his Captain Sternn segment in the *Heavy Metal* movie, his post-production work on Stephen King and George Romero's *Creepshow*, and his design work on the Reavers for the film *Serenity*. Bringing the old and new schools together, Wrightson and Steve Niles collaborated on *Frankenstein Alive!* in 2012. Unfortunately, Wrightson suffered a series of small strokes in 2014, but is on the mend. You can't keep a good ghoul down.

1.

Graham Ingels

Anyone with the nickname "Ghastly" has to be doing something right in horror art. Graham Ingels started out drawing for EC Comics's western, crime, and romance titles. Many felt his work was uninspired and disappointing, with some at the comics company requesting that he be let go. The visionary William Gaines saw something in this young artist and kept him on, just as EC was moving toward the spectacular horror line-up that would make them infamous. Ingels seemed to have found his niche, as his unnervingly creepy work appeared in *Tales from the Crypt*, *The Vault of Evil*, *Shock SuspenStories*, and, in particular, *The Haunt of Fear*. As each title had its own horror host, Ingels created the Old Witch for *The Haunt of Fear*, and never has a more antediluvian, decrepit, sinister witch appeared in comics. Ingels specialized in a unique form of modern Gothic, with crumbling settings, rotting corpses shambling down country roads, and grotesquely exaggerated characters, their mouths twisted, running toward open, well-deserved graves. His style was reminiscent of N. C. Wyeth mixed with the madness of Alfred Kubin. Something this good couldn't last, and as congressional hearings on juvenile delinquency fingered horror comics, EC was forced to cancel its horror titles. Ingels drew for EC's failed New Direction line (His work for *Piracy* rivaled Howard Pyle) and there was a slight return to horror for the blink-and-you-missed-it Picto-Fiction line. Ingels found little work after EC ceased publication in the mid 1950s and was besieged with professional, personal, and family problems. He became an art instructor in Florida and refused to acknowledge his work for EC,

THE 13 MOST GHASTLY HORROR COMIC ARTISTS

even threatening legal action against fans and historians seeking him out. It was only a few years before he died that he started to open up a bit about his work for EC, and even did private commissions of the Old Witch for a few lucky patrons. These paintings proved that he still had it and had even gotten better as he matured. Hopefully, somewhere in the Great Beyond, Ingels has found some peace and can enjoy the well-deserved kudos his work still receives.

Honorable Mention

Jack Davis
Alfredo Alcala
Jose Ortiz
Jose Gonzalez
Basil Wolverton
Richard Corben
Eric Powell
Tim Vigil
Alex Toth
Pat Boyette
Alex Nino
Frank Brunner
Vince Locke
Yoshiharu Tsuge
Shigeru Mizuki

Music

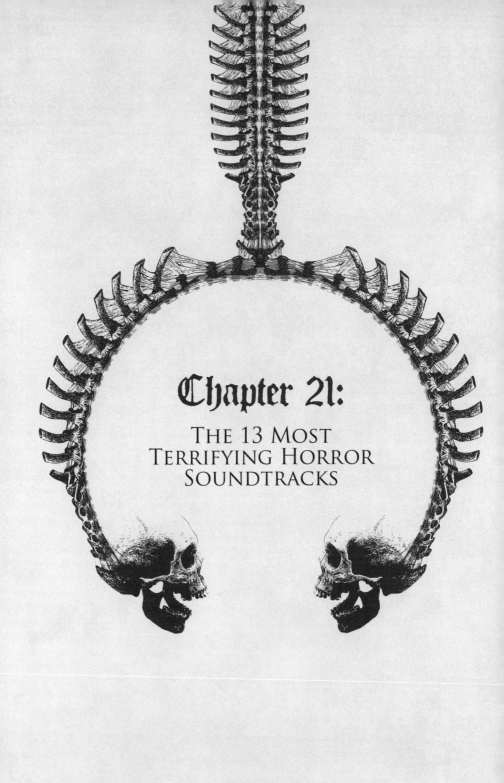

Chapter 21:

THE 13 MOST TERRIFYING HORROR SOUNDTRACKS

o other film genre is more conducive to the power of the soundtrack than horror. Suspense, anxiety, and dread are intensified by music's dizzying highs and whispered lows. The catharsis of music perfectly accentuates the expression of repressed fears and hidden desires found in every horror film. From the beginning of cinema, music was needed to give weight and meaning to many of the images that seemed to randomly pile into each other. It was an additional narrative framework that provided emotional space and interpretive cues to the perplexed viewers of this new medium.

Starting out with an accompanying pianist, live music tracked to moving pictures got more sophisticated, moving to organs, percussive sounds, sound effects, and even orchestras that added a total sensory experience to the fledgling visual novelty. Early scores were often based on classical music or popular show tunes and vaudevillian motifs, with improvised flourishes to add to the uniqueness of both the style of the musician and the makeup of the audience watching the film. Soon film studios saw the value of branding their films with music and started to supply movie houses with standardized

> The catharsis of music perfectly accentuates the expression of repressed fears and hidden desires found in every horror film.

cue sheets for the musicians to follow as they played along with the movie. For the world premiere of *The Phantom of the Opera* in 1925, Universal commissioned a special score from Eugene Conte (filled with "French airs") to be performed on a state-of-the-art organ built for the gala unveiling. Universal Films led the way with all aspects of the horror film in the '30s, especially in the use of music. *Dracula* and *Frankenstein* still used classical pieces and simple title music to add Gothic flavor, but with *The Bride of Frankenstein*, the modern horror film soundtrack was brought to life. Franz Waxman's menacing yet romantic music, punctuated with sonic asides and commentary like the tolling wedding bells to announce the creation of the bride, offered a Greek-chorus-like resonance to the film. Waxman would contribute powerful scores for Hitchcock's *Rebecca*, *Suspicion*, and *Rear Window*, and was second only to Bernard Herrmann as the master scorer of suspense. Universal would hire Hans J. Salter and Frank Skinner to track the cavalcade of horror movies that dominated the genre in the 1930s and '40s, mixing the high art of atonality, serialism, and avant-garde arrangements with the massively popular, lush orchestral music of the golden age of cinema. Max Steiner's score for *King Kong* was also influential in juxtaposing primitive sounds and melodious harmony to "ape" the archetypal struggle between beauty and beast.

By the 1950s, soundtracks had become a distinct art form rivaling both popular and modern classical music in terms of innovation. Often the first genre of music to incorporate new technologies and methods of writing, performing, and creating sound, horror's soundtracks were the perfect way to bring high aesthetic compositional theory to the proletariat (just ask Louis and Bebe Barron). Here are the thirteen most terrifying horror soundtracks. And when we say soundtrack, we mean an actual movie score, not some hodge-podge compilation of disparate tracks. I mean a sinisterly holistic experience of unsettling compositions. Listen if you dare.

13.

Shadow of the Vampire (2000)—Dan Jones

Dan Jones's work for film isn't as plentiful as it should be. He is just too busy. Jones creates music for public artworks, including the Sky Orchestra, which involves performers playing in seven hot air balloons floating above a given city, as well as the more terrestrial and tasty "Music for Seven Ice Cream Vans." His music can also be heard on several British television documentaries and dramas, and he has collaborated with the electronic group Alpha. Between jobs, Jones scored *Shadow of the Vampire*, E. Elias Merhige's fictionalized account of the making of Murnau's *Nosferatu*. Jones had an interesting predicament when it came to this soundtrack: he had to score Merhige's film, but also the film within the film. The two soundtracks had to complement but not copy each other too closely. Jones's work succeeds on both levels because he twists themes around each other. Leitmotifs pop up between the two scores, but in entirely unexpected and irrational ways as quirkiness infects the brutality and savagery colors the triumph of the artistic spirit. As if Adolf Wolfli conducted a Wagner score, tracks such as "Murnau's Vision—The Journey," "The Night Shoot," and "Schereck's Revenge" blur the lines between art and life, life and death, death and undeath. Using Jones's electro-acoustic background, the soundtrack mixes delicate Weimar whimsy with catastrophic surges of orchestral clamor. Minimalist dissonance, waltzes, music hall songs, and background exegetic sounds vie for the listener's attention. Never has the hurdy-gurdy sounded so ominous. If you've ever wondered what a Kurt Weil-Krzysztof Penderecki collaboration would be like, here is the next best thing.

12.

30 Days of Night (2007)—Brian Reitzell

Brian Reitzell wears many musical caps. He has drummed for punk-pop godfathers Redd Kross and has been Sophia Coppolas' personal composer, scoring *The Virgin Suicides*, *Lost in Translation*, and *Marie Antoinette*. He even got Kevin Shields to stop erasing and rerecording the new "My Bloody Valentine" album so that Shields could contribute music to one of Reitzell's soundtracks. Reitzell's score for the adaptation of Steve Niles's groundbreaking comic series is a dark, ambient masterpiece. Reflecting the reinvention of the vampire as portrayed in the comic and the film, Reitzell reinvents the vampire

THE 13 MOST TERRIFYING HORROR SOUNDTRACKS

film soundtrack. He experimented with alternate percussive and sound-generating devices that he constructed himself. Using silence, guttural moans, screams, deep rumblings, howls, visceral beats, and icy soundscapes, the listener not only hears but feels the nihilistic attacks on the citizens of Barrow, Alaska. Even in the still, silent moments one can detect a low-level buzzing and grinding, an effect that subtly raises the listener's nervousness and the expectation of something truly awful happening at any moment. While most traditional ambient music soothes and disappears into the background, *30 Days of Night* pierces the subconscious and violates the ear repeatedly. The tracks freeze you to the spot and then tear you to pieces. Coming off like an evil Brian Eno, Reitzell's score sounds like the end of the world or the beginning of a more savage one. Currently, Reitzell is damaging minds with his brilliantly unhinged clairaudience for NBC's elegantly brutal *Hannibal*.

11.

Buio Omega (1979)—Goblin

Helping to put both Italian prog and Italian horror on the map, Goblin has become synomous with the dark master himself, Dario Argento. Brought in because Argento felt that composer Giorgio Gaslini was too square for the sensory-overload thriller he wanted to make with *Profondo Rosso*, Goblin fit the bill perfectly with its wild but classically trained musicians. Goblin has produced some of the most mind-melting movie music ever (*Suspiria*, *Contamination*, the Italian cuts of *Dawn of the Dead* and *Martin*), but its soundtrack to Joe D'Amato's ode to cannibalism and necrophilia is just too much. *Buio Omega* was the first horror film the group worked on after composing music for the Argento cut of *Dawn of the Dead*, and it seemed as if they were chomping at the bit to get back into the horror arena after two years away. One of the problems with Goblin is that they couldn't seem to hold onto a stable lineup, and although the members who created *Buio Omega* might not be the best known of Goblin's contributors, the throbbing sound they produced can't be dismissed. In the main theme, "Quiet Drops," and "Pillage," Goblin sounds like a Gothic Giorgio Moroder pumping out pulsating disco beats, menacing synthesizer washes, and funky rock like some insane, grave-robbing DJ. Come to think of it, *Buio Omega* is kind of like *Midnight Express* if the main character had been smuggling body parts rather than drugs.

10.

Werewolves on Wheels (1971)—Don Gere

Werewolves on Wheels is the Reese's Peanut Butter Cups of horror: two great tastes that go great together. Bikers and satanists, and then a werewolf to boot? Finally, a movie that speaks to my demographic. The film is fuzzy in all the right places, even in its soundtrack. Urban legend states that composer Don Gere went "native" and delved into the hippie/occult subculture, dabbling in hallucinogenics, communes, and Lucifer. If this is true, it's certainly reflected in his sun-baked, stoned mantra of a score that sounds like Charlie Manson fronting some Krautrock band: badass acoustic guitars, chains for drums, trancey ritualistic repetition, oily grooves. One of the biker chicks in the film even looks like Susan Atkins. Songs like "Ritual," "One," "Tarot," and the simmering main theme bask in that weird post-1960s/early '70s vibe where the counterculture just wanted to bliss out and feel numb. Skip the two buckskin jacket Topanga Canyon wuss country rock tracks, though, and go straight for the occult psyche doom. Now, when will we get to hear Gere's soundtrack for *Sweet Sugar*, a film about a hooker on a chain gang who is subjected to medical experiments by a deranged doctor?

9.

Nosferatu the Vampyre (1979)—Popol Vuh

Werner Herzog's remake of the Murnau classic showcases the magic of Florian Fricke's Popol Vuh, one of the most evocative and spiritual Krautrock bands ever. Popol Vuh was a truly mystical band using instruments and sounds from all cultures to try to invoke a one world/one dream/one soul connection among listeners. Bringing together folk, rock, and electronic music, Popol Vuh treated time as a cyclical oneness, and so the past, present, and future merged in its compositions. Herzog used Popol Vuh's enchantment on many of his films, but *Nosferatu* is the epitome of the band's collaborations. Piano, sitar, and folk instruments interpret darkness becoming light as the mood shifts from despair to glory. The opening track, "Bruder des Schatten-Sohne des Licts," is an ominous yet meditative hymn, almost like a monastic plague threnody. While some pieces rejoice in hope, others, based on the frightening "Dies Irae," warn of the grave that beckons. The soundtrack was split between two albums, but the 2004 reissue collects the entire soundtrack on one CD. Unfortunately, Popol Vuh's mastermind, Florian Fricke, died in 2001, and the band passed on to the third bardo.

THE 13 MOST TERRIFYING HORROR SOUNDTRACKS

8.

7 *Note in Nero* (1977)
—Franco Bixio, Fabio Frizzi, Vince Tempera

Sometimes one Italian composer is not enough. It took three—Franco Bixio, Fabio Frizzi, and Vince Tempera—to capture the essence of mad maestro Lucio Fulci. Starting with Fulci's fierce spaghetti western *Four of the Apocalypse*, these three musicians proved that teamwork can bring out the best in all participants, even in the world of soundtracks. Bixio, Frizzi, and Tempera's score is much different than the usual giallo soundtrack. Rather than attack the viewer with the requisite stabbing strings, the music for this thriller is playfully titillating, a loungey/exotica sound with dark unsettling undertones. Okay, maybe it doesn't radically reinvent giallo music, but the distinctive use of the carillion (a keyboard that rings notes out of twenty-three bronze bells) adds a peculiar rococo motif that, when mixed with synthesizers, piano, and female vocals, creates a unique, decadent atmosphere. Pieces such as "Sucidio," "Allucinazoni," and the gentle menace of the title song prove that three composers are often better than one. Not surprisingly, Quentin Tarantino appropriated the theme song for *Kill Bill Vol. 1*. Frizzi would continue his working relationship with Fulci, creating superb scores for *Zombie*, *City of the Living Dead*, *The Beyond*, and *A Cat in the Brain*.

7.

Night of Dark Shadows (1971)—Robert Cobert

Robert Cobert is the unsung hero of horror soundtracks. If he had only scored the *Dark Shadows* TV show, his legend would have been cemented, but he also composed music for *The Night Stalker*, *The Night Strangler*, *Burnt Offerings*, *Trilogy of Terror*, *Scream of the Wolf*, *Shadow of Fear*, and *The Norliss Tapes*. If Dan Curtis made it, Cobert tracked it, hence that old philosophical paradox, "If a Dan Curtis film falls in the woods, is Robert Cobert there to score it?" Cobert's finest work coincided with Curtis's: *Night of Dark Shadows*, the criminally underrated extension of the *Dark Shadows* mythos, is given a tragically eerie score (of course, Cobert also scored the other wonderful *Dark Shadows* film, *House of Dark Shadows*). Cobert's music is elegant, gentle, and stark, using minimal piano, strings, vibraphone, and percussion enhanced by subtle electronic effects. The main instrument is, oddly, a harmonica, beseeching loneliness, melancholia, and longing. The tone is mournful, romantic, and wistful, like a half-remembered name or a feeling of déjà vu. Cobert uses a few motifs from the TV series ("Joanna" was revised into the theme of the film) and yet those repeated refrains haunt the film like revenants. The music sort of appears out of nowhere, hovers, terrifies, and dissipates like the ghostly Angelique. Truly autumnal chamber music for a Collinwood séance.

6.

Onibaba (1964)
—Hikaru Hayashi and Tetsuya Ohashi

Soundtrack composers and sound editors should have closer cooperation. Both of these artists manipulate (one through music, the other through diegetic sound) the aural to construct an auditory experience that supports, deepens, and enlivens the cinematic. When these two roles feed into each other (like the David Lynch/Alan Splet tandem for *Eraserhead*), the result is audient alchemy. For *Onibaba*, composer Hikaru Hayashi and sound editor Testsuya Ohasi terrorize the listener by creating a suffocating, all-encompassing, inescapable sonic environment. This tale of rapacious women in fourteenth-century Japan uses anachronistic mashups to express the demons of the mind and the voraciousness of greed. Ritualistic Taiko drumming is crossed with frenetic free jazz, creating a dramatic tension between the pounding, unrelenting percussion and the hysterical wailing of feverish flutes and horns, reflecting the lusts, jealousies, and animalistic survival in a post-war wasteland. Dialogue has been reduced to the barest minimum, and pure sound pummels both predator and prey. Although the film feels like a noh play, the soundtrack comes on like Grand Guignol. Hayashi was no stranger to the devastating power of noise, as he composed a choral suite entitled *Scenes for Hiroshima*.

5.

The Amityville Horror (1979)—Lalo Schifrin

Ah, the greatness that is Lalo Schifrin—the fifth jewel in the crown that represents the majesty of film composing (joining Morricone, Herrmann, Goldsmith, and Ifukube). Supposedly incorporating elements of his rejected *Exorcist* score (Friedkin's loss was our gain), Schifrin manipulates the loud/soft dynamic like the master he is. Swarms of orchestral noise and piercing, distorted notes punctuate the innocent choir voices and elegiac piano that float through the film. Schifrin offers sly homages to other iconic scores (*Psycho*, *Vertigo*, *The Omen*), and his demonic soundtrack deserves to be mentioned in the same breath. Tracks like "Father Delaney," "The Window," and the memorable main title theme are made scarier by juxtaposing the excitement and optimism of a new family in their new home with a creeping despondency and warning that explodes in ear-splitting fury. Schifrin's use of female voices and clusters of gloomy woodwinds make for an unearthly, depressing listen. Thank Satan that this score is so scary, because the film certainly isn't. *The Amityville Horror* soundtrack was nominated for an Oscar, but sadly did not receive the award. Even the devil can't win all the time.

4.

The Fog (1980)—John Carpenter

Carpenter's influence on horror soundtracks might be even bigger than his influence on horror directing (just take a listen to Symmetry, Jeff Grace, Jonathan Snipes, Rob, Jeremy Schmidt, 3:33, etc.). His epochal *Halloween* score, the minimalist beats of *Assault on Precinct 13*, the gritty-funky *Escape from New York*, and the brooding *Prince of Darkness* (many in collaboration with Alan Howarth) are almost haiku-like in their raw simplicity and austere glory. For *The Fog*, Carpenter invokes a dream within a dream using prolonged tones, sinister Satie-like piano, incessant rattling percussion, and disquieting waves of synthesizer replicating the creeping miasma. The soundtrack gives weight to the ethereal nature of the murkiness; in a strange case of synthaesia, one feels the fog through the score. The sequence where Stevie Wayne (Adrienne Barbeau) drives out to her lighthouse radio station is made starkly foreboding by the combination of wind, natural sounds, and the ambient score that never intrudes but rather seeps into our minds. Interestingly, Carpenter's first attempt at scoring *The Fog* was rejected by the composer, along with most of the film. In one month, Carpenter re-wrote, re-shot, re-edited, and re-scored the film. If you weren't convinced of the god-like stature of Carpenter before, how do you doubt him after this superhuman achievement? Adding low bass and the tidal ebbing and flowing of synthesizer waves, *The Fog* soundtrack is a ghost story without words. Not a collection of songs but a selection of moods, Carpenter's unsophisticated scoring style has stood the test of time and still reveals hidden treasures with repeated listening. But am I the only one who still wants to hear his first scrapped score?

3.

Horror of Dracula (1958)—James Bernard

The influence of James Bernard on the Hammer Film phenomenon can't be overstated. His musical motifs are just as much calling cards for British horror as anything committed to the screen. The man who brought stately grandeur to the iconic Hammer Studios brand unleashed his most bombastic, yet romantic score for the first outing of Christopher

Lee as Dracula. Embodying the ferocity and majesty of its title character, Bernard's soundtrack uses the repeated orchestral theme of sounding out "Dra-cu-laaa" and deep bassoon rumblings to invoke the count's vampiric manifestation, a constant reminder of the threat that menaces the characters in the film. Heavy when it has to be, but also light and sweet when the viewer needs a break from the undead machinations, the *Dracula* soundtrack acknowledges the past but also looks to the future. Bernard's music is just as important as the genre-changing performances of Christopher Lee and Peter Cushing in the film. Though Bernard's scores gave Hammer a distinctive identity, they certainly weren't cookie cutter in their sound or methods. His soundtracks for *The Plague of the Zombies*, *The Devil Rides Out*, *Frankenstein Created Woman*, and *Taste the Blood of Dracula* all sound different, yet all bear the irrepressible mark of the Hammer musical brand. And yet he produced his greatest score for the greatest Hammer film.

2.

Psycho (1960)—Bernard Herrmann

In a bit of egoism, a composer once remarked that "Hitchcock only finishes a picture 60%. I have to finish it for him." If it were any composer other than Bernard Herrmann, you would ask for his head to be examined. The film that launched a 1,000 thrillers has a score that influenced a thousand thriller soundtracks. Herrmann's tense, agitated, shocking music is an all-out assault on the mind and body. Using screeching strings to devastating effect, the notes viscously stab the audience's ears and penetrate into the brain. The score's driving momentum achieves a subtle psychological effect, keeping the audience in a constant state of paranoia. Herrmann was influenced by bird calls, which fits perfectly with the bird symbolism in the film. The film identifies Norman with the atonality of the score; as his madness deepens, the dissonance gets higher, sharper, and more savage—fracturing music for a fracturing psyche. Originally, Hitchcock didn't want any music during the famed shower murder scene, but Herrmann persuaded Hitchcock to let him score it. It is of some consolation that even the great Hitchcock could be wrong. Perhaps Herrmann should have upped his percentage to fifty percent?

1.

Rosemary's Baby (1968)/*The Fearless Vampire Killers* (1967)—Krzysztof Komeda

Polish jazz musician Krzysztof Komeda wrote the scores for four of his friend Roman Polanski's feature films. Two of those scores represent the finest film music ever to grace a horror film. (The other two ain't bad, either). Komeda's more European sensibilities changed the style of cinematic jazz, and his quirky, angular aesthetic transferred perfectly to Polanski's paranoiac themes. Komeda's soundtrack to *The Fearless Vampire Killers* is a swirling, ominous tempest of voices, folk music, and orchestral frenzy. Haunting wordless vocals (no doubt influenced by Morricone's use of Alessandro Alessandroni and Edda Dell'Orso) drift in and out of the score like the snow that falls on Sharon Tate as she is attacked in the bath. Some of the tracks can only be described as eerie jazz, as if Miles Davis and Gil Evans had made an album called Sketches of Transylvania. Komeda's mixing of baroque classicalism and modernist discord is unsettlingly beautiful. Other tracks sound like what The Free Design would have recorded had they been a coven rather than a sunshine pop group. Speaking of covens, Komeda's score for *Rosemary's Baby* is just as fine, if not finer. Coming across like bachelor pad music for a satanist, the soundtrack is a nightmare of disorienting sounds—blaring horns, sluggish piano, and bleary strings. The title theme is an absolute masterpiece: the infamous lullaby to the baby anti-christ. The single refrain of "La-La-La-La" (sung by Rosemary herself, Mia Farrow) never sounded so creepy and hopeless. Shards of avant-garde noise and chanting hail the new age of Lucifer as deformed trumpets pay tribute to the unholy conception and birth. Polanski remarked that *Rosemary's Baby* owes much to Komeda's empathy and creative imagination. Tragically, Komeda did not live long to enjoy his accolades. In December 1968, he fell and hit his head. Komeda slipped into a coma and never woke up.

Honorable Mention

The Omen—Jerry Goldsmith
Alien—Jerry Goldsmith
The Texas Chainsaw Massacre—Tobe Hooper and Wayne Bell
The Keep—Tangerine Dream
Horror Express—John Cacavas
Let's Scare Jessica to Death—Orville Stoeber
Jaws—John Williams
The Haunting of Julia—Colin Towns
The Evil Dead (2013)—Roque Banos
The Red Queen Kills Seven Times—Bruno Nicolai
The Legend of Hell House—Delia Derbyshire and Brian Hodgson
Session 9—The Climax Golden Twins
Beyond the Black Rainbow—Sinoia Caves
Sinister—Christopher Young, et al.

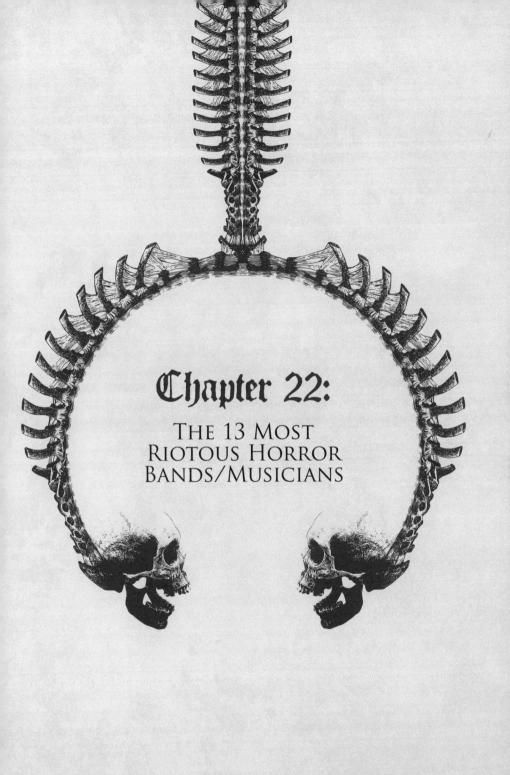

Chapter 22:

THE 13 MOST RIOTOUS HORROR BANDS/MUSICIANS

orror and rock 'n' roll, the Romulus and Remus of modern popular culture. From these two artistic founts, the best and worst of the twentieth century has been denounced, critiqued, and worshipped. Revolutions in consciousness and creativity, it is no surprise that these dual forms of expression have been attacked mercilessly by the powers that be. The connection between horror and rock music precedes the evolution of rock, as the supernatural and darker side of human nature have been perennial topics in all of rock's precursors: the blues, country, jazz, gospel, and folk. One needs only to hear Robert Johnson, Dock Boggs, G. B. Grayson, the Carter Family, or the Louvin Brothers to realize that fear and trembling are emotions that transcend any one genre of music. But it was the combination of post-WWII prosperity/Cold War angst and the explosion of that new demographic known as the teenager that created the perfect environment for horror and rock-n-roll. Both spoke to something deeper than patriotism, getting a good job, moving to suburbia, and being a loyal, upright citizen. Along with the Beats, horror and rock music offered an alternative to the capitalist myth of better living through conformist consumption and production. After losing the ability to join the Communist party to outrage their elders, America's young people needed something to rebel with that was edgy enough to produce a transgressive thrill but not too taboo that they would

Songs about hot rods and surfing mingled with raucous paeans to werewolves, vampires, witches, zombies, mummies, and the Headless Horseman.

be hauled before the House of Un-American Activities Committee. Lenny Bruce and *Mad Magazine* certainly helped funnel some of that dissenting, proto-counterculture energy in a devastatingly witty direction, but they lacked the visceral feel of Little Richard, Jerry Lee Lewis, and the King.

Just as rock 'n' roll was outraging the buttoned-down, church-going American (the same people who probably would have literally burned Elvis at the stake in the name of morality), Roger Corman and Hammer Studios ushered in the Silver Age of Horror, offering violence and terror to the sexed up teenage masses. Kids of the late 1950s and early '60s were rock 'n' roll fans, and so the horror rock song was born, fueled by *Famous Monsters of Filmland* and horror host agitators like Ghoulardi. Songs about hot rods and surfing mingled with raucous paeans to werewolves, vampires, witches, zombies, mummies, and the Headless Horseman. Monster hops and creature dances, odes to dead teenagers, and voodoo love potions expressed a morbid sensuality that fueled doomed romances, chickie runs, and rumbles. Death, fear, power, desire, and the outsider anti-hero inform both the imagery of horror film and the lyricism of horror music, as seen in such early horror rock figures as Screaming Lord Sutch and Screamin' Jay Hawkins, who used theatricality, noise, and volume to terrify and liberate. Unfortunately, rock started to take itself way too seriously, and rock musicians wallowed in the grandiose delusion that they were poets, prophets, and politicians. Horror was not topical or socially conscious enough, and so rock moved on to soundtracking the lives of spoiled middle-class teens demanding that their music justify their lifestyle. Nonetheless, there are musicians who kept (and keep) the horror/rock connection alive; subsequently, other musical genres have picked up on the notion that horror can be the perfect metaphor to push boundaries in terms of sound and lyrical content. Here are thirteen horror music artists that represent the twentieth century's finest creations.

THE 13 MOST RIOTOUS HORROR BANDS/MUSICIANS

13.

Fantômas

Mike Patton is a true enigma in contemporary music. He rose to prominence with the heavy metal/funk hybrid band Faith No More and its mega MTV hit "Epic." Later he set off for truly strange musical frontiers with his Ipecac label and his prodigious solo and collaborative works. Fantomas is an experimental collective populated with weird heavy music practitioners such as Buzz Osbourne (The Melvins), Trevor Dunn (Mr. Bungle), Dave Lombardo (Slayer), and Terry Bozzio (Missing Persons, The Mothers of Invention). As indicated by the band's name, Fantomas is influenced by fumetti and fanastique cinema, especially European and American horror soundtrack composers. Each Fantomas album has a unique concept and sound, but they all reflect the wild creativity of 1960s/'70s cinema and pop culture. The band's finest achievement is *The Director's Cut* (2001), interpretations and interpolations of theme songs from a variety of movies, mostly horror films. Styles range from orchestral to thrash, with amazing takes on Krystoff Komeda's "Rosemary's Baby," James Bernard's "The Devil Rides Out," Jerry Goldsmith's "The Omen," Angelo Badalamenti's "Twin Peaks: Fire Walk with Me," and Ennio Morricone's "Investigation of a Citizen above Suspicion." While these tributes to the great soundtrack composers are compelling, it is the versions of lesser-known themes and composers that really shine in *The Director's Cut*, such as Karl Ernst Sasses's "Der Golem," Ronald Stein's "Spiderbaby," and Harry Lubin's theme to the TV show "One Step Beyond." Obviously, Patton loves these songs, but his passion for the innovation and beauty of the originals push the Fantomas versions past reverence into truly original performances. You'll never hear the "Godfather" theme the same way again. Patton took his interest in European pop music and soundtracks to Italy, where he performed a series of concerts in 2007 under the name Mondo Cane, accompanied by a thirty-piece orchestra. The highlight of these performances was a version of "Deep Down" from Morricone's *Danger Diabolik*. Patton has also contributed to contemporary films, providing the eerie voices of the creatures in *I Am Legend* (he should have gotten the job of shrieking for the vampires in *30 Days of Night*) and composed the soundtracks for *Crank: High Voltage* and *The Place Beyond the Pines*. Patton's unique talents and vocalizing should keep him gainfully employed in the horror film world.

12.

Cradle of Filth

Black metal's debt to horror seems to be a sore spot with those who don corpse paint and pray toward Norway. Horror fashioned itself as the only truly evil genre of metal, preventing artists from acknowledging the artifice and fun of horror films and encouraging them instead to prove how kvlt they are by burning down beautiful wooden churches and killing each other. Thankfully, Dani Filth has found a way to connect the malevolent strains of black metal with the transgressive aspects of horror in a way that is powerful yet wickedly playful. One of the first British black metal bands, Cradle of Filth crawled out of the mire in 1991 and quickly evolved into epic metal grandeur, combining literary sophistication with Alice Cooper-esque shock. Following in the grand tradition of Byron, Blake, Shelley, and Keats, Filth is the Miltonian Lucifer dressed up in satanic dandyism and serial killer chic: musician, author, actor, raconteur. Following the band's debut screed *The Principle of Evil Made Flesh* (1994), each subsequent Cradle of Filth release would be informed by a central concept, usually involving some aspect of horror, whether fictional, folkloric, or historical: *Dusk . . . and Her Embrace* focuses on Gothic vampirism in the style of LeFanu, *Cruelty and The Beast* on Elizabeth Bathory, *Midian* on Clive Barker's *Nightbreed, Damnation and a Day* on "Paradise Lost," *Godspeed on the Devil's Thunder* on Gilles de Rais, and *Darkly, Darkly, Venus Aversa* on Lilith, even recruiting horror icons like Ingrid Pitt and Doug Bradley to add spoken interludes. While heavy metal had tentatively embraced orchestral and symphonic contributions, Cradle of Filth's Wagnerian odes to the dark gods effortlessly bridge the extremes of high and low musical styles. Filth's vocal prowess has aggressively developed into such a towering force that he now belongs in the pantheon of great metal vocalists like King Diamond, Bruce Dickinson, and Dio. The band's debt to horror and the tragedy of humankind extends into its videos for songs like "Mannequin" and "Babalon A.D." in which the works of Jan Svankmajer and Pasolini are invoked to stunning effect. Always courting outrage and exposing hypocrisy (through ingenious pranks like the "Jesus Is a Cunt" T-shirt controversy and the "I Love Satan" brouhaha at the Vatican), Cradle of Filth smeared the line between the artistic and the offensive with a knowing wink and a pinch of British cheek.

THE 13 MOST RIOTOUS HORROR BANDS/MUSICIANS

11.

White Zombie

If alien beings ever land on Earth and want the quickest way to understand the phenomenon of horror, just give them the collected works of Rob Zombie to listen to and watch. Zombie's musical oeuvre, expressed through his band White Zombie and his solo albums, are saturated with referents to horror films, TV shows, characters, magazines, comics, and imagery. His melodic heavy metal stylings, informed by sampling and beat-driven electronic flourishes, have proven immensely influential in the Frankensteinian cross-stitching between the heavy metal, rock, electronica, and hip hop genres. White Zombie began in 1985, recording several punk-influenced releases, but it wasn't until the 1989 album *Make Them Die Slowly* (of course referencing Umberto Lenzi's cannibal sleaze fest) that the formula coalesced and the archetype was realized. Noisy, heavy, and drenched in horrotica, the Rob Zombie persona was unleashed as a cross between Zacherele and Charles Manson. With each subsequent album, Zombie added musical and cultural influences while fine tuning the approach he brought to horror music. *La Sexorcisto: Devil Music Volume One* infiltrated the cultural consciousness in 1992 with its raucously infectious incorporation of horror samples, references, and imagery into groovy hard rock and the crushing immensity of the production. Tracks like "Spiderbaby (Yeah-Yeah-Yeah)," "Grindhouse (A Go-Go)" and the break-out single/video "Thunder Kiss "65" kept horror cool, fun, and sexy in the lean years of the early '90s. The more industrial *Astro Creep 2000* followed in 1995 to much popular acclaim, buoyed by the single/video "More Human than Human," an ode to *Blade Runner* with visuals borrowing from *London after Midnight*. *Astro Creep 2000* is chock full of horror film samples gleaned from *The Omega Man*, *The Haunting*, *The Curse of Frankenstein*, and *To the Devil a Daughter*. White Zombie ended in 1998, but Zombie certainly wasn't done with horror music, releasing three amazing solo albums: *Hellbilly Deluxe: 13 Tales Of Cadaverous Cavorting Inside The Spookshow International* (1998), *The Sinister Urge* (2001), and his masterpiece *Educated Horses* (2006) that, if anything, have expanded and enhanced the horror music genre more than White Zombie did. Zombie's solo albums have also been the conceptual breeding ground for his movies, as the tracks "House of a 1000 Corpses," "The Devil's Rejects," and "The Lords of Salem" have made the jump from sound to vision as Zombie-directed films. His significant musical and cinematic contributions to the twenty-first-century horror landscape have made him a living icon and a true friend of the genre.

10.

Goblin

Is any musical group more closely aligned with a film genre than Goblin is with Italian horror? Goblin's musicians are perhaps the only ones whose work is seen as intrinsic to a film's success. (Okay, maybe Morricone's work on Sergio Leone's films fits that description, so there must be something in Italy's drinking water.) Goblin's contributions to the works of Dario Argento helped launch his films to international acclaim, as their innovative soundtracks perfectly match Argento's audacious images. Argento recruited the band, which started out as the prog-infused Cherry Five, to give his revolutionary giallo *Deep Red* a more edgy, contemporary feel. Rechristened Goblin, the band delivered a gonzo, nuts, funky, action-painting of a score that complemented Argento's radical reinvention of the thriller. Goblin became famous in Italy, but with its classic work on Argento's *Suspiria*, the band's name became synonymous worldwide with Italian horror. The loud/soft ebb and flow dynamic of their music suggests occult rituals on windswept vistas, and the savagely throbbing rhythms connect like stabs to the heart. The classic Goblin lineup would last for one more glorious work—the soundtrack to George Romero's *Dawn of the Dead*—before splintering into rotating configurations of original and replacement players. But even with a revolving door membership, Goblin created killer horror film scores such as *Buio Omega*, *Patrick*, *Phenomena*, and *Contamination*. Their combination of synthesizer overload with technically precise prog-rock-funk pushes the already outrageous visuals into realms of absurd beauty. Core member Claudio Simonetti was the most prolific solo Goblin member in terms of horror rock, scoring such high/low lights of Italian horror as *Opera*, *Demons*, *Dracula 3-D*, *Conquest*, *Cut and Run*, *The Card Player*, *The Mother of Tears*, *Jenifer*, and *Pelts*—Argento's work for the *Masters of Horror* series. In 2000, Goblin reunited for Argento's *Sleepless*, proving that they had lost none of their magic. Unfortunately, inner band drama has resulted in competing versions of Goblin: Back to the Goblin, New Goblin, Goblin Rebirth, The Goblin Keys, with various configurations of original and new players. In 2013, most of the classic lineup reunited to tour the US for the first time ever as Goblin, bringing a taste of Italian horror to ravenous fans. The lineup barely lasted the jaunt, and the members have gone back to their contentious stances and rival bands. Only the intervention of the great communicator Dario Argento can bring these tempestuous but brilliant artists together again.

THE 15 MOST RIOTOUS HORROR BANDS/MUSICIANS

9.

Lustmord

Any horror film epicurean knows that without sound, a truly unsettling cinematic atmosphere is virtually impossible to achieve. Lustmord has been summoning chilling soundtracks to both literal films and those that I shudder to imagine could ever exist. Brian Williams is the force behind Lustmord, which began in the miserable postindustrial year 1980, and his forte is conjuring evil moods. A sometime partner of the escaped inmates of SPK and collaborator with such transgressive luminaries as Jarboe, John Balance, Monte Cazazza, Chris and Cosey, and the Melvins, Williams sculpts sounds captured in caves, abattoirs, tombs, and occult rituals into disturbingly subtle ambient music that could soothe psychopaths in their post-sex-crime bliss. Lustmord's first masterpiece was *Heresy* in 1990, a work credited with starting the dark ambient genre. Heresy seeks to simultaneously lull and frighten using field recordings of subterranean environments tortured through low-frequency amplification. His next album, *The Monstrous Soul* (1992), cemented his reputation as a shadowy sound magus. A collaboration with Clock DVA member Adi Newton, *The Monstrous Soul* is the album that Leviathan from *Hellraiser II* would make. Noise manipulation, sub-audient sounds, and film dialogue samples assault the listener, and yet the music is so intriguing that the aural ravishing is completely consensual. Pieces such as "Ixaxaar," "Protoplasmic Reversion," (both tracks use samples from *Curse of the Demon*), "The Daathean Doorway," and "The Fourth and Final Key" merge drone, roar, and quiet to invoke a spiritual world that Aleister Crowley only dreamed of. Williams's prowess with creating haunting environments has led to a lucrative career in designing sound for film and videogames and scoring movies such as *The Crow* and *Underworld*. With all this entertainment industry work, Williams hasn't neglected his sinister muse. He had a memorable live appearance accompanying a Church of Satan mass that took place on 6/6/06 and has released albums of sublime terror such as *[OTHER]* (2008), which contains the gargantuan track "Godeater,"—twenty-two minutes of tension and impenetrable gloom.

8.

Gravediggaz

The real-life violence and social injustices chronicled in rap music leave little room for the fictional frights of horror films, but allusions to Freddy Kreuger, Chucky, Leatherface, and even *Rosemary's Baby* have enlivened rap songs from the Fat Boys to the Geto Boys. While

Kool Keith is often credited for bringing the horror aesthetic to hip hop, the first masterpiece of so-called "horrorcore" was 6 *Feet Deep* (1994) by the supergroup Gravediggaz. The initial Gravediggaz lineup consisted of Prince Paul (The Undertaker), Frukwan (The Gatekeeper), Too Poetic (The Grym Reaper) and RZA (The Rzarector), effectively combining the ominous and intimidating tone of the Wu Tang Clan with the mad doctor antics of Prince Paul to create an ode to over-the-top violence, dying, and the great beyond. Funny, funky, and creepy, 6 *Feet Deep* pushed the attitude of gangsta rap to its logical conclusion: the worship of death and the fear of torments that await perpetrators in the afterlife. "1-800-Suicide" makes a number of inventive suggestions for self-defenestration such as lighting one's balls on fire like Richard Pryor or hanging oneself with barbed wire. The production is astonishing, with disturbing samples and eerie beats that replicate dirt being thrown on a grave while the not-quite-dead victim pounds on the coffin lid. The next album, *The Pick, the Sickle and the Shovel*, wasn't as dog nuts or death-obsessed as the previous album, maybe because the genius of Prince Paul was kept to a minimum, but it still conjures up a ghoulish atmosphere. More of the Wu Tang collective became involved with Gravediggaz. The death of Too Poetic from colon cancer in 2001 ended the band's original incarnation, but not before it released its most morbid album, *Nightmare in A-Minor*. Filled with references to Poetic's losing battle with cancer and the inevitability of death, the album was a fitting elegy to the Grym Reaper. Though there have been rumors of a resurrected Gravediggaz, the reanimated group has not yet unleashed its dark vision on an unsuspecting public.

7.

Necrophagia

Since its beginning in the Paleolithic era, heavy metal has explored the darker side of the human condition through its aural and lyrical assault. Death metal molests the sound and content of heavy metal and then pushes it through a meat grinder. It's no coincidence that the gore film and death metal came of age together, as they both revel in the abject reality of our own bodies and the graphic depiction of the concealed environment within us all. Death metal rubs our ears in our own disgusting existence and denies us the soothing platitudes of harmony, rhythm, and melodious vocals. Emerging from the same depths of suffering, anger, revulsion, and the awareness of the futility of our lives, death metal and horror are intricately linked, informing not only the music but the logos, band names, and cover graphics of almost every death metal band that has ever growled. Developed amongst the feverish demo tape and VHS trading days, groups

THE 13 MOST RIOTOUS HORROR BANDS/MUSICIANS

such as Possessed, Morbid Angel, and Death left legacies of brutality, but Necrophagia's *Season of the Dead* (1987) and *Ready for Death* (recorded 1986, released 1990) took death metal to the heights of horror. Necrophagia began its corpse-eating style of music in 1983, tearing through thrash to get at the black soul of metal. Songs such as "Beyond and Back," "Autopsy on the Living Dead," "Chainsaw Lust," and "Lust of the Naked Dead" fully displayed Frank "Killjoy" Pucci's obsession with low-budget mondo atrocities and z-movie gore. The band split in 1987 but was reanimated in 1997 with the help of Anton Crowley (Phil Anselmo using a pseudonym that is so stupid yet so cool), and the product of this unholy resurrection is the Italian-horror-influenced *Holocausto de la Morte* (1998). The cover is a tribute to the films of Lucio Fulci and the tracks are the sonic equivalent of an Umberto Lenzi cannibal massacre/orgy. Not content with an album of sadistic torments, Necrophagia recruited director Jim Vanbebber (of *Charlie's Family* fame) and created the *Through Eyes of the Dead* (2000) VHS tape, which is part music video, part interview, part cinematic lunacy with references to Fulci's *The Beyond*, Dario Argento, and Ruggiero Deodato's *Cannibal Holocaust*. Necrophagia is still recording and touring, proving that with strange eons even death metal may live on.

6.

Skinny Puppy

Industrial music is harsh, punishing, and often difficult to categorize. Early industrial artists used "unmusical" noise to critique politics, social inhibitions, and ideological control. Horror films seemed to be treated as part of the cultural garbage vomited out by global capital, anesthetizing bored, mindless sheep needing to see graphic violence just to get a thrill out of their desperate lives. Pornography was more relevant to industrial music than horror films were. It took a Canadian electronic band to fully embrace the transgressive aspects of horror and funnel those sounds and images into a frightening but thought-provoking body of musical work. Skinny Puppy was formed in 1982 by electronic musician cEvin Key and vocalist Nivek Ogre. Early songs such as "Smothered Hope," "Incision," and "Icebreaker" married bleak electro beats with samples from such dark film classics as *Shadow of a Doubt*, *The Tenant*, and *The Legend of Hellhouse*. The band's music and tours continually upped the ante of terror imagery and sample usage, but Skinny Puppy wasn't in it for the shock value alone: horror films were used as metaphors for social and political critiques involving such issues as vivisection, environmentalism, censorship, addiction, and war. The apotheosis of Skinny Puppy's art can be heard on *VIVIsectVI* (1988), an album that engages the horror of modern society with samples from *Evil Dead II*, mixed into a ferocious but danceable sound collage. The band's video for "Worlock" (1990) used clips from a multitude of extreme horror films such as *Deep Red*, *Suspiria*, *Tenebrae*, *Phenomena*, *Opera*, *The Beyond*, *Hellraiser II*, *Bad Taste*, *Dead & Buried*, *Combat Shock*, and *Henry: Portrait of a Serial Killer* to dizzyingly nauseating effect. After *The Process* (1996), a final album inspired by the mysterious Process Church of the Final Judgment and the entertaining Genesis P. Orridge, drugs, musical differences, and burnout brought the band's life to a close. After a one-off reunion show in 2000, Skinny Puppy re-formed in 2003 and recorded and toured, but it seems to have regressed to a more conventional industrial rock. Any hope that Skinny Puppy would return to their repulsive yet compellingly stringent sound was dashed when Ogre appeared in *Repo! The Genetic Opera*.

5.

Alice Cooper

The inventor of shock rock, Alice Cooper brought the grisly aspects of Hershel Gordon Lewis and the burgeoning gore film to the power chording of early heavy metal and glam. Beginning as an acid rock band signed to Frank Zappa's Straight label, the sensibilities of Alice Cooper (supposedly named by a Ouija board session) flew in the face of the prevailing hippie mentality: rather than peace, love, and understanding, Alice Cooper exuded hate, lust, and decadence. With each album, Alice Cooper the band became Alice Cooper the evil cabaret host, wallowing in excess, sickness, and death, extolling the interchangeable thrills of sex and murder on such tracks as "I Love the Dead," "The Black Widow" (with narration from Vincent Price), and "Dead Babies." Alice's masterpiece *Love it to Death* (1971) is a glorious mess of an album with the deathless "I'm Eighteen," "Black Juju," and especially "The Ballad of Dwight Frye," establishing the horror film ethos of Alice's whole aesthetic. As Alice became a horror rock icon, his macabre stage show became more elaborate and questionable, a Grand Guignol spectacular dedicated to the worst aspects of the human condition. Goya-esque depictions of insanity, dismemberment, torture, suicide, and capital punishment were embraced by jaded post-Vietnam audiences numbed from repeated viewings of real causalities on the nightly news. Unfortunately, the price of being the most shocking rocker led to all sorts of temptations such as alcohol, drugs, and the worst of all, commercialization and absorption into the gaping maw of the entertainment industry (notwithstanding Alice's ultracool *Nightmare* TV special and his amazing appearance on *The Muppets*, where he tried to collect souls). Through the '80s, Alice would periodically

THE 13 MOST RIOTOUS HORROR BANDS/MUSICIANS

resurface to release sleek, horror-infused songs like the ones he contributed to *Friday the 13th Part VI: Jason Lives*. Although now a spent musical force (*Welcome 2 My Nightmare*?), his acting appearances in John Carpenter's criminally underrated *Prince of Darkness, Monster Dog, Dark Shadows*, and *Freddy's Dead: The Final Nightmare*, and his slasher-cinema-infused concerts touring with his shock-rock offspring, Rob Zombie, display his rightful place in the horror pantheon of immortals. He's also in the Rock and Roll Hall of Fame, but who cares about that?

4.

The Cramps

Imagine a world in which sound movies were not invented and live music had to accompany films. The perfect band to play along with the perverted, deranged images of the grindhouse would have to be the Cramps. Reveling in all media forms that have been rejected and labeled as sick and disgusting, the Cramps celebrated bad taste as the highest art form. Since horror and rock music are the two most nefarious corrupters of youth, the Cramps had to delve into both. Though labeled as a punk band (and certainly its attitude and unhinged antics lend themselves to that appellation), the Cramps's sound harkens back to the wild and woolly days of hillbilly music, amphetamine and moonshine-fueled country and blues, and car wrecks best exemplified by the mad prodigy Hasil Adkins. The Cramps were founded by the ultimate trash culture king and queen Lux Interior (vocals) and Poison Ivy (lead guitar). Taking its passion for horror hosts, JD flicks, EC comics, sci-fi atrocities, sexy monsters, and garage rock to the illogical extreme, the Cramps mixed obscure retro covers with its own sex and violence-obsessed songs to create the genre of psychobilly, a horror-drenched version of the rollicking fun of rockabilly as funneled through Charles Manson and Wild Man Fischer. The perfect venue for the Cramps music is an insane asylum, which the band played in 1978 at the California State Mental Hospital in Napa for the worked-up inmates. Early psychotronic singles like "Human Fly" and "Surfin' Bird" set the stage for the first album *Songs The Lord Taught Us* (produced by the legendary Alex Chilton), containing such mind-melters as "I Was a Teenage Werewolf" and "Zombie Dance." The Cramps would rampage for thirty years, releasing such stone-cold classics as *Fiends of Dope Island*, "I'm Just a Gorehound," "Bikini Girls with Machine Guns," "Burn She-Devil, Burn," "The Creature from the Black Leather Lagoon," and its contribution to the immortal *The Return of the Living Dead* soundtrack "Surfin' Dead." The band's outrageous live shows were powered by Ivy's Link-Wray-meets-Johnny-Ramone buzz saw guitar and Lux's lunatic front-man antics that would make Iggy Pop blush. Alas, Lux's premature death ended the reign, but no other band has combined horror, rock, humor, and good times better than the Cramps.

3.

Electric Wizard

Some contemporary bands just weren't made for these times. Electric Wizard would have been the perfect house band for a '70s Eurocine discotech. As Lina Romay and Brigitte Lahaie perform a lesbian sex show, Jack Taylor and Howard Vernon read *Man Myth and Magic* and *Witchcraft* magazines, and Jess Franco and Jean Rollin smoke hash, Electric Wizard's droning, volume-crushing doom epics could accompany the sleazy occult atmosphere. Inspired by pulp writers, drugs, and fumetti, The Wizard channels Black Sabbath through layers of bong resin and quaaluded sex magick. Guitarist, singer, cult leader Jus Oborn started the band in 1993 as a way to justify his obsession with heavy metal, horror, and getting stoned. Their first masterpiece was *Dopethrone* (2000), a lurching, lumbering behemoth with odes to *Weird Tales*, *Conan the Barbarian*, and *Mark of the Devil*. Other heavy doses of Wizard insanity include *Come My Fanatics* (1997) and the *Supercoven* E. P. (1998), which bludgeon the listener through the density of the sound but entice with references to late '60s/early '70s trash horror culture. After some band member shake-ups and problems with the law, Electric Wizard added doom goddess Liz Buckingham and in 2007 released *Witchcult Today*, the greatest occult rock record of all time. By turning the volume down a bit and speeding up tempos a half-step, Oborn found the magick formula for horror rock. Every track on the album is a tour de force, starting with the dirty, humming siren call of the title track, beckoning the "chosen few" who have joined the Electric Wizard coven. The album creates a hazy, drugged-out atmosphere ripe for summoning Yog Sothoth and feeling the shiver of the vampires. A plethora of euro-cult horror touchstones pervade the songs, such as references to *The Devil Rides Out* and the foxy vampire Zora, but Oborn creates his own mythos with the Bobby Liebling-inspired character Drugula. The album is heavy as hell but grooves like Soledad Miranda in *Vampyros Lesbos*. *Black Masses* (2010) and 2014's *Time to Die* signaled a shift to a more proto doom metal sound but still hit all the right horror rock buttons with songs about Franco's *Venus in Furs* and satanism. The Wizard has inspired other occult rock bands such as the witchy Blood Ceremony, the Devil's Blood, Orchid, Uncle Acid and the Dead Beats, Bloody Hammer, Satan's Satyrs, and pretty much the entire Swedish doom scene.

THE 13 MOST RIOTOUS HORROR BANDS/MUSICIANS

2.

Roky Erickson

The father of horror rock (he even coined the term), Roky Erickson's life reflects the horror films his songs celebrate and use as metaphors for his mental and metaphysical struggles. As a member of the 13th Floor Elevators, Roky combined bluesy garage rock with the dawning psychedelic consciousness and counterculture imperative to experiment with music and lifestyle. His willingness to put his art, health, and freedom on the line in order to embrace mind-altering chemical explorations (a truly heroic diet of LSD, mescaline, and DMT) and philosophical alternatives resulted in mental breakdowns, incarceration in psychiatric hospitals, and involuntary electroshock and thorazine therapies. After four years in a hospital for the criminally insane, Roky was released, but he was significantly changed by his harrowing experiences. No longer a naïve flower child, Roky believed he was inhabited by an alien and tried to exorcise the terrors he endured by writing lyrics that dealt with horror and sci-fi films, the supernatural, and the occult. His first solo single, backed by the Blieb (an anagram of "Bible") Alien band, was the unbelievably raw and uncomfortably sincere "Two Headed Dog (Red Temple Prayer)," a ferocious track that must have shocked those who were used to the Elevators's more benign hippie sentiments. On the strength of this single, Roky and the Alien band recorded a session produced by CCR's Stu Cook that established the genre conventions for horror rock, which have not been bettered. Songs such as "I Walked with a Zombie," "Creature with the Atom Brain," "White Faces," "I Think of Demons," and "Bloody Hammer" mixed blistering hard rock with Buddy Holly melodies and bizarre lyrics that on paper make absolutely no sense ("Spanning your theory/ Alien I creator"?) but when sung by Roky take on the gravity of Old Testament truths. The tracks were split between two albums—*The Evil One* and *I Think of Demons*—but really should have been one cohesive, mighty work that would have redefined rock music. Every song is a classic, haunted by ghosts, devils, vampires, aliens, and alligators that stood in for the mental patients, cops, judges, and doctors that made Roky's life a living hell. Surely his madman vocals and nightmarish imagery inspired cow punk bands such as the Dicks and the Butthole Surfers. After the album *Don't Slander Me*, Roky's metaphoric demons seemed to be losing to his actual psychotic episodes and for a while he was living in poverty in a squalid apartment with dozens of radios and TV's blasting to drown out the voices in his head. The tribute album, *Where the Pyramid Meets the Eye*, kept Roky on the hipster radar, and with the help of family and friends he received enough treatment to return to recording and touring. His latest album, *True Love Cast Out Evil*, is a testament to the life and art of Roger Krynard Erickson.

1.

The Misfits

The undisputed kings of horror punk, the Misfits crafted an iconic look and sound that has spawned a multitude of imitators. Melding the excitement of punk with B-horror movie thrills, the Misfits released some of the most memorable singles in the history of punk: Ramones-ian explosions of spook show delights contained within picture sleeves that resembled the coolest horror movie posters never made. The first incarnation of the band started in 1977, led by the highly controversial but undoubtedly hugely influential Glenn Danzig. While their earliest work deals with the darker side of American culture (the Patty Hearst kidnapping, the assassination of JFK), it was with 1979's "Horror Business" single (the Crimson Ghost logo graced the cover for the first time) that horror punk was born. Whether about Hitchcock's *Psycho* or Nancy Spungeon's murder, "Horror Business" (backed with the ferocious medley "Teenagers from Mars/Children in Heat") finally united the two most controversial pop culture commodities of the '70s. From this auspicious beginning, the Misfits churned out most of horror punk's greatest hits from hell: "Night of the Living Dead," "Ghoul's Night Out," "Halloween I & II," "Vampira," "Die, Die My Darling," barely scratching the surface of Danzig's genius. The albums *Walk Among Us* and *Earth A.D./Wolfs Blood* are stone cold classics as well, adding rockabilly and hardcore to their already impressive repertoire. (Though I still think that if the Misfits had been able to release *Static Age* when they wanted to, it would have been their crowning glory.) The Misfits were not just singing about horror, but were a living embodiment of it: executioner garb, skeleton gloves, sinister devil lock hairdos, and coffin stage props were their album cover graphics writ large. Danzig moved on to new pastures following an acrimonious split with the Only brothers (the Misfits's bassist and guitarist) in 1983 and kept the horror rock flame alive with outstanding releases from Samhain (*November Coming Fire* is an underrated masterpiece) and his solo project Danzig. After a long legal battle, Jerry Only revived the Misfits in 1997, and though he gave it a good try with new vocalist Michale Graves, it wasn't the same. Though their look was great, the songs just weren't there, again proving that Danzig's arrogance is entirely justified.

THE 13 MOST RIOTOUS HORROR BANDS/MUSICIANS

Honorable Mention

King Diamond
Jacula
The Ghastly Ones
Venom
Hooded Menace
Marilyn Manson
GWAR
The Caretaker
Flatlinerz
Ulver

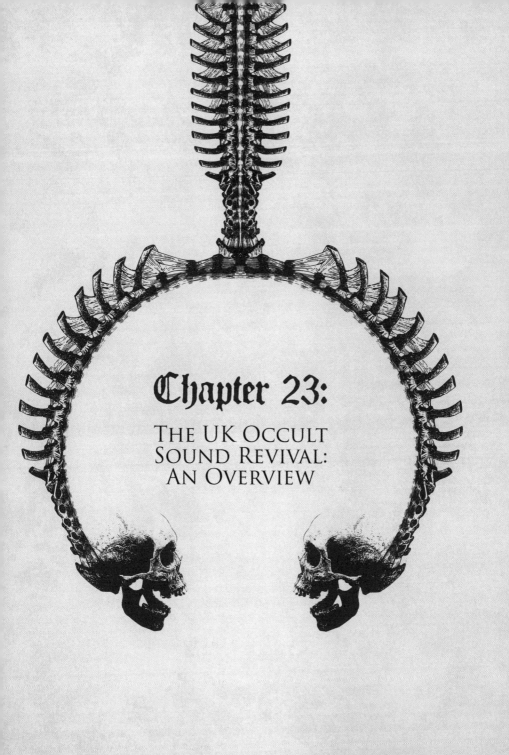

Chapter 23:

The UK Occult Sound Revival: An Overview

t is the morning of the drone magicians. The Sonic Age of Horus manifested itself on November 9, 2013, at the Star and Shadow Cinema in Newcastle, UK, through a magickal working entitled Unearthing Forgotten Horrors. A loose artistic/esoteric/experimental collective of musicians, travelers, and eccentrics convened to share their music, experiences, and interest in the supernatural. Invoking the Exploding Plastic Inevitable if it were conducted by Kenneth Anger and Alex Sanders, the cinematic backdrop of *Blood on Satan's Claw* and *The Stone Tape* channel the deep heritage of British horror, helping to set the atmosphere for the musical conjurings of artists such as Culver, the Psychogeograpical Commission, and the Tempel of Sekhmet, sounds that summon the anguished spirits of persecuted covens, Druid sacrifices on blood drenched stones, and lonely revenants in haunted

Over the last decade, this mystical network of musicians-artists-writers-filmmakers-scholars has collaborated, explored, and presented their uniquely powerful creations to those whose tastes run to the night side.

abbeys. The creations of James, Machen, Kneale, and Hodgson, the visuals of Hammer, Amicus, and Tigon, the philosophies of Crowley, Spare, and Grant, and the environs of the Seven Witches Stone Circle, Borley Rectory, and Dunwich are felt through the musical performances. Combining ritualistic noise, moody hums and whirls, resonant samples, and eerie field recordings, these artists are not just musicians or aesthetes; they are mages, researchers, wanderers, surveyors, and historians: psychogeographers wielding sound, vision, and the uncanny to warp time, space, and consciousness.

Unearthing Forgotten Horrors was the apotheosis of a growing underground movement that shares some core interests but expresses them in diverse, highly creative multi-media permutations. Over the last decade, this mystical network of musicians-artists-writers-filmmakers-scholars has collaborated, explored, and presented their uniquely powerful creations to those whose tastes run to the night side. In 2004, Julian House and Jim Jupp founded Ghost Box Music to document these excursions into the haunted audient and house a musical occult collective consisting of core groups Belbury Poly, yhe Focus Group, and the Advisory Circle. Other artists have followed their own artistic familiars into the strange, idiosyncratic world of hauntology—esoteric sound anachronisms influenced by the UK's spectral geography and T. C. Lethbridge's theories of "'residual haunting" (best articulated in his extraordinary book *Ghost and Ghoul*), all filtered through the BBC Radiophonic Workshop. Four key participants in the Unearthing Forgotten Horrors and the Occult Wave project are English Heretic, Black Mountain Transmitter, the Dead End Street Band, and Joseph Curwen. These horror-infused voyagers are poised to enlighten weird music acolytes in this world and the next.

English Heretic (Perdurabo)
A self-described "creative occult organisation dedicated to the reification of malefic energy spectres and the adumbration of a modern qliphoth," Andy Sharp's English Heretic is a mind-melting information overload of *Man, Myth, and Magic* meets *Re/Search* meets *Apocalypse Culture*. Using music, lectures, performances, literary journalism, and field reports from the outer limits, the English Heretic agenda encompasses witchy electronics, folk skullduggery, absurdist wit, and preserving the weird currents of British supernatural history. And yet English Heretic is not only focused on the marvels of a distant age. Contemporary alchemists like Michael Reeves, J. G. Ballard, and Ian Sinclair are connected in the cosmic continuum that unites past, present, and future as overlapping, recursive realities. The British soil is inseparable from the personalities and experiences of these magickal icons, and so the energies stored in their blessed plot, their earth, their realm are unlocked through English Heretic's multi-media projects. Site-specific musical/literary/visual/spoken word workings as well as artifacts such as *The Sacred Geography of British Cinema: Scene One, Radar Angeology—A Drone For Joe Kennedy, Tales of the New Isis Lodge, Anti-Heroes, Mondo Paranoia*, and *The Underworld Service* are proof that English Heretic is the illuminated hierophant of this new day dawning for the hidden mysteries of UK occult music.
https://www.facebook.com/EnglishHereticOfficialOrgan
http://englishheretic.blogspot.com/

The following is an interview with English Heretic's Andy Sharp.

WB: When did your interest in horror and the occult begin?

AS: My interest in horror began as a child in the late '70s in the UK. During the summer, the BBC would show a horror double bill every Saturday night. The shows consisted of a classic oldie and a modern horror (*Satanic Rites of Dracula*, *Dracula AD 1972*, etc.). After that, when home video became available—around 1981—we'd rent films every night. Interest in the occult started in my early teens and was very much influenced by the countercultural movement constellated around industrial music. Crowley was the obvious entry point, but I soon became more interested in his protégé, Kenneth Grant. His work was so strange and otherworldly—quite early I figured out that these books weren't about occult practice, but were, in fact, *Necronomicons*. There were also all the references to fiction and film—"Cults of the Shadow" is dedicated to Bela Lugosi—so there was the fascinating interplay with horror in his work. I argue that the blind atavisms of the preternatural world might not discriminate between a "genuine" ritual and a suitably staged cinematic presentation—in fact they'd probably prefer a cinematic one because it's more ornate!

WB: Who are your musical influences?

AS: Certainly the whole underground music scene that was spawned from Industrial Records (Cabaret Voltaire, Throbbing Gristle, Psychic TV, etc.) influence the content, but I see that as a cultural inheritance. I am interested in the idea that these folks were following a path of autodidactic learning—and it affected my development, so I feel I am honoring that tradition. However, stylistically, in terms of music, there's a lot influence from other, probably less expected, sources: I love the layering, epic sounds of folks like Mono, for instance. Electric Wizard, for both sound and content. Nurse with Wound, Robert Ashley's "Automatic Writing" in terms of the use of voice and queasy ambience. Again, working in a different idiom, I was certainly inspired by DJ Shadow and his use of sampling.

WB: How does English Heretic work? What are your goals?

AS: Well, the goals were pretty much set out about ten years ago. The general idea was to illustrate the fecundation of the imagination by a kind of revved-up hyper-association of fiction and historical fact using people and place. I hoped to plant all this information I was connecting in the subconscious and see what happened to my imagination. There are three parts to the project—people (Black Plaques), places (Sites of Heresy), and *Wyrd Tales* (which I hoped would be the imaginative result—in other words, fictions derived from the first two facets).

However, what's happened is that the English Heretic has become this very broad project concentrating on the first two aspects, and rather less on the third. I think the reason is that in order for something to emerge from the subconscious, you have to distance yourself from the conscious matter. I hope the fictions will develop more over the next few years.

WB: How do your occult interests and musical influences come together in your work?

AS: I've always been interested in making creative sigils, and many years ago, particularly when working with Kenneth Grant's books— *Nightside of Eden*, for example— I was creating sound pieces very much as mean of exploring occult subject matter. That work has really carried on into English Heretic: It's why there are a lot of repetitive voice samples. That said, I've also wanted to explore ceremonial narratives in terms of sound—a very good example of this being GRS Mead's interpretation of a gnostic liturgy, which has sonic elements—popping hissing, thunder crashes, etc. Grant himself interprets Mead's analysis in a Lovecraftian light, saying that the proximity of the Old Ones is accompanied by a hissing sound. So naturally I am interested in the extrapolation of the occult significance of such sounds to create a symbolic but also a theatrical and hopefully dramatic point of access to alien realms!

WB: English Heretic is an incredibly multi-modal band. Is music the most important medium you create in?

AS: Creating music is slightly less intense than writing, but writing was very important. I do a lot of the work for EH in the evening after a full day's work, and I find it more relaxing to do music in the evening than to write—so it's only more important for pragmatic reasons.

WB: Place plays an enormous role in your work. How does your environment affect your artistic process?

AS: It's very important. I visit almost every location that I portray in music or writing. I always take recordings, whether it be ambience or some heuristic interplay with the place. I've also recorded music on location, but that process has changed from essentially improvising to a more recent concept in which reality becomes the recording studio. So now I take a laptop out and will compose the bare bones of a piece on site. I did this recently at the Kennedy memorial at Runnymede. The process of concentrating as if in a studio, but on site, creates the quite intensive feedback loop. I first noticed the effect when taking a lot of photographs on site and scanning through the picture on the LCD display of the camera while on site. I seemed to get in this hyper-real state of mind and wondered what would happen if I used other digital technologies in the same way. I noticed the same effect years ago when using radio to do sound experiments; there is a quite powerful feedback loop as you use a technology in an obsessive and iterative way. It is akin to the state of mind that I feel EVP experimenters like Raymond Cass were experiencing. A kind of over-connectedness with the cosmos that becomes exhilarating and frightening—two of my favorite states of mind.

WB: Why is packaging and ancillary releases (*Wyrd Tales*, English Heretic dossiers, visitor guides, English Black Plaque presentations) so intrinsic to the English Heretic project?

AS: The packaging is an important way of creating a cohesive and well-defined aesthetic. English Heretic began very much as a subversion of the government quango English Heritage that is so heavily branded—tea towels, jams, jigsaw puzzles—you name it, and English Heritage has branded it. So I wanted to create this otherworld where the rampant consumerism of history is subverted. Packaging and serialized products are a natural way to present this subverted, surrealised attack on historical sanity.

WB: *Mondo Paranoia* devolves into the arcane synchronicities between the assassination of JFK, James Shelby Downard's "Preface to King-Kill/ 33," and the counterculture dementia of the '60s. What are your thoughts on the connections between occult phenomenon and conspiracy theories?

AS: My argument in *Mondo Paranoia* is that conspiracy theory is a form creative therapy stemming from paranoia. The incredulous nature of the Warren Commission Report seemed to create a great suspicion with authoritarian reality. That suspicion mixed with the mass shock and mass grief generated by the Kennedy assassination created this powerful and deranged way of rationalizing reality. But occultism and magic is by nature paranoid. To practice magic, you have to accept a paranoid stance. Indeed, the occultist Kenneth Grant views the paranoiac-critical method of Salvador Dali as magical formula, rather than, say, a Freudian method. My particular interest is in how you can use paranoid narratives as an aesthetic and poetic means of creating a powerful myth; similar in a way that, say, Robert Graves weaves a poetic truth in his "White Goddess," or indeed as Shelby Downard does in "King Kill." The truths of conspiracy and magic may not be literal truths, but they are poetic truths.

WB: How crucial is performing live to English Heretic?

AS: Important, but I feel it's a part of the project that needs a lot of work to be effective. The performances have varied wildly from the earlier exercise in Ritual electronics to more conventional band setups. Mixed with that, there have been more conceptual performances—for example, we did a performance with the Blue Tree based on Polanski's Apartment Trilogy. Our performance attempted to re-imagine the soundtrack to Polanski's *The Tenant* as some kind of psychiatric documentary, with readings from scientific papers on schizophrenia overlaying the music. It's what I call "the inner cinema"—a kind of personalized rendering of a film. I am very interested in developing this idea.

WB: What is the future of English Heretic?

AS: More releases and research. That's the real strength, I feel; it was always designed to be woven into the fabric of my life—my travels and learning. In terms of releases, there are two projects well under way: *Wish You Were Heretic*, which follows on from both *Anti-Heroes* and *Tales of the New Isis Lodge*. It looks at cinematic connections with place—what I call the sacred geography of British cinema. Second, I am working on *Mondo Paranoia 2*, which uses Polanski's Apartment Trilogy to explore the mid to late-1960s in much the same paranoiac vein as *Mondo Paranoia*. I'll also be talking about *Mondo Paranoia* in Gettysburg in March at a conference called "Exploring the Extraordinary."

Black Mountain Transmitter (De Profundis Ad Lucem)
Belfast-based musician and artist James R. Moore is a true multi-tasker. When not creating abstract videos, drawings, paintings, or photos, Moore composes music under various names, the most evil-sounding coming out under the Black Mountain Transmitter moniker. A throbbing beacon calling supplicants to the Sabbath, Black Mountain Transmitter's releases *Theory & Practice*, *Black Goat of the Woods*, and *Playing with Dead Things* buzz like the Mi-Go in Lovecraft's "The Whisperer in the Darkness," summoning Shub Niggurath and her thousand young. Moore likens his music to "the soundtrack from some lost low budget horror movie, rediscovered on an old and faded VHS cassette found moldering in a deserted house in the depths of the woods," which should quicken the pulse of any true epicurean of eldritch sounds. Black Mountain Transmitter's aesthetic goes deeper than horror's typical histrionics into an EVP trance where past lives, Elder Gods, and other spiritual entities are channeled and break through into the earthly sphere. Moore's own Lysergic Earwax distributes his recordings, but a few other lucky labels have been able to spread the terrifying gospel of Black Mountain Transmitter as well. Black Mountain Transmitter rends the veil of the mundane, opening terrifying vistas of a new sonic dark age.
www.lysergicearwax.bandcamp.com
http://jamesrobertmoore.tumblr.com/

261

WB: When did your interest in horror and the occult begin?

JRM: It began at a very young age. I grew up during the late 1970s and early '80s, a time when there seemed to be a lot of references to the paranormal and general strangeness in mainstream culture. It was a delightful treat to be allowed to stay up past bedtime for double bill screenings of Universal and Hammer horror films (though a mixed blessing, as sleepless nights often followed). "Scream" comic delivered a weekly dose of gruesome delights for its unfortunately short existence from March to June 1984. The local library had a well-stocked paranormal section groaning with ghosts, haunted houses, and screaming skulls. I can't underestimate the influence of seeing the lurid covers of the VHS Nasties displayed in video shops and deliriously imagining the contents of the films, even though finally seeing many of them often ended in disappointment. Regardless, I was drawn to it all. Something about the strangeness that stood in stark contrast to daily life. All that material suggested alternatives, other possibilities opening up, plus the good old unpretentious thrill of a tingling spine. The fact that adults were always trying to discourage any interest in those sorts of things made it even more of a magnet.

WB: Who are your musical influences?

JRM: There is too much of a range to boil down to a representative list, though it's mostly music that is textural rather than melodic or "verse-chorus-verse" in structure. I think my all-time favorite album is Miles Davis' *Bitches Brew*, and currently I'm listening to a lot of Morton Feldman. Join the dots. Much of the music that has influenced me has been an impetus to wanting to make music, without having had a direct effect on the sound of my own work.

WB: How does Black Mountain Transmitter work? What are your goals?

JRM: The process always starts with a feeling or particular atmosphere and some sort of conceptual or narrative element. Recording is experimentation and exploration combined with happy accidents— layered, distressed, manipulated, mixed. I still use analog tape as a recording medium, which I feel encourages one to live with and build on mistakes; this often takes a piece in an unexpected direction. I've never come to grips with the infinite editing possibilities of software, which to me becomes a prison of indecision. Likewise, most of my equipment is physical, from analog synthesizers to bass guitar, fx pedals, contact mics, and other bits and pieces of junk. Most of the gear is cheap and nasty and often used in ways they weren't designed for.

I've never had any serious goals with Black Mountain Transmitter, at least not in respect to something as mundane as making money or gaining critical attention. It's simply something I enjoy doing. Entertainment. The fact that other people derive pleasure from what I do is often enough reason to do it.

WB: How do your occult interests and musical influences come together in your work?

JRM: The Occult, and by that I mean stuff like Crowley, Magick, etc., is something I've lost interest in over the years, something I have no use for personally, and to be honest now find rather tedious. I am still interested, though with a more skeptical approach, in the paranormal world of ghosts, UFOs, and other high strangeness. I've always made the distinction that Black Mountain Transmitter is predominantly influenced by a world of atmospheric horror films, weird fiction, and a particular strain of grotesque black humor.

WB: Black Mountain Transmitter has composed soundtracks for "photographic diaporamas." Is soundtrack work an area that you want to explore more? Who are your favorite soundtrack composers?

JRM: I'd be delighted to be offered an opportunity to do some soundtrack or sound design work. Film has had such a huge influence on what I do musically, and here I'm not just speaking about horror films. Like my musical influences, there is so much to draw on that falls outside that sphere. Rather than making a list of favorite soundtrack composers (as I'm sure many would be blindingly obvious), I will simply say that my favorite soundtrack—an abstract, almost proto-Industrial clanking and groaning soundscape filled with terror—was created by Tobe Hooper and Wayne Bell for *The Texas Chainsaw Massacre*, which in my humble opinion is the most perfect of horror films. Seeing it for the first time in my early teens made a huge impact. I doubt it will ever be bettered.

WB: Your work references weird fiction writers like Lovecraft, Ligotti, and James. Is the written word an important influence on your musical compositions and artwork?

JRM: Very much so, though any influence would be mostly felt in any music I make rather than visual work. I've been a voracious reader since childhood and have always taken much inspiration in the written word, whether it's a concept, a phrase or a general atmosphere, and the three writers you mention are adept purveyors of potent atmospheric landscapes—Lovecraft and James's haunted and eerie rural locations, Ligotti's entropic nocturnal townscapes. I live at the northerly tip of Strangford Lough in County Down, Northern Ireland, and the surrounding countryside is rife with woods, old farms, crumbling abbeys, lonely coastal walks, and depressed seaside towns, which over the years have gradually intermingled in my mind with the locations described by those writers. Innsmouth is only a short drive down the coast.

As a side note, horror or weird fiction makes up only a small percentage of what I read these days. I would genuinely love to have some ability as a writer. For me, no other media provides such a personal and immersive experience.

WB: You have released works in multiple media. Do you have a preference for a certain medium? Do you consider yourself more of a musician or a visual artist?

JRM: Engaging in any creative activity is an essential part of my life, regardless of its basis. I studied fine art at university in the 1990s and have wanted to be a painter since my early teens (that's longer than I've had a serious interest in making music). I consider myself simply an artist, but even though I enjoy a wide range of creative activities, I find it difficult to work across different disciplines at the same time. For the first time in many years, I've been producing more visual art, and because of that, music making has currently slipped into the background.

WB: Your artwork suggests a minimalist abstract expressionism and your music can be categorized in a similar way. Does your visual/video work feed into your music, or are they separate entities?

JRM: Abstract certainly, though always starting out with a seed of something concrete: a landscape, a phrase in a book, a sound. I wouldn't engage with the idea that my work is "expressionist" in a sense that conjures up images of personal angst—the clichéd idea of the tortured or tormented artist, which I'm most definitely not (I'm lucky enough to live a relatively untroubled existence). The work, both visual and music, is always about the conjuring and transmission, or you could say expression of, an atmosphere.

As I noted in response to the previous question, I don't usually work across different disciplines at the same time, so to say there was much, if any, cross-fertilization between the different media would be misleading. I see the visual work as completely distinct from and drawing on very different sources from the music. However, I do have at least one project brewing in the back of my mind that would hopefully unite my interests in visual art, sound and film.

WB: How important to Black Mountain Transmitter is performing live?

JRM: When I began releasing music in 2008, I had no interest in the project becoming a live act. It took a few years of being repeatedly asked before I first performed in 2012, and since then I've only played four additional live sets. I've been honored that three of those were as part of lineups at the consistently excellent Outer Church (in Dublin, Glasgow, and Edinburgh), and the Unearthing Forgotten Horrors event in Newcastle was also an absolute pleasure to perform at.

There isn't much scope for playing live, or even much of an audience for what I do at home in Northern Ireland. I also find any travel involving airports to be an almost unbearable chore, especially when carrying music equipment, which limits my enthusiasm for playing at some of the more distant gigs I've been offered. I don't go out of my way to seek live performance opportunities, but if I'm offered a gig at a particularly interesting event, I'll consider it, if only because performing live has offered me the chance to meet and socialize with some absolutely lovely people. It still beats faceless internet-based communication hands down.

WB: What is the future of Black Mountain Transmitter? Will we hear the third installment of the "Trilogy of Terror?"

JRM: The "Trilogy of Terror" will certainly see completion, possibly later this year. No guarantees. I have a concept and a body of material that needs editing and refining. It's just about finding the time to bring it all together in a satisfying manner. When it is completed, I'll likely self-release it, as I've missed the aspect of designing and creating a physical package for a recording. After that I'm not sure what the future holds for the project. It may have run its course, so one needs to move on and explore other ideas. I have released music under different aliases in the past (some of which should have stayed unreleased, to be brutally honest) and I'm sure I will do so again regardless of the status of Black Mountain Transmitter.

The Dead End Street Band (Demon est Deus inversus)
Imagine an alternative world where Doctor Who is a series of drugged out, sexed-up '70s euro-sleaze sci-fi/occult epics starring Howard Vernon as a Crowley-esque doctor and Lina Romay and Brigitte Lahaie as his foxy sex-magick-empowered companions combatting sadistic alien dominatrices and lustfully insatiable satanists from the sixty-ninth dimension. The soundtrack to these futuristic witchcult films would have been provided by the Dead End Street Band. It would be psych-damaged noise and synth torture that manages to crash ancient pagan ecstasies into dystopian metal machine nightmares. Emerging from the scratched up, jump cut, washed out exploitation movie aesthetic, the Dead End Street Band's releases are micro limited dispatches from porno scuzz hell unleashed by three hauntologists (trash cinema personas Victor Janos, A. M. Frank, and Joseph Curwen) ritually abusing their equipment. Releases like *Songs of Aiwass*, *Microscopic Liquid Subway to Oblivion*, and *Bombs Rain Down on Innsmouth* sound like Hawkwind lead by Krug and Company and transmogrified by William Bennett, Fabio Frizzi, and Alan Splet. Their music smears evil dissonance all over drug-induced, sexual cannibalistic freak-outs. Experience the bloody exorcism of the Dead End Street Band and keep telling yourself it's only an album, it's only an album, it's only an album . . .
www.facebook.com/scumelectronics
https://thedeadendstreetband.bandcamp.com/

Following are separate interviews with the Dead End Street Band's Victor Jano, A. M. Frank, and Joseph Curwen.

WB: When did your interest in horror and the occult begin?

VJ: When I was a kid, my cousin had an impressive collection of horror film books, mostly by Alan Frank. When I visited, I spent hours soaking up every word of *Monsters and Vampires*, *Horror Movies*, Dennis Gifford's *A Pictorial History of Horror*, etc., and developed an obsession with the macabre at an early age. In the 1970s, when these books were published, you could only dream beyond the imagery the illustrations in these books hinted at.

Within a few years, the home video industry boomed.In those magical, unregulated early days I tracked down every horror film I could lay my hands on, and the transition from reading about Hammer and Amicus films to spending weekends in front of *Cannibal Ferox*, *Unhinged*, *Nightmares In a Damaged Brain*, *Death Bed*, *The Erotic Rites of Frankenstein* was complete. Old habits die hard.

WB: Who are your musical influences?

VJ: Richard Einhorn's superb (and criminally unreleased) scores to the films *Shock Waves* and *Don't Go in the House*, Hive Mind, Demons/Wolf Eyes, Burial Hex, Haare, Atrax Morgue, Sewer Goddess, and in no particular order: Failing Lights, Popol Vuh, Klaus Schulze, Coil, Redrot, Neuntoter der Plage, Hair Police, Luasa Raelon/Envenomist, Dead Body Love, Prurient, Maurizio Bianchi, Emeralds, Demonologists, Culver, Aun, The Rita, The Cherry Point, Deathpile, Gnaw Their Tongues/Aderlating, Astro, Merzbow, T.O.M.B. Crimson, Cadaver in Drag, Wold, Sylvester Anfang, Disclose, Discard, Mob 47, Atrocious Madness, No Fucker, Skitsystem, Antisect, SWANS, Eyehategod, Tackhead, Sunburned Hand of the Man, Birchville Cat Motel, Suicide, Porter Ricks, Thomas Koner, Experimental Audio Research, GAS, Pole, Circle, Glenn Branca, Howard Shore, and countless electronic scores to 1970s and '80s horror cinema.

WB: How does grindhouse cinema and euro-horror inspire the Dead End Street Band? Do you feel a kinship to such outsiders like Roger Watkins, Jess Franco, and Jean Rollin?

VJ: Absolutely. The band was named after *Last House on Dead End Street* and apart from our mutual love of Demons (especially their *Frozen Fog* album), and a couple of other musical nods, our primary influences are the dank, morbid atmospheres created by bleaker, realistic horror films. Atmosphere is paramount in genre films, and the mood/tone of *Don't Go In the House* was one of my key points of reference when exploring the concept for this band. There are a small number of films that, while gory, are not about the gore for me. They are about mood and are particularly downbeat, dark works: *Don't Go in the House, Last House on Dead End Street, Combat Shock, Deadbeat at Dawn, Shock Waves, Don't Answer the Phone,* Walerian Borowczyk's *Doctor Jekyll et les Femmes.*

We are outsiders 100 percent—we aren't gonna be playing anywhere big soon. It's funny how the directors you mention were blasted by critics in their day. However, they enjoyed a renaissance when their work was seen with a fresh set of eyes and reappraised as genius. Their influence cannot be underestimated.

WB: How does the Dead End Street Band work? What are your goals?

VJ: We have a laid-back approach. We develop concepts during lengthy discussions before trying sounds. Once we've agreed on the parts each of us will play, we layer and layer sounds until they build to a crescendo. There is a pattern, and we plan each stage before letting rip in the rehearsal studio or at a gig. From my perspective, any goals would be about trying to create the kind of music I would want to listen to myself. If anyone else likes it—great! I will continue as long as I enjoy doing it.

WB: How do your occult interests and musical influences come together in your work?

VJ: It is one and the same. A lifelong passion for horror films, books, and generally outsider interests, combined with an increasingly specific musical taste over the years overlap to the point of being neck-deep in pitch blackness.

WB: Does your environment affect your artistic process?

VJ: Once playing with the band, the environment is in my head and I drift off into intense concentration/relaxation. Otherwise, there is little environmental influence, except in the artwork that employs a lot of local photography. The sleeve design for our *Murder* CDr was drawn from its title scraped into the plaster of the bathroom wall at our rehearsal studio. Right down the side of the toilet. I have no idea why.

267

WB: Do you have a preference for disseminating your music? Why such limited editions?

VJ: I prefer physical formats. The effort that goes into many DIY-released editions cannot be re-created by downloads—hand-assembled artwork, painted CDr, and cassette releases are items that really connect you with the artists who create these items. For many years I collected theatrical posters for the films I love. These artifacts are primary source materials from the days when such films were actually playing in cinemas, and as such are first-hand evidence of the amazing films of yesteryear. There is something very appealing to me in actually holding a release that the artists have lovingly created themselves, rather than accumulating mp3 after mp3 of tracks that may be flicked through on a laptop. Ideally, the wider the audience an artist can reach, the better. Therefore, attracting many listens on Bandcamp may increase the exposure of a band. However, my personal preference is for the hand-assembled edition. Just look at the amazing releases on Crucial Blaze—limited CDr runs in DVD sized cases with chapbooks, stickers, badges, etc. Fabulous!

The Dead End Street Band does limited runs not because we try to be "exclusive," which would be pretentious in the extreme. The quantities are based on economics. To date, most of our releases have been funded out of our own pockets.

WB: How important to the Dead End Street Band is performing live?

VJ: It's always interesting—we get together for a three-hour jam every two weeks, where we devise concepts for tracks, then have time to build upon them. In the live environment, you do not have that luxury, so you have to hit the ground running, and this can lead to performances being somewhat more "abrasive" than our CDr releases. We had fun at Unearthing Forgotten Horrors—an event where we played with Black Mountain Transmitter, The Psychogeographical Commission, Culver, a solo Joseph Curwen set, and The Temple of Sekhmet. It would be very cool to host this again.

There are many positive things to say about Newcastle—there are loads of gigs. The Dead End Street Band is a bit of a niche, though, so we rarely play to a live audience. The city does boast some amazing acts, though: Culver, Charles Dexter Ward, Bong, Foot Hair, Transylvanian Sex Pest, I Torquemada, Depletion, Dressed in Wires, to name a few. You just have to scratch the surface . . .

WB: What is the future of the Dead End Street Band?

VJ: Pitch-black electronics and doomy scores to the never-made sleaze and horror flicks of the 1970s, and perhaps mood music for Edward Lee novels.

A. M. Frank

WB: When did your interest in horror and the occult begin?

AMF: I have been a fan of horror for as long as I can remember, watching Hammer classics on TV as a youngster and reading anthologies of short stories by the likes of Roald Dahl, M. R. James, Edgar Allan Poe, H. P. Lovecraft, and Ambrose Bierce. At the end of the 1970s there was a massive shift and suddenly my interest was piqued by a whole new world of literature. Stephen King, James Herbert, and Ramsey Campbell had begun to appear on the shelves of the local Sainsbury's, and along with the movie tie-ins, novels such as *The Omen* and *The Brood* showed me a darker, more realistic side to the horror story.

My interest in the occult developed during my teenage years. A school friend introduced me to the writing of Aleister Crowley, which opened up a whole new world and was the catalyst for leaping headlong into the study of the occult. I read everything I could lay my hands on, including Eliphas Levi, Kenneth Grant, Israel Regardie, John Dee, Carlos Castaneda, Gerald Gardner, and dozens of other mystics.

WB: Who are your musical influences?

AMF: There are so many varied musical influences: Black Sabbath, Trouble, Candlemass, Metallica, Slayer, St. Vitus, Mercyful Fate, Celtic Frost and Witchfinder General, Electric Wizard, Sleep, Sunn O))), Neurosis, Yob, The Pixies, Swans, Hawkwind, Gong, Can, Ash Ra Tempel, The Cure, Sly Stone, Burial Hex, Fairport Convention, Coven, Black Widow, Dead Kennedys, Misfits, Black Flag, Adrenalin OD, Circle Jerks, Dag Nasty, Electro Hippies, The Stupids, Dr. and the Crippens, Goblin, Kate Bush, Ennio Morricone, Fabio Frizzi, Expo 70, Acid Mothers Temple, Mellow Candle, Forest, The Dark, Atomic Rooster, Sergius Golowin, Tudor Lodge, Loop, Mudhoney, Tad, Green River, Joy Division, Soft Cell, and Kraftwerk, to name just a few.

WB: How does grindhouse cinema and euro-horror inspire the Dead End Street Band? Do you feel a kinship to such outsiders like Roger Watkins, Jess Franco, and Jean Rollin?

AMF: Grindhouse cinema is a huge influence on the Dead End Street Band. Everything from those wonderful old VHS covers and cinema posters to the cheap electronic soundtracks, splashy gore effects, and creepy atmosphere that oozed from the nth-generation video cassettes that almost looked like someone's home movie. This has all become infused into what we do.

I sincerely feel that we share a kinship with people like Franco, Rollin, and Watkins. We all believe in doing things our own way and we've all become adept at doing things on infinitesimal budgets. We like to work that way, and I think they did, too. It allows for greater freedom of expression.

WB: How does the Dead End Street Band work? What are your goals?

AMF: Our goals are to enjoy what we do and make music for like-minded individuals. If it stops being fun, we'll stop doing it. It's really quite free; we don't have any set way of doing things and tend to just go with the flow. We will usually start with an idea or concept that is central to the piece we're working on, and go from there.

WB: How do your occult interests and musical influences come together in your work?

AMF: Sometimes the occult interests inform what we do. Our *Songs of Aiwass* CD, which we recorded for Altar of Waste, was heavily influenced by Aleister Crowley's *Magick in Theory and Practice*. In fact, it was so infused with magick that when we sent the finished recordings to Cory Strand, he immediately understood where we were coming from and his artwork featured Crowley.

Musically I think there is a big kosmiche influence in almost everything we do—long, drawn-out psychedelic jams make up a large proportion of our music. Bands like Can, Popol Vuh, and Amon Duul are great influences on each of us, and I think they can always be heard in our recordings. Other major influences range from '90s techno to doom metal and crust punk.

WB: Does your environment affect your artistic process?

AMF: Yes, any number of variables affect the artistic process, not just the environment. Wherever and whenever you record, everything from the weather outside, to the day you've had, to what you had for tea has an effect on your mental state. The same can be said for what you're reading, what you've been watching, and the music you're listening to at any given time. These factors always have an impact on the creative process. Sometimes we can sit down in the rehearsal studio with an idea and by the time we leave we've veered in a completely different direction.

WB: Do you have a preference for disseminating your music? Why such limited editions?

AMF: We release our product in limited editions because our music has a very niche market. As we generally fund our own CDr releases, we can't afford to gamble on large print runs.

WB: How important to the Dead End Street Band is performing live?

AMF: It's imperative. The sound of the Dead End Street Band really comes into its own in a live setting. Our music is not just to be listened to; it's meant to be felt. Our aim has always been to create an unsettling atmosphere, and we do that best in a live setting.

WB: What is the future of the Dead End Street Band?

AMF: Dark horror drones and sinister kosmiche jams, all played out on a Jean Rollin movie set.

Joseph Curwen

WB: When did your interest in horror and the occult begin?

JC: I've been a horror movie fan since I was a child. I remember watching Hammer Horror Movies, which could be described as eerie rather than scary, with my Gran. My parents had an extensive bookcase, and I read up on everything from true crime anthologies to Edgar Allan Poe collections at a very young age. My Mam had a voluminous record collection, including a lot of late '60s, early '70s psychedelic rock stuff. I remember one record in particular featuring the infamous "Come to the Sabbat" by Black Widow, and putting that on repeat whenever I could.

In my teenage years I remember my friends and I going through an extended period of acquiring video nasty VHS tapes off older brothers and friends in the loop, and devouring them at a great pace. This coincided with an interest in black metal, which resulted in me getting copies of *The Satanic Bible* by Anton Lavey and *Moonchild* by Aleister Crowley. These had a big impact on my impressionable mind and made me start to appreciate the good and evil forces in everyone.

WB: Who are your musical influences?

JC: Aphex Twin, Autechre, Early '90s rave and jungle, Gabba, John Carpenter, Slayer, Meshuggah, King Crimson, Brian Eno, Yes, Tad, Sunn O))), Goatsnake, Burning Witch, Bong, Mr. Bungle, Roxy Music, Black Sabbath, and '80s horror soundtracks.

WB: How does grindhouse cinema and euro-horror inspire the Dead End Street Band? Do you feel a kinship to such outsiders like Roger Watkins, Jess Franco, and Jean Rollin?

JC: They influence us a lot. If I'm describing the Dead End Street Band to friends who aren't necessarily into abstract music or noise, I say we're improvised '70s horror soundtracks. This often results in a bemused look, but it's certainly the atmosphere we go for. I guess we have a kinship with any creative people considered to be making outsider art.

WB: How does the Dead End Street Band work? What are your goals?

JC: We usually decide on a basic premise, be it a particular horror film or weird noises from space. For my parts, I make a basic template on my laptop that gives me space to improvise around the material when I perform. My role in the Dead End Street Band is a lot more intuitive than my solo work as Joseph Curwen. Work with the band allows me to elaborate and manipulate ideas on the fly to suit the vibe in the room when we're playing together.

WB: How do your occult interests and musical influences come together in your work?

JC: I have been told on a number of occasions that using my music as accompaniment to reading H. P. Lovecraft stories is a very rewarding experience, which means a lot to me. I try to channel a genuine sense of unease and dread into my music, which was something H. P. Lovecraft was excellent at evoking.

The first music I got into without parental influence was dance music, so this will always be a massive influence on any music I make. I played bass in various heavy metal bands a few years back, which taught me how to appreciate crippling volume. One band, BERK, was a doom metal power trio that subscribed to the "more amps equals better music" idea, and I learnt how to utilise low frequencies for maximum results. That knowledge has certainly served me well in my electronic adventures. I'm into the idea of deconstructing the music of my youth and pushing it into new and more abstract directions.

WB: Does your environment affect your artistic process?

JC: I grew up in the wilds of County Durham. Next to my house was a giant forest that stretches for miles. I would spend countless hours exploring my surroundings as a child. County Durham is an ancient place, with a lot of spiritual and psychogeographical history. I have spent a lot of time wandering through the woods surrounding old ruins. There is a sense of the genuine unknown around such archaic spaces, and I guess that rubbed off on me in my formative years. That ethereal feeling you get when you're miles away from anyone is certainly something I try to bring to my music.

WB: Do you have a preference for disseminating your music? Why such limited editions?

JC: The internet is a powerful tool for exposure to a lot of new music, which has both positive and negative connotations. I like the immediacy of services such as Bandcamp. You can upload an album and instantly share it with the world, and offering Joseph Curwen albums digitally has been one of my most rewarding and successful musical ventures. Social media platforms such as Facebook and Twitter are extremely useful for disseminating music to a wide audience, and a lot of my contact with fellow weird noisemakers is via the internet. A couple of times, music heroes of mine have got in touch to say they appreciate my music, which has meant the world to me.

That being said, there is nothing finer than seeing a physical release of your own "in the flesh." I have released various cassettes and CDrs, and always enjoy interacting with folks at gigs who are interested in my music in physical formats that they can enjoy on their own time later. People wanting to have my music in physical form gives me a greater sense of musical validation than just watching the download numbers on Bandcamp. Limited editions are cool.

WB: How important to the Dead End Street Band is performing live?

JC: I always enjoy playing live with the Dead End Street Band. Our particular brand of oppressive noise seems to go down really well with live audiences, especially when we have the luxury of a good sound system. Our live performances tend to evolve a lot more quickly than when we're practicing. I guess the tension of performing in public pushes us further. We don't gig that often, which I am perfectly happy about. It makes gigs feel special, which allows us to go hell for leather when we do play.

WB: What is the future of the Dead End Street Band?

JC: I am happy just seeing how things pan out. We'll always be a niche market sort of band, so I don't expect us to get famous any time soon. We're always coming up with new concepts and ideas, which results in more and more music. I think we're in the fortunate position of being quite laid back about it, so our sound will evolve naturally as we play with each other. Our roles within the band evolve and grow with each new performance, which means the creative process is always fresh and exciting. We regularly comment that we're getting better as a band, and my knowledge of DSP and sound design is increasing at an exponential rate, so I don't see us stopping any time soon. I am happy for it to continue as long as we enjoy it.

Joseph Curwen (Resurgam)
In addition to participating in the Dead End Street Band, Newcastle-upon-Tyne sonic sorcerer Alexander Roberts conjures his own malevolently haunted tones under the guise of Joseph Curwen. In 1771, Joseph Curwen was killed during a raid on his Pawtucket, Rhode Island, farmhouse. Curwen had been a merchant, a member of the Providence elite, and a necromancer. It was whispered that he had conquered the aging process and had the ability to resurrect the dead, brutalizing them for their secrets. Worst of all were the rumors of his worshipping the Great Old Ones, invoking Yog-Sothoth to acquire the power to step outside of time. Joseph Curwen is the avatar for the wizard's second resurrection, this time manifested through the essential

drones of ambient dust inspired by the works of the prophet H. P. Lovecraft. Joseph Curwen's ominous soundscapes reflect what the earth will sound like when it is cleared off; it is the key, gate, and guardian of the spaces between. Discordant and yet oddly soothing, his prolific releases are some of the most sinister and dark ambient pieces to emerge from the UK occult wave movement. His newest release is *Gates of Oblivion*, a powerfully dreary amalgam of early Tangerine Dream, Cabaret Voltaire, and Alan Howarth, all transmogrified through JC's sonic alchemy. A warning to the curious: Joseph Curwen's sounds call up things that can't always be put down.
https://www.facebook.com/JosephCurwenDrone
http://josephcurwen.bandcamp.com/
http://www.youtube.com/user/JosephCurwenDrone
http://josephcurwendrone.tumblr.com/

WB: Obviously, the first question has to be: why H. P. Lovecraft? How has his work and thought informed your music? Have you ever taken a pilgrimage to Providence or Arkham country?

JC: I have been a fan of H. P. Lovecraft for a long time. His work instantly captivated me; I don't think I've ever read anyone else that describes the genuine weird better than him. The aspect of his tales that seems to resonate most with me is that of seemingly normal people being thrown into truly berserk situations. I feel like Lovecraft had a genuine fear of the unknown, and I attempt to re-create that atmosphere in my music.

I have never been to Providence or Arkham country; it is certainly a pilgrimage I would like to take. When I read Lovecraft stories, I imagine them to be set in landscapes similar to those in my native County Durham.

WB: How does Joseph Curwen work? What are your goals?

JC: Joseph Curwen initially started as an experiment in electronic bass weight. I love heavy music of any genre, and I'm very much an audio technology geek, so I thought combining the two would be perfect foil for my creativity. I take tiny samples of sound; stretch, manipulate, and reprocess them to the point of insanity; and then layer them on top of each other to create something new. A lot of it is based on mathematics, working out how frequencies react to each other using calculations. Joseph Curwen is my attempt at making ethereal and weird music to soundtrack ethereal and weird situations.

WB: There seems to be a difference between your earlier, darker Lovecraft-inspired pieces (*Essential Salts of Human Dust, The Thing on the Doorstep*) and your current more environmental and cosmic works (*Antediluvian Forest, Reflections in the Lake*, live performances). How has Joseph Curwen evolved?

JC: Joseph Curwen is constantly evolving as I learn more and more about modern music technology. I am constantly experimenting with sound design and production methodology. My earliest works were purely about digital oppression and saturated waveforms. As time has gone on, I've tried to incorporate more textures and musicality into my music.

For my Unearthing Forgotten Horrors set I deliberately set out to create a piece that celebrated the feeling I get when I'm in the forests of County Durham. I really enjoyed the experience of going back to Cocken Woods and Finchale Priory to film footage and take field recordings, and this inspired me to research the history of the area, including the choir of St. Godric. I hope I re-created the atmosphere of the forest on the day of the performance.

I had some time away from my solo stuff to concentrate on the Dead End Street Band over the winter. A good friend of mine, artist Robin Megannity, recently asked me to soundtrack an exhibition he is planning. After some time away, I relished the opportunity to experiment with the idea of soundtracking a film that never got made. I've tried to emulate authentic horror synth tones and atmospheres, using cutting edge audio technology. I'm proud of the results, and genuinely think it is above and beyond what I have created before. I am looking forward to sharing it with the world soon.

WB: How important is performing live to Joseph Curwen?

JC: I like keeping live appearances a rare treat. There is an almost ritual aspect to live gigs, sitting behind a laptop and slowly doing digital filter sweeps, etc., and it's cool to share the hypnotic quality of the music with others at sometimes oppressive volumes.

WB: What is the future of Joseph Curwen?

JC: Post-Rave Hauntology Rituals and Radiophonic Occult Synth Horror Soundtracks.

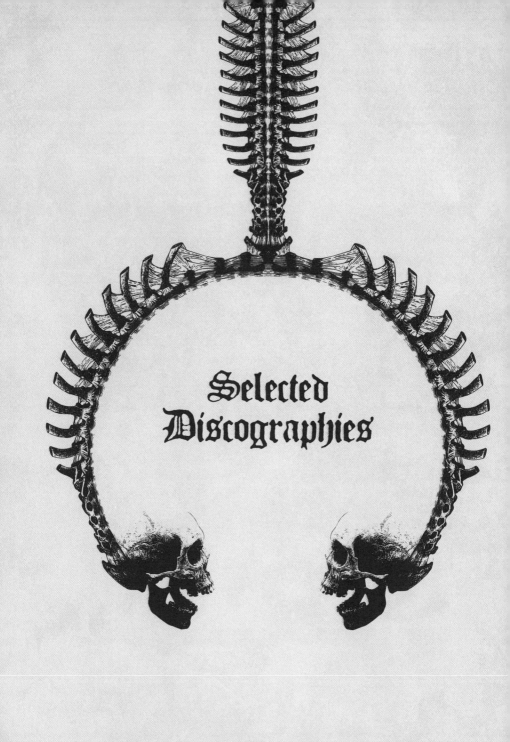

Selected
Discographies

UK Occult Revival Artists

Advisory Circle: *Other Channels, As the Crow Flies, From Out Here*

Belbury Poly: *The Willows, The Owl's Map, From an Ancient Star, The Belbury Tales*

Black Channels: *Oracles*

Black Mountain Transmitter: *RedShift, Black Goat of the Woods, The Unsettled Dust, Theory & Practice, Playing with Dead Things, Stille Nacht, Palimpsestes, Deathdream! Live in Edinburgh*

Culver: *Dead Winter Blood, House of Black Flowers*, various split releases with Seppuku, Werewolf Jerusalem, Electric Omen, Onco, La Mancha Del Pescado

Joseph Curwen: *Pale Watching Moon, At the Mountains of Madness, Essential Salts Of Human Dust, Dreams in the Witch House, The Dunwich Horror, Reflections in the Lake, Forest Night, Vengeance of the Infinite Abysses, The Freedom of Dreamless Sleep, The Cold Room, Shunned House, Blasphemous Alliance, Exham Priory, Flight Through Goblin Space, Subterrene Arcana, Atomic Disturbances 1–5*

Dead End Street Band: *Microscopic Liquid Subway to Oblivion, Songs of Aiwass, Nosferatu on Acid, In the Forest . . . They Wait!, Satan's Claw Sessions, Black Christmas, Bombs Rain Down on Innsmouth, The Kosmische Curse, The Dark Heart*

Charles Dexter Ward: *Past Lives*

English Heretic: *Temple Of Remembrance : In Conversation with Michael Reeves: An English Heretic Black Plaque Presentation, The Sacred Geography of British Cinema: Scene One, Wyrd Tales, Visitor Guides: Your Passport to the Qliphoth, Radar Angeology—A Drone for Joe Kennedy, Tales of the New Isis Lodge, Anti-Heroes, Mondo Paranoia, Outré Bound—Live and Unreleased, The Underworld Service, A Study of Lunar Research Flights*

Focus Group: *The Elektrik Karousel, Sketches and Spells, We Are All Pan's People, Broadcast and The Focus Group Investigate Witch Cults of the Radio Age.*

Hare and the Moon: *The Hare and the Moon, Grey Mulkin, Wood Witch*

Haxan Cloak: *Haxan Cloak, The Men Parted the Sea to Devour the Water, Excavation*

Melmoth the Wanderer: *The Insomniacs Almanac, The Curious Episode of the Wizard's Skull, The Legent of the Demon Tree, The Ghost of Winters Past, The Hell Fire Caves, The Whispered Nightmare, A Fireside Companion*

Mount Vernon Arts Lab: *The Seance at Hobs Lane*
Pye Corner Audio: *Black Mill Tapes 1–4*
Eric Zann: *Ouroborindra*

Influences/Fellow Acolytes

Aghast: *Hexerei Im Zwielicht Der Finsternis*
Aphex Twin: *Selected Ambient Works I* and *II*
Autechre: *Incunabula, Tri Repetae, Chiastic Slide, EP 7*
BBC Radiophonic Workshop: *The Soundhouse: Music from the BBC Radiophonic Workshop, BBC Radiophonic Music, Out of This World, Dr. Who Sound Effects, Fourth Dimension*
Black Sabbath: *Black Sabbath*
Black Widow: *Come to the Sabbat*
Boards of Canada: *Twoism, Music Has the Right to Children, Geogaddi*
Broadcast: *Berberian Sound Studio*
Cabaret Voltaire: *Mix Up, Voice of America, Red Mecca, 3 Crespuscule Tracks*
John Cameron: *Psychomania*
Candlemass: *Epicus Doomicus Metallicus*
John Carpenter: *Halloween, The Fog, Halloween II* (with Alan Howarth), *Halloween III* ((with Alan Howarth), *Escape from New York* (with Alan Howarth), *Prince of Darkness* (with Alan Howarth)
The Caretaker: *Selected Memories from the Haunted Ballroom, A Stairway to the Stars, Deleted Scenes/Forgotten Dreams, Patience (After Sebald)*
Wendy Carlos: *A Clockwork Orange, The Shining*
Coil: *Scatology, Horse Rotorvator, Gold Is the Metal (with the Broadest Shoulders), Love's Secret Domain, Stolen and Contaminated Songs, Musick to Play in the Dark I and II*
Comus: *First Utterance*
Coven: *Witchcraft Destroys Minds & Reaps Souls*
Current 93: *Dogs Blood Rising, Nature Unveiled, In Menstrual Night*
Philippe D'Aram: *Fascination*
Delia Derbyshire and Brian Hodgson: *The Legend of Hell House*
DJ Spooky: *Songs of a Dead Dreamer*
Richard Einhorn: *Shock Waves*
Electric Wizard: *Come My Fanatics, Supercoven, Dopethrone, Witchcult Today*
Brian Eno: *Ambient 4 (On Land)*
Experimental Audio Research: *The Koner Experiment, Data Rape*
Fabio Frizzi: *Zombi 2, Paura Nella Citta Dei Morti Viventi, L'Aldila*
Edgar Froese: *Epsilon in Malaysian Pale*

Goblin: *Profundo Rosso, Suspiria, Buio Omega, Phenomena, Tenebre* (Simonetti/Pignatelli/Morante)

Hawkwind: *In Search of Space, Space Ritual, Warrior at the Edge of Time*

Tobe Hooper and Wayne Bell: *The Texas Chainsaw Massacre*

Manfred Hubler and Siegfried Schwab: *Vampyros Lesbos*

Tim Krog: *The Boogey Man*

Lustmord: *A Document of Early Acoustic and Tactical Experimentation, Heresy, The Monstrous Soul*

Magnet and Paul Giovanni: *The Wicker Man*

Fred Myrow and Malcolm Seagrove: *Phantasm*

Nurse with Wound: *Homotopy To Marie, Soliloquy For Lilith, Thunder Perfect Mind*

Popol Vuh: *Affenstunde, Aguirre, Brüder Des Schattens—Söhne Des Lichts*

Psychic TV: *Force the Hand of Chance, Dreams Less Sweet, Themes, Ov Power, Live 23* Series

Scanner: *Scanner, Spore, Sulphur*

Klaus Schulze: *Irrlicht, Cyborg, Black Dance, Angst*

Howard Shore: *Videodrome*

Skullflower: *From Destroyer, Xaman, Last Shot at Heaven, Obsidian Shaking Codex*

Sleep: *Holy Mountain, Dopesmoker*

Giuliano Sorgini: *The Living Dead at the Manchester Morgue*

Sunn O)): *The Grimmrobe Demos, ØØ Void*

Tangerine Dream: *Zeit, Phaedra, Rubycon, Hyberborea, Thief, Sorcerer, The Keep*

Throbbing Gristle: *The Second Annual Report, D.O.A. The Third and Final Report, Heathen Earth, Mission of Dead Souls*

Mike Vickers: *Dracula A.D. 1972*

White Noise: *An Electric Storm*

Marc Wilkinson: *Blood on Satan's Claw*

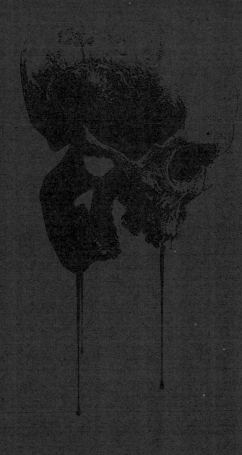

William Burns is an English professor at Suffolk County Community College. He teaches classes on horror films and horror literature as well as on experimental films, graphic novels, postmodernism, and surrealism. He has lectured on horror films in Chicago, New York City, and Washington, DC (right down the block from the infamous stairs featured in *The Exorcist*).

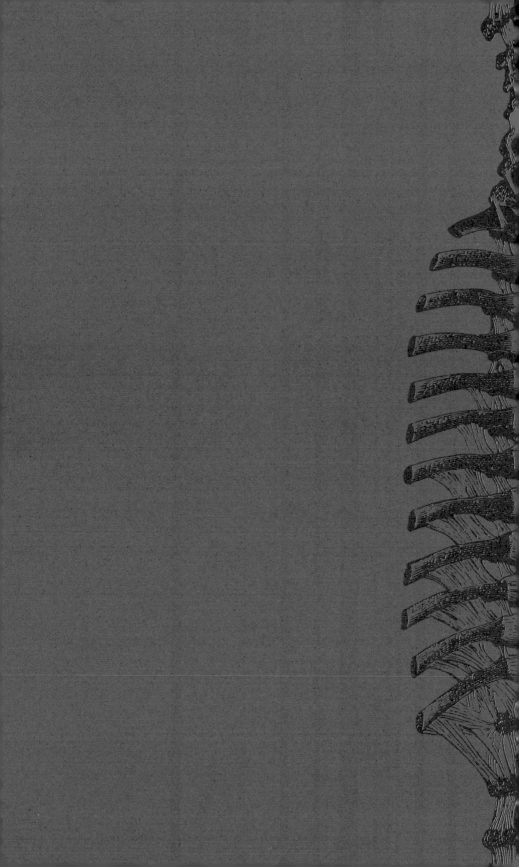